FIFTY MAJOR CITIES OF THE BIBLE

From the ruins of the ancient seaside city of Acco to the small but archaeologically important town of Yokne'am, *Fifty Major Cities of the Bible* provides readers with a comprehensive guide to the ancient cities that played a vital role in the world from which the Bible originated.

Included are not only well-known cities such as Jerusalem and Jericho, but also lesser-known towns like Aroer, Beth-Zur, and Gibeah, which have all provided their own valuable contributions to the way in which we now understand the biblical world.

Includes:

- the biblical context of each city or town
- a summary of its known archaeological history
- non-biblical references to the site
- photographs and illustrations
- a concise bibliography for further reading

Also provided is a handy reference map to the major archaeological sites in Israel, as well as chronological tables for easy reference.

Concise, informative and highly accessible, *Fifty Major Cities of the Bible* is a superb overview of the cities and towns that made up the biblical world, and an essential resource for students and enthusiasts.

John C. H. Laughlin is Professor of Religion and Chair of the Department of Religion, Averett University in Danville, Virginia. He is an experienced field archaeologist who has served on the staff of several excavations, and is also the author of *Archaeology and the Bible* (Routledge, 1999).

Also available from Routledge

Fifty Key Christian Thinkers
Peter McEnhill and George Newlands
0–415–17050–8

Eastern Philosophy: Key Readings
Oliver Leaman
0–415–17358–2

Fifty Key Jewish Thinkers
Dan Cohn-Sherbok
0–415–12628–2

Key Concepts in Eastern Philosophy
Oliver Leaman
0–415–17363–9

Fifty Eastern Thinkers
Diané Collinson, Kathryn Plant and Robert Wilkinson
0–415–20284–1

Who's Who in Christianity
Lavinia Cohn-Shenbok
0–415–26034–5

Who's Who in Jewish History
Joan Comay, new edition revised by Lavinia Cohn-Sherbok
0–415–26030–2

Who's Who in the New Testament
Ronald Brownrigg
0–415–26036–1

Who's Who in the Old Testament
Joan Comay
0–415–26031–0

The Bible in Western Culture
Dee Dyas and Esther Hughes
0–415–32618–4

Archaeology: The Key Concepts
Colin Renfrew and Paul Bahn
0–415–31758–4

Archaeology: The Basics
Clive Gamble
0–415–22153–6

Ancient History: Key Themes and Approaches
Neville Morley
0–415–16509–1

FIFTY MAJOR CITIES OF THE BIBLE

FROM DAN TO BEERSHEBA

John C. H. Laughlin

Routledge
Taylor & Francis Group

LONDON AND NEW YORK

First published 2006
by Routledge
2 Park Square, Milton Park, Abingdon, Oxon OX14 4RN

Simultaneously published in the USA and Canada
by Routledge
270 Madison Avenue, New York, NY 10016

Routledge is an imprint of the Taylor & Francis Group

Typeset in Bembo by Florence Production Ltd, Stoodleigh, Devon
Printed and bound in Great Britain by
TJ International Ltd, Padstow, Cornwall

British Library Cataloguing in Publication Data
A catalogue record for this book is available from the British Library

Library of Congress Cataloging in Publication Data
Laughlin, John C. H. (John Charles Hugh), 1942–
Fifty major cities of the Bible/John C.H. Laughlin.
p. cm.
Includes bibliographical references.
1. Israel – Antiquities.   2. Middle East – Antiquities.   3. Cities and
towns, Ancient – Israel.   4. Cities and towns, Ancient – Middle East.
5. Bible. O.T. – Antiquities.   6. Middle East – Civilization – To 622.
7. Excavations (Archaeology) – Israel.   I. Title.
DS111.1.L38 2006
220.9'1 – dc22
2005014271

ISBN10: 0–415–22314–8 (hbk)
ISBN10: 0–415–22315–6 (pbk)

ISBN13: 978–0–415–22314–0 (hbk)
ISBN13: 978–0–415–22315–7 (pbk)

CONTENTS

FIGURES

ABBREVIATIONS

AASOR   *Annual of the American Schools of Oriental Research.*

ABD   *The Anchor Bible Dictionary.* Six volumes. David Noel Freedman, ed., New York: Doubleday, 1992.

ANET   *Ancient Near Eastern Texts Relating to the Old Testament* Third Edition. James Pritchard, ed., Princeton: Princeton University Press, 1969.

AOTS   *Archaeology and Old Testament Study.* D. Winton Thomas, ed., Oxford: Clarendon Press, 1967.

ASHL   *The Archaeology of Society in the Holy Land.* T. E. Levy, ed., New York: Facts on File, 1995.

BA   *Biblical Archaeologist.*

BAR   *Biblical Archaeology Review.*

BAReader   *Biblical Archaeologist Reader.*

BASOR   *Bulletin of the American Schools of Oriental Research.*

BAT   *Biblical Archaeology Today: Proceedings of the International Congress on Biblical Archaeology Jerusalem, April 1984.* Janet Amitai, ed., Jerusalem: Israel Exploration Society, 1985.

BAT 90   *Biblical Archaeology Today, 1990: Proceedings of the Second International Congress on Biblical Archaeology Jerusalem, June–July, 1990.* A. Biran and J. Aviram, eds, Jerusalem: Israel Exploration Society, 1993.

EAEHL   *The Encyclopedia of Archaeological Excavations in the Holy Land.* Four volumes. M. Avi-Yonah and E. Stern, eds, Jerusalem: Israel Exploration Society and Massada Press, 1977.

FNM   *From Nomadism to Monarchy: Archaeological and Historical Aspects of Early Israel.* I. Finkelstein and N. Na'aman, eds, Jerusalem: Israel Exploration Society, 1994.

IEJ   *Israel Exploration Journal.*

JBL   *Journal of Biblical Literature.*

NEA *Near Eastern Archaeology* (formerly *Biblical Archaeologist*. The first issue of the *NEA* is Vol. 61 No. 1, March, 1998).

NEAEHL *The New Encyclopedia of Archaeological Excavations in the Holy Land.* Four volumes. Ephraim Stern, ed., Jerusalem: Simon & Schuster, 1993.

OEANE *The Oxford Encyclopedia of Archaeology in the Near East.* Five volumes. Eric M. Meyers, ed., New York: Oxford University Press, 1997.

PEQ *Palestine Exploration Quarterly.*

REI *Recent Excavations in Israel: Studies in Iron Age Archaeology.* S. Gitin and W. G. Dever, eds, Winona Lake, Indiana: Eisenbrauns, 1994.

SAIA *Studies in the Archaeology of the Iron Age in Israel and Jordan.* Amihai Mazar, ed. Journal For the Study of the Old Testament Supplement Series 331, Sheffield: Sheffield Academic Press, 2001.

TA Tel Aviv.

PREFACE

In volume one of the *NEAEHL* (published in 1993), the editors list the names of 365 archaeological sites which are discussed as separate entries in this multi-volume work (1: xvii–xix). Most of these sites are located in modern-day Israel; a minority are located in Trans-jordan. Today, these latter sites are in the state of Jordan. However, as valuable as this encyclopaedia is, it is now some twelve years old (as of 2005) and is out of date in many places where archaeological work has continued or begun since its publication (Megiddo, for a former example; Jezreel, for a latter one). Thus, in the chapters that follow, I have tried to include the most recent results of current excavations, at least where results have been published.

While this volume was written for the "Fifty Series" published by Routledge, the title has been bothersome. Many of the places described below would hardly qualify to be called a "city." Most, at best, were little more than "towns" and some probably should be called "villages." Nevertheless, for each city/town chosen, I have provided a description of its occurrence in the Bible as well as its known archaeological history. The latter more often than not includes periods of habitation that long preceded any "Israelite" occupation of the site (Jericho is a prime example). I have done this to impress upon the reader the fact that, archaeologically speaking, "Israel" was a late arrival upon the Ancient Near Eastern stage. Furthermore, I have used the word "Israel" to refer to the geographical location of these sites (except for Damascus, of course, which is in Syria), despite the problems created by doing so (Jericho was hardly an "Israelite" city in the Neolithic periods!). As the map will clearly demonstrate, these cities/towns literally stretched from Dan in the north to Aroer in the south. This was also done with deliberate intent.

Furthermore, while I think that the archaeological realia, properly identified and interpreted, can, at times, correlate with the world of biblical texts, this is not an attempt to engage in "Biblical Archaeology," whose demise has long been celebrated by most archaeologists and biblical historians. But if an archaeological site can be identified with any degree of certainty with a biblical place name (which is not always easy), what is known archaeologically about that site should at least contribute to how we understand the society/culture into which the biblical writers have placed their discussion, whether this discussion is considered historically accurate or not.

At the end of the book, I have included three appendices. These include a brief discussion of one of the most intriguing peoples mentioned in the Bible, the Philistines. Four Philistine cities known from the Bible have chapters devoted to them (Ashdod, Ashkelon, Ekron/Tel Miqne and Gath; the fifth Philistine city mentioned in the Bible is Gaza). A second appendix contains a chronological chart of archaeological periods. While some of these dates are still debated, the chart is included simply for the convenience of the reader. Dates are important, even when they cannot always be precise. A third appendix is a chart listing the names and dates (again, these are not with absolute certainty) of the kings of Judah and Israel. I hope it too will prove useful to the reader, especially one to whom a lot of the discussion is new or unfamiliar.

Discussing 50 "cities" of the Bible in one small volume is a daunting task. Most of the difficult decisions centered around two questions: what cities/towns should be included, and what information should be provided for the sites that were selected? Some places were picked because they are well known and visited by most tourists. These include Jerusalem, Megiddo, Hazor, Caesarea Maritima, Capernaum, and Banias (Caesarea Philippi). The names of other cities/towns may be far less familiar to some readers: Yokne'am, Azekah, Beth-Zur, Aroer, and others. Thus, what follows should be considered only the beginning of the study of these places, and certainly not the end. To help in a reader's desire for further study, I have included a highly selected bibliography at the end of each chapter. In addition, the reader can find discussions of most of the sites described below in two major encyclopaedias: the *NEAEHL* and the *OEANE*. Consequently, out of space consideration, in some instances, I have assumed the information in these resources without listing specifics in the bibliography. For the sheer sake of convenience, the entries are arranged alphabetically regardless of chronological, geographical, and/or other considerations that might have suggested a different scheme.

ILLUSTRATION CREDITS

Bolen, Todd (BiblePlaces.com) 4, 5, 6, 8, 10, 11, 12, 15, 17, 38, 39, 40, 41, 42, 43, 44, 49, 55, 59, 61, 62, 68, 70, 72, 73

Fitzgerald, Jenne 7, 37, 46, 60

Israel Antiquities Authority, courtesy of Vassilios Tzaferis 25, 28

Israel Museum ©, courtesy of Staff Archaeological Officer in the Civil Administration of Judea and Samaria 69

Laughlin, John 2, 3, 9, 13, 14, 16, 18, 19, 20, 21, 22, 23, 24, 26, 27, 29, 30, 31, 32, 33, 34, 35, 36, 45, 47, 48, 50, 51, 52, 53, 54, 56, 57, 58, 63, 64, 65, 66, 67, 71

Oxford University Press. Adapted from *Oxford Encyclopedia of Archaeology in the Near East*, edited by Eric M. Meyers (c) 1997. Used by permission of Oxford University Press 1

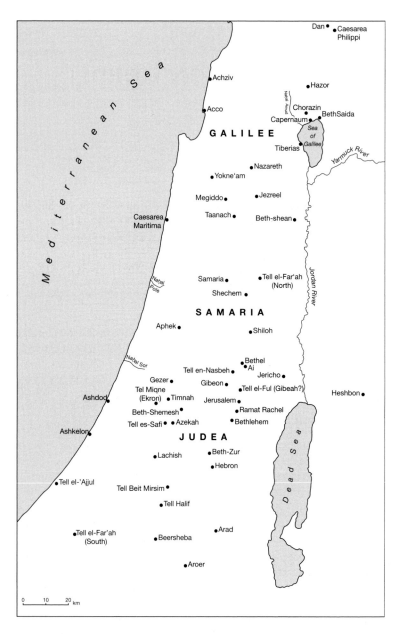

Figure 1 Map: main excavations in the Holy Land.

INTRODUCTION

Out of all the villages, towns and cities mentioned in the Bible, this book describes fifty. Furthermore, as mentioned in the Preface, the title of the book is somewhat misleading to an unsuspecting reader. While there were urbanized areas in the Bible that may deserve the title of "city," and are, in fact, called so in the Bible (Jerusalem, Dan, Hazor, and so forth), most people most of the time lived in small hamlets, villages, or towns. In fact, it has been suggested recently that during the main biblical period (called "Iron Age II" by archaeologists and dated from around 1000–587 BCE) somewhere between 66 percent and 95 percent of the population of Israel and Judah lived, not in cities, but in villages and farmsteads (Herzog, 1997). In a fairly recent survey of Samaria (Broshi and Finkelstein, 1992), 428 Iron Age II sites were identified. Of these, 84 percent were estimated to be less than 2.5 acres in size. Obviously, in many instances it is a stretch to refer to some places as "cities" (for examples: Bethel, Bethlehem, Capernaum, Nazareth), but the importance given to these sites in the Bible merits their inclusion in this book. In fact, it has been common in discussions of this sort to use the words "city," "town," and "village" interchangeably (whether justified or not).

In the current literature (and there is a lot of it!) an ancient city is usually defined or described, in part, as a form of permanent human settlement with political, social, economic, and religious relationships with its immediate surroundings. Thus cities, as opposed to villages and/or towns, were composed of a very diversified population that could include rulers (palaces), priests (temples), merchants (shops), artisans (various artifacts), warriors (weapons), and no doubt the ubiquitous peasants and slaves. The economic base of all cities in the ancient world was agriculture. Thus a kind of symbiotic relationship developed between the cities which provided such needs as security, religious and political leaders, trade networks, storage and distribution

1

facilities and the surrounding villages and hamlets that provided the agricultural products. Furthermore, while the Bible may provide valuable information about a "city," that is usually not the primary purpose of a text.

Consequently, in this book particular attention will be given to the archaeological history of the cities/towns discussed. Problems still exist nevertheless. From the very beginning of archaeological excavations in Israel (late nineteenth century CE), very little attention was paid to how most people lived, hoped, dreamed, and died. Archaeologists simply did not dig where most people lived. The attention was focused on the "cities," the impressive tells (ruins) where the wealthier and more powerful people were believed to have lived. The result is that while we now know a lot about fortification systems, water resources, architectural styles, temples, diets, weapons of choice, ceramic production and even some of the names of the more prominent players on the ancient stage, only recently have efforts been made to understand the daily life of most of the people who lived in the past. This is especially true concerning the roles of women (King and Stager, 2001; Borowski, 2002; Meyers, 2003).

The history of the origin(s) and development of cities in the Ancient Near East is complex, and there is a growing literature on the subject. For a long time it was traditional to trace the origin of city life to the Neolithic period (c.8000–4500 BCE). Sites such as Jericho were cited as examples of the beginning of urbanization. While important changes in human lifestyles did occur during this long period (see Mithen, 2004), it is now a consensus among authorities that the first true "cities" emerged in Syria at the end of the fourth millennium BCE (the Chalcolithic period). During the following Early Bronze Age, cities spread throughout Mesopotamia reaching sizes of nearly a thousand acres (Uruk, Mari, Ugarit, Alalakh, and so forth).

In Israel three major periods of urbanization have been identified:

1   the Early Bronze Age I–III (3300–2200 BCE);
2   the Middle Bronze Age to the Late Bronze Age (2000–1200 BCE; although during the latter period, decline of city life is clearly evident in the archaeological remains);
3   the Iron Age II (1000–587 BCE).

It should not come as a surprise that evolving with the emergence of cities was writing. The oldest known texts date to around 3200 BCE and were found in Uruk (Sumer), written in cuneiform (wedged-shaped symbols). All of these periods of city development have different characteristics and are not part of a monolithic culture. Furthermore, compared to the cities of Mesopotamia, cities in Palestine were quite small. Early Bronze Age cities varied in size from around 15 acres (Megiddo) to some 60 acres (Khirbet Kerak); Early Bronze Aphek was about 30 acres and 'Ai (et-Tell) 27.

During the Middle Bronze Age, cities were, on the whole, larger. The largest Middle Bronze Age city yet discovered in Israel is Hazor which reached nearly 200 acres. By comparison, other cities, such as Laish (Dan) enclosed about 50 acres while Ashkelon, on the Mediterranean coast, reached a size of nearly 150 acres. By 1200 BCE, the long Bronze Age culture in Israel (and elsewhere) came to a sudden end. The causes of this cultural disintegration have long been debated and may have included a combination of ecological disaster, foreign invasion (the Philistines?), decline of Egyptian regional control and economic collapse. Whatever the cause, there would be a two-hundred-year hiatus before new cities began to emerge in the tenth century BCE.

During the Iron Age II, the archaeological period of most of what takes place in the Hebrew Bible, cities were the center of administrative, religious, and political control. By the ninth century BCE, the two royal cites, Jerusalem (in Judah) and Samaria (in Israel), ruled over their respective "empires." All of this came to an end when Israel was destroyed by the Assyrians in 722/21 BCE, and Judah by the Babylonians in 587/86 BCE.

Each of these developments in the long history of urbanization in Israel is unique and in no case is there cultural continuity. The ethnic identities of the people(s) in each period, and even during different phases of the same period, are often difficult to establish beyond general categories (e.g. "Canaanites," "Philistines," "Israelites"). The cities from these time periods have their own histories of occupations and in some instances were re-occupied by different people(s) in different periods (Jerusalem, Hazor, Dan, Gezer, Shechem, just to cite a few clear examples). Furthermore, the size of a city could also vary from period to period – sometimes increasing (Tel Dan), other times decreasing in size ('Ai).

Cities in Israel and Judah during the period of the so-called "Divided Monarchy" also seem to have existed in a kind of hierarchy. There were obviously "royal" cities, such as Jerusalem and Samaria, where kings lived and in which power was concentrated. How much contact "the people of the land," living in hamlets or farmsteads, had with these cities is uncertain. Other cities served "administrative" roles and probably included such sites as Dan and Megiddo in Israel and Lachish, on the edge of the Shephelah, in Judah. Perhaps smaller towns served secondary administrative or military functions of some sort such as Beersheba in Judah and Jezreel in Israel. Some seem to have been used primarily for residential purposes, while others were major market centers. By New Testament times, the cities of the Ancient Near East had been greatly influenced by Greek/Roman models.

In a book of this nature, there is always the problem of what to include, and by inference, to exclude. Some cities, such as Jerusalem, Capernaum, Jericho, and other famous biblical places, were obvious choices. Other selections will probably be seen as more arbitrary reflecting the personal interests and biases of the author. In any event, even though some places, no doubt, were omitted that one could argue should have been included, hopefully, none have been included that should have been excluded.

Site identification has been, and still is, a major concern for archaeologists and biblical historians. How do we know that Tell es-Sultan really is Jericho and so forth? This is a very legitimate question that needs always to be part of the discussion. In the descriptions that follow, I accept the identifications between the archaeological sites and the biblical place names where (for the moment at least) there seems to be agreement among the majority of authorities. Where there are still serious questions, I have adopted a more cautious approach and noted such uncertainties (Tell Beit Mirsim, for example, whose biblical name is still uncertain).

There is another caveat that needs to be carefully noted. Archaeological excavations are continuously occurring in Israel as well as other parts of the Middle East (especially Jordan: Tall Jalul, Petra, and Kirbet Iskander, for examples). In Israel, excavations are currently underway at Hazor, Megiddo, BethSaida and Kursi; Dor, Kadesh, Gath (Tell es-Safi) and Ramat Rachel, to cite just a few. No one really knows what will be discovered tomorrow, next week, next year, or ten or fifty years from now that will require significant modification, if not outright rejection, of "conclusions" held to be all but certain today. Thus, most, if not all, conclusions in this study should be held with a certain amount of tentativeness.

A note on the bibliography

The publications on the archaeological/biblical histories of the sites discussed in this book defy logic. They appear in a wide range of forms including journals, technical and popular, in dictionary and encyclopaedia articles and, of course, whole books. The primary sources for any excavation are always the field publications by the excavator(s). However, all too often the original excavator has died before final publications have been published (three major twentieth-century examples: Kathleen Kenyon, Jericho and Jerusalem; Joseph Callaway, 'Ai (et-Tell); and Yigal Shiloh, Jerusalem). In some instances (Jerusalem, for one), so much has been published it is unlikely that anyone has the time or motivation to read it all. It is also impractical, if not nearly impossible, to list all relevant publications. (The complete listing of all publications on Jerusalem, for example, would take a book in itself. In fact, *two* such volumes have been published on this city. See bibliography accompanying the entry on "Jerusalem.") Consequently, only highly selected bibliographical information is provided.

In addition to the *NEAEHL* and the *OEANE* mentioned in the Preface, the reader may also find entries in the *Anchor Bible Dictionary* helpful. All of these sources contain their own bibliographies and are a convenient place to start for more study. I have also avoided footnotes to make this book as readable as possible to the uninitiated. Whether that was a desirable action or not, the reader will have to judge.

Bibliography

Amiran, Ruth. "The Beginning of Urbanization in Canaan." In *Near Eastern Archaeology in the Twentieth Century: Essays in Honor of Nelson Glueck.* James A. Sanders, ed., Garden City, NY: Doubleday, 1970: 83–100.

Bonine, Michael E. "Cities of the Islamic Period." *OEANE 2.* Eric M. Meyers, ed., NY: Oxford University Press, 1997: 35–36.

Borowski, Oded. "The Biblical Identity of Tell Halif." *BA* 51.1 (1988): 21–27.

—— *Daily Life in Ancient Israel.* Atlanta: Scholars Press, 2003.

Broshi, M. and I. Finkelstein. "The Population of Palestine in Iron Age II." *BASOR* 287 (1992): 47–60.

De Geus, C. H. J. *Towns in Ancient Israel and in the Southern Levant.* Peeters: Leuven, 2003.

Dever, W. G. "The Middle Bronze Age: The Zenith of the Urban Canaanite Era." *BA* September (1987): 149–177.

DeVries, LaMoine F. *Cities of the Biblical World.* Peabody, MA: Hendrickson Publications, 1997.

Finkelstein, Israel. "The Great Transformation: The 'Conquest' of the Highlands Frontiers and the Rise of the Territorial States." *ASHL:.* T. E. Levy, ed., NY: Facts on File 1995: 349–365, especially 354–356.

Freyne, Sean. "Cities of the Persian Period." *OEANE 2*. Eric M. Meyers, ed., NY: Oxford University Press, 1997: 29–34.

Frick, Frank S. *The City in Ancient Israel*. Missoula: Society of Biblical Literature, Dissertation Series, No. 36, 1977.

—— "Cities: An Overview." *OEANE 2*. Eric M. Meyers, ed., NY: Oxford University Press, 1997: 14–19.

Fritz, Volkmar. "Cities of the Bronze and Iron Ages." *OEANE* 2: 19–25.

Hammond, Mason. *The City in the Ancient World*. Cambridge, MA: Harvard University Press, 1972.

Herzog, Ze'ev. *Archaeology of the City. Urban Planning in Ancient Israel and Its Social Implications*. Tel Aviv: Tel Aviv Monograph Series, No. 13, 1997.

—— "Israelite City Planning Seen in the Light of the Beer-Sheba and Arad Excavations." *Expedition* 20 (1978): 38–43.

—— "Cities in the Levant." *ABD* 1: 1032–1042.

Kempinski, Aharon. *The Rise of an Urban Culture: The Urbanization of Palestine in the Early Bronze Age*. Jerusalem: Israel Exploration Society, 1978.

King, Philip J. and Lawrence E. Stager. *Life in Biblical Israel. Library of Ancient Israel*. Louisville: Westminster John Knox Press, 2001.

Meyers, Carol. "Engendering Syro-Palestinian Archaeology: Reasons and Resources." *NEA* 66.4 (2003): 185–197.

Mithen, Steven. *After the Ice: A Global History, 20,000–5000 BC*. Cambridge, MA: Harvard University Press, 2004.

Rohrbough, Richard L. "The City in the Second Testament." *Biblical Theology Bulletin* 21 (1991): 67–75.

Shiloh, Yigal. "Elements in the Development of Town Planning in the Israelite City." *IEJ* 28 (1978): 36–51.

—— "Cities of the Persian Period." *OEANE 2*. Eric M. Meyers, ed., NY: Oxford University Press, 1997: 25–29.

FIFTY
MAJOR CITIES
OF THE BIBLE

ACCO
CITY WITH A VIEW

Described as "one of the most prominent coastal cities in Canaan" (Dothan, *ABD* 1992: 50), the ruins of ancient Acco (also spelled "Akko") are located some eight miles north of the modern city of Haifa. The Arabic name of the site is Tell el-Fukhar ("ruin of potsherds"). During much of its long history, Acco was the largest city in the area – between thirty and fifty acres (Dothan, *NEAEHL* 1993, 1: 17). Rising some 115 feet above sea level, the tell provides a panoramic view of the Mediterranean Sea to the west. Today's visitors can easily miss this tell because the modern city of Acco is located west of the mound and runs up to the sea itself (the ancient tell is about half a mile from the coast). Furthermore, the Old City of Acco,

Figure 2 Tel Acco with excavation in progress.

with walls dating no later than the eighteenth century CE, looks far more like an ancient city than the abandoned tell (see Figure 2, p. 9). Nevertheless, from around 2000 BCE down to Ottoman times (sixteenth–early twentieth centuries CE) the tell was occupied. However, much of the occupational details, especially from the Hellenistic period onwards, have been lost to robbery, cultivation, and perhaps natural erosion when the sea level was higher than it is today.

The importance of Acco is belied by the fact that the city is mentioned only once in the Bible (Judg. 1: 31; however, in some Greek texts of Joshua 19: 30, "Acco" appears instead of "Ummah"). While the biblical writers may have felt no need to refer to the city (it is doubtful that Acco was ever controlled by Israel), Egyptian texts mention it as early as the Execration Texts dating to the nineteenth–eighteenth century BCE. The city is also among the sites claimed to have been conquered by Thutmose III in the fifteenth century. In the famous Tel el-Amarna letters of the early fourteenth century BCE, Acco appears at least thirteen times (*ANET*, 1969: 484, 485, 487). The city will suffer destruction at least one more time by the Egyptians in the thirteenth century BCE, or so claimed Ramses II.

Following the Egyptians, the Assyrians had their turn, attaching and destroying the city in both the eighth and seventh centuries BCE. While there is little archaeological evidence of a Babylonian presence on the site, the Persians turned Acco into an administrative center. Alexander the Great conquered it in the fourth. Acco was prominent in the struggle between the Seleucids of Syria and Ptolemies of Egypt in the third–second centuries BCE. In fact, during this period, its name was changed from "Acco" to "Ptolemais." The latter was still its name when, centuries later, the Apostle Paul spent a day there (Acts 21: 7). Hellenistic (332–37 BCE), Roman (37 BCE–324 CE), and Byzantine (324–638 CE) remains were recovered in the excavations. In addition, occupational evidence for the Umayyad through the Ottoman periods was also discovered (seventh–early twentieth centuries CE). Thus, Acco, like **Jerusalem** and **Damascus**, is one of the oldest continuously occupied cities in the world. It can also "boast" of having been besieged by Napoleon in 1799.

While some biblical texts imply that the city may have been under Israelite control during the time of David and Solomon (see 2 Sam. 24: 7; 1 Kgs. 9: 11–13), there is no supportive archaeological evidence for such a claim. In fact, in a recent survey (conducted in 1993–1996) of Acco's surrounding rural countryside, the city was identified as a major urban center that supported the settlement patterns that existed during the Late Bronze Age, Iron Age II, and the Persian Periods (Lehmann, 2001). This lack of control by "Israel" may explain, partially, at least, why this important coastal city is mentioned only once in the Hebrew Bible.

Before 1973 only salvage work, including surveys and tomb excavations, had been carried out here. From 1973 until 1989, Moshe Dothan (Haifa University) directed twelve seasons of systematic excavations. The work was sponsored by Haifa University, the University of Marburg (Germany), the Israel Exploration Society and the Israel Department of Antiquities and Museums.

While evidence of a Late Chalcolithic–Early Bronze Age farming community was found on the southwestern part of the mound (pottery, pits, wall foundations), the first major fortified city was not built until over a thousand years later during the Middle Bronze Age. To this period belong a series of complicated defensive earthen ramparts, one above the other, and a "sea gate," discovered in 1978. Its name comes from the fact that the gate faced the Mediterranean. This gate, which was almost sixty feet long, consisted of two chambers and three pairs of asymmetric pilasters. Partially constructed of mud brick, the gate went through three stages of construction, all of which were dated to the Middle Bronze Age I (Dothan's II A). In the last stage, it was filled with sand and covered with clay, and made part of the city's defensive rampart. It was this filling that preserved the gate for thousands of years. The same fate befell the Middle Bronze Age mud brick gate at Tel Dan, discovered in 1979 (see p. 39). This gate, too, was filled in and incorporated into the city's defensive rampart. Thus, a long-standing controversy among archaeologists over whether or not rampart defensive fortifications were built in Canaan during the first part of the Middle Bronze Age should now be settled (other examples of similar Middle Bronze Age fortifications are known from such sites as Tel **Dan**, **Aphek**, and **Achziv**). While the Canaanite city seems to have declined by the end of the period, pottery remains clearly indicate that the city had contacts with the broader Mediterranean world.

During the Late Bronze Age (1550–1200 BCE), Acco seems to have been a thriving city with various supportive industries including a purple dye industry evidenced by a pit full of crushed murex shells. In the survey mentioned above, Acco was found to be a regional center during this time. This pattern changed during the Iron Age I (1200–1000 BCE), when disruptions in settlement patterns were evident. However, in the following Iron Age II and Persian Periods, the area was once more centered around Acco, which was the largest urban center in the region. According to a relief at Karnak (Egypt), the city gate of the Late Bronze Age was destroyed by Ramses II (thirteenth century BCE). However, the excavator failed to discover any Late Bronze Age fortifications.

Based on archaeological remains alone, the city entered a period of decline during Iron Age I and the beginning of the Iron Age II periods (twelfth–early ninth centuries BCE). The excavator concluded that the inhabitants of Acco during the early part of Iron Age I may have been the Sherden, identified as part of the "Sea Peoples." But more recent studies in ethnicity have shown that such identifications are simplistic, though the city's inhabitants may have been part of the general "Sea People" movement.

By the end of the eighth century BCE, Acco was once more a flourishing and regional center (Lehmann, 2001: 90ff.). According to Assyrian records, the city was attacked both by Sennacherib (701 BCE) and later by Ashurbanipal (mid-seventh century). The latter boasted that he "killed those inhabitants of Accho, who were not submissive, hanging their corpses on polls which I placed around the city" (*ANET*, 1969: 300).

What happened to this city immediately following the Assyrian period is not too clear archaeologically. In fact, there is little evidence of activity until the Persian occupation beginning in the fifth century BCE. During this time, Acco became once more an important administrative center and began to expand towards the sea. Evidence of its importance as a port city is seen in the Greek pottery reflecting trade with the Mediterranean region.

While the archaeological history of Acco reflects little that can be correlated with its mention in the Bible, its long occupational history, located on the northwestern border of Israel, is testimony to the cultural mix that was part of the world of the Israelites. It is one of the few cities of the biblical period (Jerusalem is another one) that is still very much alive today (although not on the ancient tell). It also serves as a prime example of a city that existed throughout the biblical period about which we would know very little were it not for the efforts of archaeologists.

Further reading

Arie, Kindler. "Akko, a City of Many Names." *BASOR* 231 (1978): 51–55.
Dothan, Moshe. "A Sign of Tanit from Tell 'Akko." *IEJ* 24 (1974): 44–49.

—— "Akko: Interim Excavation Report, First Season 1973/74." *BASOR* 224 (1976): 1–48.

—— "A Phoenician Inscription from 'Akko." *IEJ* 35 (1985): 81–94.

—— "Acco." *ABD*, Vol. 1. David Noel Freedman, ed., NY: Doubleday, 1992: 50–53.

Lehmann, Gunnar. "Phoenicians in Western Galilee: First Results of an Archaeological Survey in the Hinterland of Akko." *SAIA*. Amihai Mazar, ed., Sheffield: Sheffield Academic Press, 2001: 65–112.

Stern, Eliezer. "'Akko, the Old City." *Hadashot Arkeologiyot – Excavations and Surveys in Israel*. 109 (1999): 10★–13★.

ACHZIV

THE CITY OF CEMETERIES

Another important Bronze Age town hardly mentioned in the Bible is Achziv (also spelled with a 'b': Achzib). The tell is located on the Mediterranean coast about nine miles north of **Acco**. This town is mentioned only twice in the Hebrew Bible: once where it is allotted to the tribe of Asher (Josh. 19: 29), and again when it is announced that this tribe was unable to drive out the "Canaanites" who lived there (Judg. 1: 31). However, Achziv is mentioned in sources post-dating the biblical period (Josephus, *WAR* I. 257; Eusebius, *Onomasticon* XXX, 12), but the major archaeological remains date to the Bronze and Iron Ages.

During 1963–1964 excavations sponsored by the Oriental Institute of the University of Rome were conducted on the mound. Directed by Moshe W. Prausvitz, an eighteenth-century BCE city (Middle Bronze Age I/II) was discovered that was protected by an earthen rampart surrounded by a deep fosse (moat). Water springs feeding the moat created, for all practical purposes, an island. This Middle Bronze city was destroyed at the beginning of the Late Bronze Age. These architectural remains are very important in any attempt to understand the Middle Bronze Age culture that existed here. However, much attention has been focused on the incredible cemeteries discovered here. Salvage excavations of these burial sites began as early as 1941 and continued (with interruptions) for nearly 50 years. Four cemeteries have been identified: "Central," "Northern," "Eastern," and "Southern."

Achziv is an important ruin not only because the archaeological history of the site greatly supplements the sparse biblical references, but also because there was a flourishing city here during the heart of the "biblical period" (Iron Age II), when the town reached a size of some 20 acres. Achziv is an excellent example of how archaeologists have given us most of what we are likely to ever know about this place. Like Acco to the south, Achziv seems to have been an urban center for surrounding villages and hamlets.

Much work has focused on the four cemeteries, all of which contained burials that could be dated to the Iron Age. Only the "Central" and "Southern" ones contained remains from the Middle Bronze Age (a Middle Bronze Age II grave was found in the Southern cemetery in 1990). Evidence that these cemeteries were reused over long periods of time was found in the Eastern and Southern sites where the remains of an estimated 200–300 bodies were found in each. In the Eastern Cemetery, these remains were piled to the ceiling in a burial chamber. The excavator concluded that the cemeteries had been used by the same families over a period of several generations (tenth–seventh centuries BCE). Along with the human remains, the cemeteries contained rich deposits of grave goods, especially pottery vessels. Other goods consisted of bronze objects, clay figurines and, in some cases, stelae (especially in the Southern site). In addition, jars and kraters containing ashes of the deceased witness to the practice of cremation (Northern Cemetery) and, in one instance, a tophet (usually associated with child sacrifice), was discovered. These cemeteries were not just used for burials, however. There is evidence that cultic rituals of some nature also occurred here. This is especially true in the Northern Cemetery.

The grave goods indicate that Achziv was a prosperous Sidonian city with ties to the larger Mediterranean region. What kind of interaction, if any, existed between Achziv and the "Israelites" during the Iron Age II period is not clear. It is doubtful that Israel ever really had political control of this city on the Phoenician coast.

Further reading

Oren, Eliezer D. "The Pottery from the Achzib Defense System, Area D, 1963 and 1964 Seasons." *IEJ* 25 (1975): 211–225.

Prausnitz, M. W. "Israelite and Sidonian Burial Rites at Akhziv (*sic*)." In *Proceedings of the Fifth World Congress of Jewish Studies*. Jerusalem: Israel Exploration Society, 1972: 85–89.

—— "The Planning of the Middle Bronze Age Town of Achzib and Its Defences." *IEJ* (1975): 202–210.

'AI (ET-TELL)

IF ET-TELL IS "'AI", THE CONQUEST OF JOSHUA ISN'T

Few stories in the Bible are more dramatic than that told about the city of 'Ai in Joshua 7–8 ('Ai is mentioned in the Bible a total of 31 times. All but five of these references are in Josh. 8–12. The site is mentioned twice in Genesis (12: 8; 13: 3), and once each in Ezra 2: 28; Neh. 7: 32; and Jer. 49: 3). Biblical 'Ai is identified by most scholars with Khirbet et-Tell ("ruin of the tell") which is located about nine miles northeast of **Jerusalem**. The story of the battles between the Israelites and the citizens of 'Ai seems on the surface to be straightforward and matter-of-fact. After an initial humiliating defeat in which "about thirty-six" Israelites were killed (Josh. 7: 5), Joshua prepared and carried out a ruse (Josh. 8: 3ff.) that resulted in drawing the men of 'Ai out of the "city" where they were ambushed and slaughtered. In all, counting men and women, we are told that 12,000 people were killed (8: 25). The "city" was burned, and the body of its king, who had been hung, was cast into the "city" gate, implying that the "city" was fortified (Josh. 8: 24–29). The story of 'Ai is told within the larger context of the "conquest" of Canaan by the "Israelites," who after a "forty"-year wandering in the wilderness invaded Canaan from the Transjordan opposite **Jericho**. The destruction of 'Ai thus serves as a paradigm of "Holy War" reflecting the theology of the biblical writer(s).

The archaeological history of et-Tell, however, suggests a very different story. Though the British archaeologist, John Garstang, briefly dug at et-Tell in 1928, the major archaeological work conducted here was by J. Marquet-Krause (1906–1936) during three seasons from 1933 to 1935, and later by Joseph A. Callaway (1920–1988) in several seasons from 1964 to 1976. Both excavators concluded that et-Tell had two major periods of occupation: the Early Bronze Age (c.3100–2400 BCE) and Iron Age I (c.1220–1050 BCE). Of ten strata that were identified, eight belong to the Early Bronze Age.

Figure 3 et-Tell ('Ai) with remains of Iron Age I pillared building.

During most of its Early Bronze Age history, et-Tell was a large (*c*.27.5 acres) fortified city. Architectural remains from this period include cultic buildings, industrial remains and residential buildings. The Early Bronze Age phase of the city's history came to a violent end around 2400 BCE. Callaway believed that the Egyptians may have been responsible for this destruction.

The site was abandoned for almost 1200 years to around 1220 BCE when a small (*c*.6 acres) unwalled farming village was built here. While two phases of Iron Age I occupation were identified by Callaway, et-Tell remained a very small farming community during its entire Iron Age I history. The archaeological data from this period – remains of pillared houses (see Figure 3, p. 17); arches built into house walls; water cisterns; stone farming tools (such as querns, mortars, and pestles) as well as sheep and goat bones – clearly indicate that et-Tell was an agricultural/pastoralist community very similar to other Canaanite farming villages. The end of the Iron Age I village came around 1050 BCE when the site was abandoned. Houses were left standing and no evidence was found of burning as told in the biblical story. Callaway estimated the population at this time to be no more than 150 people, as opposed to the 12,000 mentioned in the Bible.

Because the archaeological history of et-Tell does not "fit" at all with the biblical story, various scenarios have been suggested. Many years ago, the famous W. F. Albright argued that a story of the destruction of Bethel, which did occur at the end of the Late Bronze Age, somehow got transferred to et-Tell. This seems most unlikely and a desperate attempt to reconcile archaeology and the Bible. Others have maintained that biblical 'Ai was someplace else, not et-Tell. In fact, Callaway, well aware of the problem, conducted soundings at the nearby sites of Khirbet Heiyan and Khirbet Khudriya but found nothing older than Late Hellenistic times. Still other sites, such as Khirbet el-Hay, a few miles southeast of et-Tell, have been suggested but must be rejected also on archaeological grounds. Furthermore, the geographical description of 'Ai in the Bible fits et-Tell better than any suggested alternative. In fact, in his comparison of the topography of et-Tell with the biblical description of 'Ai, Z. Zevit concluded that: "These topographical details reinforce the conclusion reached on general geographic considerations that et-Tell is to be identified with 'Ai. In fact, *they guarantee that the 'Ai story in the Bible was told about Khirbet et-Tell*" (emphasis mine; Zevit, 1985: 62).

Thus, though the identification of 'Ai with et-Tell has never been absolutely proven, I know of no real reasons to doubt the current archaeological identification. While the name "'Ai" (in the Hebrew

Bible the name is almost always preceded by a definite article, thus "The 'Ai") has traditionally been understood to be the Hebrew equivalent of the Arabic "et-Tell," meaning "the ruin" or "heap," Zevit (in the above mentioned article) has argued that this association is incorrect. He concluded that the initial letter of the word (an *'ayin* ' in Hebrew) was most likely pronounced as a *ghayin* in biblical times rendering the pronunciation of 'Ai as "*gay*" (meaning "extreme limit," or "utmost extremity"). Thus the name "'Ai" probably referred to some topographical feature of the tell (Zevit, 1985: 62).

When the archaeological history of 'Ai is added to additional data now known from other Late Bronze Age/Iron Age I sites in Israel, very serious questions regarding the historicity of the biblical story of the 'conquest' of Canaan by 'Israel' must be faced. While these questions cannot be addressed here, suffice it to say that the biblical story of 'Ai seems to have a lot more to do with the theological concerns of its author(s) than with the actual history of the site. Whether the biblical story teller inherited this narrative full-grown with all of its dramatic details, or greatly embellished a popular folk-tale, may never be known.

Further reading

Marquet-Krause, J. *Les Fouilles de'Ay (et-Tell), 1933–1935*. Paris: Bibliotheque Archeologique et Historique 45, 1949.

Callaway, Joseph A. *Pottery from the Tombs at 'Ai (et-Tell)*. London: Colt Archaeological Institute, Monograph Series 2, 1964.

—— "The 1964 'Ai (et-Tell) Excavations." *BASOR* 178 (1965): 23–40.

—— and M. B. Nicol. "A Sounding at Khirbet Haiyan." *BASOR* 183 (1966) 12–19.

—— "New Evidence on the Conquest of 'Ai." *JBL* 87 (1968): 312–320.

—— "The 1966 'Ai (et-Tell) Excavations." *BASOR* 196 (1969): 2–16.

—— "The 1968–1969 'Ai (et-Tell) Excavations." *BASOR* 198 (1970): 7–31.

—— *The Early Bronze Age Sanctuary at 'Ai (et-Tell)*. London: Colt Archaeological Institute, 1972.

—— and Kermit Schoonover. "The Early Bronze Citadel at 'Ai (et-Tell)." *BASOR* 207 (1972): 41–53.

—— *The Early Bronze Age Citadel and Lower City at 'Ai (et-Tell): A Report of the Joint Archaeological Excavations to 'Ai (et-Tell) 2*. Cambridge, MA: ASOR Excavations Reports, 1980.

Zevit, Ziony. "The Problem of 'Ai: New theory rejects the battle as described in Bible but explains how story evolved." *BAR* 11.2 (1985): 58–69.

APHEK (RAS EL-AIN)
THE CITY OF PALACES

The name "Aphek" ("riverbed") appears eight times in the Bible but refers to several different places (1 Kgs. 20: 26–30 refers to an "Aphek" near Syria, while Josh. 19: 29–30 lists an "Aphek" in the tribal territory of Asher; in Josh. 13: 4, "Aphek" is in Lebanon). The "Aphek" described in this chapter is sometimes called "Aphek of Sharon" and is located some four miles east of Tel Aviv, close to the modern town of Petah Tikva (see Figure 4). Its importance in antiquity was precisely its location because the site guarded a major crossroads in Israel. The tell is about thirty acres in size and is today universally identified with Ras el-Ain.

Figure 4 Aphek with Crusader fort.

Aphek is first mentioned in the Egyptian Execration Texts of the nineteenth–eighteenth centuries BCE (*ANET*, 1969: 329), and is on the topographical list of Thutmose III (fifteenth century BCE). In fact, it is the description of the location of the city on this latter list that convinced earlier biblical historians that Aphek is to be identified with Ras el-Ain. The city is also mentioned in numerous texts dating from the seventh century BCE and later. In the Bible, this Aphek is mentioned only three times (Josh. 12: 18; 1 Sam. 4: 1; 29: 1). In the Joshua text, Aphek is listed among the cities conquered by Joshua during the "Conquest." However, there is a textual problem with this reading. In the Hebrew Bible the text reads: "the king of Aphek one, the king of Lasharon one." The Septuagint (the Greek Bible), on the other hand, reads "Aphek of the Sharon one." The Samuel passages clearly indicate that early in the history of "Israel," Aphek was under the control of the Philistines. It was used by them as a staging ground for preparation for a war against Israel (1 Sam. 4: 1), and later, for an attack on **Jezreel** (1 Sam. 29: 1).

Archaeological interest in Tell Ras el-Ain dates as early as 1923 when W. F. Albright conducted a survey of the mound, but the first excavation was not until 1935–1936 when J. Ory dug on the north side of the tell. In 1961, Abraham Eitan excavated along the south-eastern foot of the mound. Based on his findings, he concluded that the site was inhabited during the Early Bronze Age I, the Middle Bronze Age I (called Middle Bronze Age II by the excavator) and the Hellenistic, Roman, and Byzantine periods. From the Roman period, Ory discovered a mausoleum which was used for 150–200 years before being destroyed in the late third or early fourth century CE.

The first systematic excavation of Aphek would be left to Moshe Kochavi of Tel Aviv University. Beginning in 1972, and lasting thirteen seasons down to 1985, Kochavi and his team opened eight areas and showed archaeologically that Ras el-Ain was occupied almost continuously for 5,000 years, beginning with the Early Bronze Age I period (*c.*3300–3000 BCE; pottery from the preceding Chalco-lithic period, fifth–fourth millennium BCE, was found on the site, but no architectural remains). During the Early Bronze Age II period (*c.*3000–2700 BCE) the city, typical of other Early Bronze Age cities, was walled and enclosed nearly 30 acres. It is one of the earliest walled cities known in Israel. The Early Bronze Age city was followed by a gap in occupation which lasted for some 300 years (*c.*2300–2000 BCE).

Kochavi distinguished six Middle Bronze Age phases (or "stages"), the second of which witnessed the zenith of the material culture of

Aphek. Remains from this time were found scattered over the entire mound and include what the excavator identified as three "palaces," the last of which enclosed an area of some 43,000 square feet. Aphek was a major fortified Canaanite city at this time, witnessed by both the archaeological remains and its appearance in the Execration Texts. In the latter part of the Middle Bronze Age the city began to decline until its violent destruction in the middle of the sixteenth century BCE, perhaps by the Egyptians.

Two phases of occupation during the Late Bronze Age were found. The first one, dating to the fifteenth–fourteenth centuries BCE, included the remains of yet another "palace". The last phase (thirteenth–twelfth century BCE) also included significant material remains including "palace" VI, identified as an Egyptian governor's house. This Late Bronze Age city was violently destroyed sometime during the thirteenth century, though by whom is not known. The excavator suggested the aggressors my have belonged to one of the groups making up the so-called "Sea Peoples" who were entering the area at this time.

The presence of so many "palaces," during both the Middle and Late Bronze Ages indicates that control of towns such as Aphek was no longer under the religious elite (which would be indicated by the remains of large temples, as is the case from Early Bronze Age remains), but the politically powerful.

One of the most significant discoveries from the Late Bronze Age is a corpus of textual remains. Among these is the only known trilingual text (written in Akkadian, Sumerian, and Canaanite) from Israel, as well a bilingual text written in Sumerian and Akkadian (although some have suggested that the second language may be Canaanite). Another important document is an entire letter, written in Akkadian, from the city of Ugarit to the Egyptian governor of Aphek named "Hoya." This letter was discovered in the destruction debris of the governor's house and helped date the destruction to the thirteenth century. Other Late Bronze Age discoveries include tombs and two well-preserved winepresses.

Most of the significant Iron Age I remains came from the excavator's Area-X. Here two domestic areas were uncovered. The houses were built square-shaped, a technique found elsewhere in Israel only at Tell Abu Hawam, which was an ancient harbor on Haifa Bay. The existence of a local fishing industry at Aphek is likely, given the lead weights and fishing hooks recovered from this period (twelfth century). The ethnic identity of these inhabitants is unknown, but once more the "Sea Peoples" are suspected.

The identity of the next Iron Age I phase (eleventh century BCE) inhabitants is believed to have been the Philistines. Though few architectural remains were found, much characteristic Philistine pottery was retrieved along with "Ashdoda"-type statuettes. Some pits dated to this time were also found. An inscription written in an unknown language (Philistine?) belongs to this period.

From the tenth century are remains of four-room houses, identified as "Israelite." This town suffered a violent destruction toward the end of this century. Pharaoh Shishak of Egypt is the usual culprit suspected of carrying out the destruction. Kochavi suggested that the inhabitants of the town during this time were Israelites who settled here when David became king. Very few material remains could be dated to the Iron Age II. Part of the problem is the extent of the destruction of the mound due to the fortress built here in the sixteenth century CE by the Ottomans (see Figure 4, p. 20).

No remains from the Persian period were found, though some 850 feet to the north of the mound, a "farmhouse" was dated to this period. However, there were extensive Hellenistic remains indicating that during this time the city comprised a significant settlement. Three occupational phases were differentiated, the last one containing a fortress. Kochavi argued that it is this Hellenistic city that should be identified with the "Pegae" mentioned in the literature from this period and not nearby Fejja ("the springs"), whose excavation has turned up no Hellenistic remains.

Herod the Great is credited with re-building the site, beginning in 9 BCE. However, he changed the name of the town to "Antipatris," in honor of his father. This Roman city sported a cardo (30 feet wide) lined with shops and exceeded the size of the Hellenistic city. Antipatris is mentioned only once in the New Testament, in relation to the life of Paul (Acts 23: 31). This Early Roman city was destroyed by Cestius Gallus and Vespasian. During the Late Roman period, the city prospered again only to be destroyed by an earthquake usually dated to the last half of the fourth century CE. This Late Roman city is mentioned many times in the two important Jewish writings: the Mishnah and the Talmud.

While some remains were found dating to the Byzantine and Ummayad (seventh–eighth CE) periods, the most significant construction on the mound following the Roman era was built in the sixteenth century by the Turkish Sultan, Selim II. In 1571 Selim built yet another fortress on top of the mound. It is called in Turkish, *pinar bashi*, ("fountain-head"). The walls of this fort enclosed the ancient acropolis and it was in use for nearly 200 years. The remains of this structure are still visible today (see Figure 4, p. 20). Unfortunately, during its construction, considerable damage was done to earlier strata.

The ancient mound of Aphek contains some 5,000 years of human activity. Located on one of the main crossroads of ancient Israel, major cities existed here from the Early Bronze Age through the Roman era. During other times it served more as a fort or way-station. The primary reason for its importance was, with little doubt, its location, which enabled whoever controlled it to protect the crossroads associated with it. However, the sparse remains from the Iron Age II period leaves unclear any "Israelite" associations with this place.

Further reading

Feldman, Steven. "Return to Aphek." *BAR* 28.5 (2002): 52–59.

Kochavi, Moshe. *Aphek-Antipatris 1: Excavation of Areas A and B. The 1972–1976 Seasons*. Moshe Kochavi, Pirhiyah Beck and Esther Yadin, eds. Monograph Series of the Sonia and Marco Nadler Institute of Archaeology, Number 19. Tel Aviv: Sonia and Marco Nadler Institute of Archaeology, Tel Aviv University, 2000.

—— "The History and Archaeology of Aphek – Antipatris: Biblical City in the Sharon Plain." *BA* 44 Spr. (1981): 75–86.

—— "Tell Aphek (Ras el-Ain)." *Review Biblique.* Jan. (1976): 80–87.

ARAD

FROM ANCIENT CANAANITE CITY TO JUDEAN "TEMPLE"

Few sites are more important for understanding the Early Bronze Age in the southern part of Israel than Tell Arad. Located some 18.5 miles northeast of **Beersheba** in what is called the "Negev," the city witnessed its zenith during the Early Bronze Age II period. Two separate excavations have been conducted on the site. The first one, directed by Ruth Amiran, focused specifically on the Early Bronze Age city and consisted of 18 seasons 1962–1984. The second excavation was directed by Y. Aharoni (1919–1976) and concentrated on the Iron Age II fortress that was built on the northeastern side of

Figure 5 Arad: Early Bronze Age wall and tower with Iron Age fortress in background.

the site (see Figure 5, p. 25). This archaeological phase took place between 1962 and 1965, and again in 1967. Z. Herzog, on behalf of the Institute of Archaeology of Tel Aviv University, directed a small-scale excavation on the Iron Age site in 1976 and 1977.

The identification of Tell Arad with biblical Arad has been confirmed by most authorities and will be assumed secure for the discussion that follows. Part of the supporting evidence for this identification is the name, "Arad," which was found written several times on a pottery sherd. In the Bible, Arad is mentioned only four times (Num. 21: 1; 33: 40; Josh. 12: 14; Judg. 1: 16). An important non-biblical reference to the site is believed to be on Pharaoh Shishak's campaign list dated to the fifth year of King Rehoboam (c.925/6 BCE; see 1 Kgs. 14: 25).

R. Amiran identified five strata of occupation dating from the Chalcolithic through the Early Bronze II (c.4000–2650 BCE). The most important of these is Stratum II when the urbanization of the site reached its pinnacle. This phase of the city's life is estimated to have lasted some 150 years (c.2800–2650 BCE). During this time the city was protected by a wall whose circumference stretched for some 4,000 feet. This massive structure measured between 6.5 and 8 feet thick and is estimated to have stood 13–16 feet high (see Figure 5, p. 25). Protected by an estimated 35–40 towers, 11 of which were excavated, the city was accessed by two major gates as well as two postern gates. A "postern" gate is a narrow opening in a city wall that allowed for individual passage but could be easily blocked up during a time of outside threat.

Early Bronze II Arad was a well-planned city indicative of a central-ized government of some sort. In addition to a domestic quarter, Amiran uncovered what she believed to be the remains of a palace, suggesting the presence of a king or "priest-king" since she also found the remains of a sacred area with temples near by. Amiran also excav-ated a large open pool area (over 10,000 square feet) which she identified as a water reservoir designed to collect rain water.

The people who lived at Arad during this period enjoyed a diversified economy that included agriculture (charred grain, seeds of various species, sickle blades), animal husbandry (sheep, goats, ass, and cattle bones), and crafts of various types (spindle whorls, bone needles and shuttles, beads, shells, copper and flint drills and awls). The ceramic repertoire and copper items suggested trade with both the peoples to the north and the Sinai and Egypt to the south and southwest.

Some of the most interesting finds came from the "sacred area." Among these is what has been identified as a *massebah* (sacred stone pillar; such pillars are mentioned many times in the Hebrew Bible) and a large altar with an adjacent basin. Animal figurines made from stone or clay were also found. A broken stela made from chalk contained two human figurines: one standing, the other lying down. Curiously their heads were represented by what looks like either a plant of some sort or an ear of grain. All of these finds suggested to the excavator that the people of Arad engaged in some type of nature worship, perhaps associated with the myth of the god Tammuz so well known from the ancient Near East.

This major Negev urban center came to an end around 2,700 BCE, either from environmental and/or political causes. Following a brief use by "squatters," the site was abandoned for some 1500 years until the eleventh century BCE. The importance of Arad for understanding the Early Bronze Age in general, as well as the daily lives of the people who lived there, is difficult to over-estimate. The well-preserved state of so many of the remains provides an archaeological "snap shot" of everyday life as well as the degree of urban sophistication attained by its inhabitants.

After a 1500-year gap in occupation, the northeastern hill of the site was rebuilt beginning in the eleventh century BCE. To investigate this development, a separate excavation was conducted here in the 1960s by A. Aharoni, mentioned above. Some of his conclusions, such as the date of the construction and use of the Iron Age "temple," have been modified by the later efforts of Z. Herzog. Herzog conducted further archaeological investigation on the site between 1976 and 1977 and re-examined, during 1995–1996, all of the stratigraphical evidence available from the excavations. Based on his study, he concluded that the temple existed during two periods only, the tenth and ninth strata, and not some four or five strata as originally thought. The dates of strata ten and nine are not certain, however, due to similarities in the pottery remains. What seems clear is that the temple was first constructed in either the tenth or ninth century BCE and abandoned towards the end of the eighth. The temple was found inside a fortress compound.

In all, twelve strata were recognized and were dated from the twelfth–eleventh century BCE (Str. XII) to a Bedouin cemetery (Str. I). The latter was used for hundreds of years (thirteenth–nineteenth centuries CE). Herzog disputed a previous claim that in the first period of occupation, Stratum 12, a "Kenite" high place was built here. In his view, this conclusion reflects the older "biblical archaeology" approach that has now been discredited (see Herzog's discussion *SAIA*, 2001: 171–174). The "Fortress" was basically square (164 × 164 feet) and showed evidence of having been destroyed several times: the first time by Pharaoh Shishak around 926 BCE. The structure is believed to have served not only military but also administrative, commercial, and religious functions. The latter two can be seen especially in the many ostraca discovered and in the so-called "temple" remains.

For students of the Bible, one of the most interesting discoveries at Arad is a tripartite construction that has been identified as a temple of YHWH, the god of Israel. If this interpretation is correct, and most authorities seem to concur, it may be the only known YHWH temple ever discovered (however, more recent discoveries at Beersheba and **Dan** may be from such "temples"). Located in the northwest corner of the fortress, the structure contained a courtyard measuring some 33 × 33 feet, a holy place (called the *hekal*) and a *debir*, the "Holy of Holies." This latter element consisted of a niche in the back of the building which measured 6 × 7 feet (1.80 × 1.10 m). At the entrance to the *debir* were two limestone altars. In the back of the niche was a *massebah* or sacred pillar. Aharoni claimed that two other *massebot* (pl.) were found in later walls, indicating that originally more than one deity was worshipped here. However, Herzog concluded that these stones were for constructional purposes only and did not have a religious function (2001: 166). Furthermore, he also concluded that the shape of the Arad temple was not like that of the "Solomonic" temple described in the Bible (1 Kgs. 6). Finally, according to Herzog, the Arad temple was not destroyed by Josiah in the last half of the seventh century BCE as previously claimed, but was most likely abandoned during the reign of Hezekiah (*c*.715 BCE).

Another important discovery from Arad are the dozens of ostraca (inscribed pot sherds) coming from different periods. Some 223 were found, 131 of them written in Hebrew. There are 85 written in Aramaic and dated to the Persian period (fifth–fourth centuries BCE). Two are in Greek (perhaps from the Roman period), and five are written in Arabic and are thought to date to the ninth century CE. While the stratigraphy of the site is still not totally clear, the Hebrew inscriptions are assigned to Strata XI (tenth century BCE) through VI (sixth century BCE). Several of these ostraca contain messages sent to a man named "Elyashib," the commander of the fort during its last days of existence (early sixth century). Most are orders to provide food to a group of people identified as the "Kittim," believed to be Greek or Cypriot mercenaries fighting for Judah. In fact, many of these ostraca have been dated precisely to the invasion of Judah by the Babylonians under Nebuchadnezzar around 597 BCE. Three seals or stamps from this period bearing the name of Elyashib were also found. This collection of inscriptions is one of the largest ever found dating to Iron Age II. The ostracon with the name of "Arad" written several times has already been mentioned.

Because this Iron Age II fortress at Arad existed throughout most of Judah's history (with relatively short periods of interruption), the discoveries here give archaeologists and biblical historians an excellent opportunity to study many aspects of Judean daily life that occurred in the context of a biblical town whose primary function seems to have been military in nature.

Further reading

(Note: There are many publications on various aspects of the Arad excavations. The following all contain their own bibliographies and can lead the interested reader to many other publications.)

Aharoni, Yohanan. "Arad: Its Inscriptions and Temple." *BA* 31.1 (1968): 2–32.

—— and J. Naveh. *Arad Inscriptions*. Jerusalem: Israel Exploration Society, 1981.

Amiran, Ruth and Ornit Ilan. *Early Arad I: The Chalcolithic Settlement and Early Bronze Age City, First–Fifth Seasons of Excavations, 1962–1966*. Jerusalem: Israel Exploration Society, 1978.

Amiran, Ruth, Ornit Ilan, and M. Sebbane. *Early Arad II: The Chalcolithic and Early Bronze IB Settlements and the Early Bronze II City – Architecture and Town Planning; Sixth to Eighteenth Seasons of Excavations, 1971–1978, 1980–1984*. Jerusalem: Israel Exploration Society, 1996.

——, ——, and ——. *Early Arad III: Finds of the Sixth–Eighteenth Seasons, 1971–1978; 1980–1984*. Jerusalem: Israel Exploration Society, forthcoming.

Herzog, Ze'ev. "The Date of the Temple at Arad: Reassessment of the Stratigraphy and the Implications for the History of Religion in Judah." in *SAIA*. Amihai Mazar, ed., Sheffield: Sheffield Academic Press, 2001: 156–178.

——, M. Aharoni, A. F. Rainey, and S. Moshkovitz. "The Israelite Fortress at Arad." *BASOR* 254 (1984): 1–34.

AROER (IN JUDAH)
WHERE DID DAVID REALLY GO?

The name "Aroer" is thought to mean something like "crest of a mountain," or even to refer to the "juniper" plant. Thus it is a common name in the Bible and refers to three or four different places, all but one located east of the Jordan River. This short chapter is concerned with the "Aroer" west of the Jordan which is a five acre site located in the northern Negev about 14 miles southeast of **Beersheba** (see Figure 6). In the Masoretic Text (Hebrew) the town is mentioned only once in context of the activities of David (1 Sam. 30: 28). In the Septuagint (the Greek Bible) there may also be a reference to the place in Joshua 15: 22.

In 1838 Edward Robinson identified this tell as biblical Aroer. However, archaeological exposure of the site did not occur until

Figure 6 View east from Aroer with ruins in the foreground.

1975–1982. The excavations were conducted by A. Biran of the Nelson Glueck School of Biblical Archaeology of the Hebrew Union College Jewish Institute of Religion, Jerusalem, and R. Cohen of the Israel Antiquities Authority. Their work failed to find any archaeological evidence that the site was occupied any earlier than the late eighth–early seventh century BCE. Consequently, Aroer can not be a town existing during the presumed time of David (first half of the tenth century BCE).

Overall, four strata were identified: three from the Late Iron Age and one from the Early Roman (Herodian) period. The excavators concluded that the two major periods of occupation were the late seventh–early sixth century phase (Str. II), and the first century BCE to the first century CE (Str. I). Biran also speculated that the town may have been founded by an influx of refugees from Samaria who fled the Assyrian onslaught of the late eighth century. However, there is some ambiguity over whether or not the initial occupation of the place occurred during the reign of the Judean king, Hezekiah, or his son Manasseh.

In any case, Edomite pottery was found in abundance from this period indicating that Aroer's residents had contacts with this Transjordanian neighbor to the southeast. In fact, Aroer was probably a designated stop-over for traders who made their way back-and-forth from Edom to the Mediterranean coast.

Since Aroer has no tenth century BCE remains, Biran suggested that perhaps the biblical town should be identified with a site some one-and-a-half miles north of Aroer known as Tell Esdar. Esdar was excavated in 1963–1964 by Moshe Kochavi and remains dating to the late tenth century were found. However, according to Kochavi, the remains reflect little more than the existence of a farmstead during this time.

All of this discussion points to the difficulty often encountered when an attempt is made to correlate archaeological data with biblical stories. Even if Aroer had contained tenth-century material, the problem would still exist. But this does not detract from the archaeological significance of the site. D. Ilan, in his article on Aroer published in the *OEANE*, suggested three major contributions that Biran's and Cohen's excavation have made to the field:

1 The excavation of Aroer has helped to refine our understanding of three discrete Iron Age periods, especially so due to the splendid pottery assemblages recovered from these periods.

2   The results of the excavation have also clarified the political picture of the Negev during this time, especially between Judahite, Edomite and Assyrian factions.

3   The rich artifactual remains, especially the pottery, have a very practical utility of helping to clarify the history of other sites containing poorer ceramic material.

The Iron Age life of the town was brought to a close by the Babylonians in 587/586 BCE. It then lay dormant for some 500 years before being re-occupied sometime during the first century BCE. From this latter period, a large (38 × 35 feet) building was discovered containing an underground storage facility. The excavator interpreted it as a Herodian fortress. Supporting this interpretation are two "Revolt-era" coins. One bears the inscription: "for the freedom of Zion."

Further reading

Biran, Avraham. "'And David Sent Spoils . . . to the Elders in Aroer' (1 Sam. 30: 26–28): Excavations Bring Life to Ancient Negev Fortress but Find no Remains of David's Time." *BAR* 9.2 (1983): 28–37.

—— "Aroer (in Judah)." *NEAEHL* 1. Ephraim Stern, ed. Jerusalem: Simon & Schuster, 1993: 89–92.

Feldman, Steven. "Return to Aroer: a Trip Through the Ages with the Ageless Avraham Biran." *BAR* 28.1 (2002): 50–54.

ASHDOD

HOME OF THE "ASHDODA"

One of the five Philistine cities mentioned in the Hebrew Bible (the other four are **Ashkelon, Ekron, Gath,** and Gaza: see Josh. 13: 3; on the Philistines themselves see Appendix A), Ashdod is located about ten miles north of Ashkelon and some two miles inland from the Mediterranean Sea. By ancient standards, Ashdod was a fairly large site, covering over 70 acres (the exact dimensions of the mound are unknown due to cultivation of local fields and modern construction). The city is mentioned 19 times in the Bible, with most references coming from the books of Joshua (11: 22; 13: 3; 15: 46, 47) and 1 Samuel (5: 1, 3, 5, 7; 16: 17). In Joshua (15: 47) we are told that Ashdod, along with "its towns and villages," were given to Judah. However, both the date and the historical significance of this text are disputed. The latest biblical reference to the city is a derogatory comment found in Zechariah 9: 6, where the inhabitants of Ashdod are referred to as a "mongrel people."

Perhaps the most important biblical story about Ashdod is found in 1 Samuel regarding the capture of the "Ark of God," and the resulting consequences for the Philistines (1 Sam. 5–6). Somewhat puzzling, the Chronicler mentions a tradition not found in the Book of Kings recounting how Uzziah, the eighth century BCE king of Judah, destroyed the "wall" of Ashdod. Whether this means that Ashdod at this time was under the control of Judah is not clear. Other biblical references to the city are found in the prophetic books of Amos (1: 8), Isaiah (20: 1) and Jeremiah (25: 20).

Ashdod is well-documented outside of the Bible, mentioned for the first time in a Ugaritic text dating to the Late Bronze Age II. This text describes a merchant who bought a large amount (2,000 shekels in weight!) of purple wool at Ashdod, indicating that the city was a textile center. The city is also mentioned in Assyrian texts from the time of Sargon (722–701 BCE) down to the time of Ashurbanipal

Figure 7 The "Ashdoda."

(668–633 BCE; *ANET*, 1969: 284, 287–288, 291, 294). Nebuch-adnezzar II (605–562 BCE), the Babylonian king, also claimed to have attacked Ashdod (*ANET*, 1969: 308). Such references indicate that throughout most of Iron Age II, Ashdod, along with other Philistine cities, was a viable and politically important city.

The archaeological excavation of Ashdod began in 1962 under the direction of Moshe Dothan, and continued, off and on, until 1972. In addition to the Israel Antiquities Authority (then named the Israel Department of Antiquities and Museums), the project was also sup-ported by Pittsburgh Theological Seminary during the 1962, 1963, and 1965 seasons. In all, Dothan identified 23 strata of occupation ranging from the Middle Bronze Age II C (seventeenth–sixteenth century BCE) down to the Byzantine Period (fourth–fifth centuries CE).

The first fortified city, consisting of walls, a rampart and a two-entryway gate, was built during Middle Bronze Age III. However, from an archaeological perspective, the main periods of occupation were during the Late Bronze and Iron Ages. In particular, Strata

XII–XI (twelfth century BCE) represent the major Philistine period. Among other things, Philistine presence was indicated by the distinctive Bichrome Ware recovered from the site. A unique discovery belonging to this phase of occupation is a small terracotta female figurine seated on a table or stool. The excavator interpreted the object as representing a Philistine goddess of a type known as the "Mycenaean Great Mother" and nicknamed it the "Ashdoda" (see Figure 7, p. 34). Tourists can now view this remarkable object in the Israel Museum in Jerusalem. From the same occupational period belong two seals containing what have been identified as examples of "Philistine" writing, which still have not been deciphered.

Following this important Philistine phase, the political fortunes of Ashdod seem to have rested with Judean and Assyrian aggressiveness. Strata IX–VI are dated to Iron Age II and associated with this period is a new four-entryway gate traditionally compared with similar gates from **Hazor**, **Megiddo**, and **Gezer**. However, questions regarding the dates of their constructions and their implications for any "United Monarchy" have been at the center of a major discussion between various archaeologists and biblical historians. Another significant discovery from Iron Age II Ashdod are the remains of a temple (Str. VIII) in which were found many cult objects including animal and human figurines. Libation vessels were also recovered. Discoveries such as inscribed weights, a *lmlk* stamped jar handle, and Hebrew inscriptions indicate that the citizens of Ashdod had contact (trade?) with Judah during Iron Age II.

However, there was no evidence to support the biblical claim that early in the eighth century BCE, Uzziah destroyed the "wall" of Ashdod (2 Chron. 26: 6). On the other hand, a major destruction did occur towards the end of the century (712 BCE, according to Dothan) credited to the Assyrians under Sargon II. Part of the archaeological evidence for this destruction are three fragments of a stela (an ancient "historical marker") of Sargon. A rather horrific discovery belonging to the same destruction level are the skeletal remains of over 3,000 people, suggesting a massacre by the Assyrians.

While evidence of later occupation was uncovered, including remains from the Byzantine period, after the Persian phase (Str. V), Ashdod entered a time of steady decline from which it never recovered. In the excavator's words: "Ashdod, which for two thousand years had been the capital of a kingdom, a province, and an independent city, lost its importance in the Byzantine period and never regained its previous splendor" (Dothan, *NEAEHL* 1: 102).

Further reading

Dothan, Moshe. *Ashdod II–III: The Second and Third Seasons of Excavations (1963, 1965)*. *'Atiqot 9–10*. Jerusalem: Department of Antiquities, 1971.

—— and David Noel Freedman. *Ashdod I: The First Season of Excavation (1962)*. *'Atiqot 7*. Jerusalem: Department of Antiquities, 1967.

—— and Yosef Porath. *Ashdod IV: Excavations of Area M*. *'Atiqot 15*. Jerusalem: Department of Antiquities, 1982.

—— *Ashdod V: Excavations of Area G, the Fourth–Sixth Seasons of Excavations (1968–1970)*. *'Atiqot 23*. Jerusalem: Department of Antiquities, 1993.

Ussishkin, David. "Notes on Megiddo, Gezer, Ashdod, and Tel Batash in the Tenth to Ninth Centuries BCE." *BASOR* 227–278 (1990): 71–91.

ASHKELON

HOME OF THE MIDDLE BRONZE AGE SILVER CALF AND A PERSIAN DOG CEMETERY

The ruins of ancient Ashkelon lie on the Mediterranean coast some 35 miles south of modern Tel Aviv and about 18 miles west of Tell **Lachish** (see Figure 8, p. 38). The name, "Ashkelon," has been interpreted to mean "to weigh," from which the Hebrew word, *shekel*, comes. In antiquity the region was apparently famous for producing a variety of onion, which is preserved in the modern word, *scallion*, which was derived ultimately from *Ascalon*.

Occupational history

The earliest occupational debris go back thousands of years to the Neolithic period (*c*.8000–4200 BCE), but the first major city built on the site dates from the Early Bronze Age (3300–2200 BCE). The city at this time is believed to have served both as a port city as well as an overland trade crossroads. After an occupational hiatus at the end of the third millennium BCE (*c*.2200–2000 BCE), a large fortified Canaanite city was constructed here. The massive rampart wall enclosed some 150 acres and was entered through a gate that contained the oldest monumental arch yet discovered in the Near East (see Figure 8, p. 38 and Figure 9, p. 39). The only other Canaanite city to rival the size of Ashkelon at this time was **Hazor**, located north of the lake of Galilee, which was some 200 acres in size.

One of the most sensational discoveries dated to this period is a small (*c*.4″ × 4.5″) silver-coated calf found in 1990 in a room cut into the rampart material. This object probably represented the Canaanite god, El, or Baʿal, and later the Israelite god, YHWH. This period of the site's history was brought to an end by the Egyptians around 1550 BCE.

Egyptian influence on, if not control of, Ashkelon persisted throughout the Late Bronze Age. Texts from this period indicate that

Figure 8 Ashkelon from the northwest.

a temple to the Egyptian god, Ptah, was in use then. An important discovery dated to the beginning of the Late Bronze Age (c.1500 BCE) is the grave of a young woman found in a mud-brick-lined vault. Among the grave offerings are Egyptian scarabs, toggle pins and ceramic vessels. It is not yet clear from excavations if the city from this period was fortified.

From the first half of the twelfth century BCE (c.1180), the city was occupied by the famous Philistines, who would continue to inhabit it until its destruction by the Babylonians in 604 BCE. The contribution of the current excavations to Philistine history should be enormous. Already much has been recovered relevant to their foodstuffs, ceramics, industries, architecture, and even perhaps their language.

One of the richest archaeological periods preserved at Ashkelon is the Persian (c.540–300 BCE). Evidence of their presence was found in deposits up to nine feet thick in some places. Several phases of occupation were identified with many interesting discoveries. None was more surprising and puzzling than that of dog burials. Hundreds of dog graves were found dating to this period. Over 60 percent of the graves contained the remains of puppies only a few weeks old. Since each burial was interpreted to be a singular event, it would appear that all of the dogs died from natural causes, especially since no grave markers were found nor were any goods buried with the animals. These factors militate against the excavator's conclusion that the burials had something to do with dog-worship by the Phoenicians.

Following a brief Hellenistic phase of influence (third–second centuries BCE), a significant Roman city was constructed here. In fact, the largest building yet discovered at Ashkelon comes from this period. Discovered by John Garstang (1876–1956), who erroneously dated it to the Herodian period, the structure measures over 360 feet long and some 115 feet wide. It was flanked by 24 marble columns on each side and six on each end. Roman burials have also been found, including one that consisted of a painted tomb. A most interesting, if somewhat risqué, discovery from this period are several oil-lamp sherds on which are depicted explicit sexual scenes, both homosexual and heterosexual. Such discoveries, both at Ashkelon and elsewhere in the ancient Roman world, clearly illustrate that the Romans enjoyed a more lenient attitude toward sexual activity than did the Jews and Christians.

The final chapters of the long history of Ashkelon were written during the Arab–Crusader periods (tenth–twelfth centuries CE). During the Arab occupation the city witnessed a major refortification program. It was then briefly occupied by the crusaders until its destruction by Saladin in 1191 CE.

Figure 9 Middle Bronze Age gate.

History of archaeological excavations

The excavation of Ashkelon began more as a treasure hunt in 1815 by a woman, Hester Stanhope. Among other things, she found a statue of a soldier that she had smashed, for whatever reasons. The first "scientific" exploration of the site was conducted by John Garstang with the aid of W. J. Pythian-Adams in 1921–1922. Significant discoveries from the Bronze and Iron ages, as well as the Roman period, were made. In the 1930s, several salvage operations were carried out by the Mandatory and Israel Department of Antiquities. Among other items, the remains of two basilican churches were found, one of which was excavated by V. Tzaferis in 1966–1967. But the first large-scale excavation of Ashkelon was not begun until 1985 under the direction of Lawrence E. Stager (see Figure 9, p. 39). Sponsored by the Harvard Semitic Museum of Harvard University, this undertaking is called "The Leon Levy Expedition," named after the dig's primary benefactor. As of this writing, this excavation is still in progress, though its work, like many others, has been stopped or slowed due to the contemporary political turmoil now taking place in Israel.

Ashkelon in ancient texts

The place is mentioned in several ancient texts, including, of course, the Bible where it is referred to some 13 times in 12 verses (Josh. 13: 3; Judg. 1: 18; 14: 19; 1 Sam. 6: 17; 2 Sam. 1: 20; Jer. 25: 20; 47: 5, 7; Amos 1: 8; Zeph. 2: 4, 7; Zech. 9: 5 ("Ashkelon" occurs twice in this last verse)). The city was forever immortalized in David's lament over the deaths of Saul and Jonathan (2 Sam. 1: 20). However, it has been suggested that the traditional translation: tell it not in the "*streets* . . ." should more accurately be read as "*markets*" or "*bazaars*." A noteworthy reference to Ashkelon is found in the prophetic book of Jeremiah (47: 5–7). The prophet wails that Ashkelon has been "silenced." Some authorities have suggested this may be in reference to the destruction of the city by the Babylonians in 604 BCE. An interesting discovery by the current excavation may also be alluded to in Jeremiah. The remains of a collapsed roof were found on the floor of a building destroyed by Nebuchadnezzar. On the roof debris was a small incense altar which apparently had been used on the roof top. According to the current excavator, this is the only known stratified evidence for the existence of roof-top altars. The prophet

Jeremiah (32: 28–29) told the people of Jerusalem that YHWH was sending the Chaldeans under Nebuchadnezzar to burn the city "on whose roofs offerings have been made to Baal and libations have been poured out to other gods. . . ." Whether or not the prophet had in mind anything similar to what was found at Ashkelon cannot, of course, be archaeologically determined.

The last reference to Ashkelon in the Hebrew Bible is a late (fourth–third century BCE) text found in Zechariah (9: 5). The passage speaks of the fate of Ashkelon (and the other Philistine cities, Gaza and Ekron) as having become an "uninhabited place." This may reflect the destruction of these cities by the Greeks at the end of the fourth century BCE.

Given its political and economic position in the region, it is no surprise to learn that Ashkelon is mentioned in several important extra-biblical texts. The oldest reference is in a nineteenth–eighteenth century BCE Egyptian Execration Text. Execration texts are inscriptions written on ceramic vessels or figures and then smashed in a ritual ceremony believed, apparently, to bring about the defeat of the names written on the object. Ashkelon also appears on the famous "Merneptah," or "Israel" stela dated to the end of the thirteenth century BCE. The text reports that during Merneptah's raid on Canaan, Ashkelon was "carried off." The propaganda commemorating Ramses II's (c.1300–1234 BCE) capture of the city claims that Ashkelon was "wretched" and "wicked."

Ashkelon also figured in the political machinations of the four Assyrian kings: Tiglath-Pileser (744–727), Sennacherib (704–681), Esarhaddon (680–669), and Ashurbanipal (668–633). The texts speak of revolts by the local kings, their replacements, of tributes paid to the Assyrians in various forms, and, at least in one instance, how the king of Ashkelon, "Mitinti," "kissed the feet" of Ashurbanipal (just to confuse the issue, there are also kings named "Mitinti" from the time of both Tiglath-Pileser and Esarhaddon).

Conclusions

From both the textual and archaeological evidence it is clear that Ashkelon was considered an important city for many years by friend and foe alike. The major excavation now underway has already made significant discoveries pertaining to all periods of the site's occupational history. Who knows what future seasons in the field will reveal?

Further reading

Stager, Lawrence E. "When Canaanites and Philistines Ruled Ashkelon." *BAR* 17: 2 (1991): 24–34, 40–43.

—— "Why Were Hundreds of Dog Buried at Ashkelon?," *BAR* 17.3 (1991): 26–42.

—— "Eroticism and Infanticide at Ashkelon." *BAR* 17.4 (1991): 34–52; 72.

—— with a contribution by Paula Wapnish, *Ashkelon Discovered from Canaanites and Philistines to Romans and Moslems*. Washington, DC: Biblical Archaeological Society, 1991. (This monograph is a reprint of the three articles mentioned above.)

—— "The Fury of Babylon Ashkelon and the Archaeology of Destruction." *BAR* 22.1 (1996): 56–69; 76–77.

Wapnish, Paula and Brian Hesse. "Pampered Pooches or Plain Pariahs?" *BA* 56.2 (1993): 55–80.

AZEKAH

WHERE THE FIRE WENT OUT

Biblical Azekah is identified with modern Tell Zakariya, a one-acre site located some ten miles north of **Lachish** and about four miles southwest of **Beth-Shemesh** (see Figure 10). Azekah is mentioned only seven times in the Bible (Josh. 10: 10, 11; 15: 35; 1 Sam. 17: 1; 2 Chron. 11: 9; Neh. 11: 30; Jer. 34: 7), but it is also mentioned in a famous Lachish Letter, and an Assyrian inscription. The latter is now in the British Museum and is believed to refer to the time of Sargon II's (*c.*712 BCE) attack against **Ashdod**. In this reference, Azekah is

Figure 10 Azekah.

43

described as ". . . located on a mountain ridge like a pointed dagger" (Tadmor, 1958). Eusebius (*Onom.* 18: 10) also described the site, though some experts think he may have been referring to Khirbet el-'Almi, located to the east of Tell Zakariya. Azekah is also believed to be shown on the sixth-century CE Madaba Map.

But perhaps the site is most famous for its occurrence in one of the letters found in the destroyed remains of a guardhouse at Lachish. The destruction is credited to the Babylonians and took place early in the sixth century BCE. The ostracon is believed by most scholars to have been written by an officer in charge of an outpost located somewhere between Azekah and Lachish. The letter reads: "And let (my lord) know that we are watching for the signals of Lachish, according to all the indications which my lord has given, for we cannot see Azekah" (*ANET*, 1969: 322; however, for a different interpretation of the Lachish Letter, see Yadin, 1984). Related to this extra-biblical text is Jeremiah 34: 7. This prophetic passage claims that except for Jerusalem, the only two fortified cities left in Judah are Lachish and Azekah.

Azekah is also mentioned in the "conquest" story of the destruction of the Amorites in Joshua (10: 10–11). This is the well-known story where the Israelites are aided in their slaughter by divine hailstones. The theological implications of such a story must be left up to others. Azekah is also said to have been among the towns given to Judah (Josh. 15: 35), and it was involved in a conflict with the Philistines (1 Sam. 15: 7). Rehoboam, the King of Judah (*c.*922–915), is said to have re-fortified the town (2 Chron. 11: 9) and, finally, some of the returning exiles apparently re-settled here (Neh. 11: 30).

The only excavation of Tell Zakariya was conducted between 1898 and 1899 by F. J. Bliss and R. A. S. Macalister (1870–1950; see Bliss and Macalister, 1902). While they discovered various material remains described as "towers" and a "fortress," due to excavation methods of the time, no clear stratigraphy of the site was forthcoming. The excavators did identify four broad "occupational phases": Early pre-Israelite; Late pre-Israelite (*c.*1550–800 BCE); "Jewish" (*c.*800–300 BCE); and Seleucid (*c.*300 BCE). However, revisions of this outline have been suggested by later authorities. Until an excavation using contemporary field techniques is carried out here, more detailed analysis of the occupational history of the site is unlikely. To this author's knowledge, no archaeological evidence was found, or recognized, as evidence of a Babylonian destruction implied by both the Lachish Letter and the passage in Jeremiah.

Further reading

Albright, W. F. *The Archaeology of Palestine.* Harmondsworth, 1960: 30–31.

Bliss, Frederick J. and Robert A. S. Macalister. *Excavations in Palestine during the years 1898–1900.* London, 1902.

Tadmor, H. "The Campaigns of Sargon II of Assur." *Journal of Cuneiform Studies* 12 (1958): 80–84.

Yadin, Yigael. "The Lachish Letters – Originals or Copies and Drafts?" In *Recentury Archaeology in the Land of Israel.* H. Shanks and B. Mazar, eds, Washington, DC: BAS/Jerusalem/IES, 1984: 179–186.

BEERSHEBA
AN IRON AGE II JUDEAN TOWN "MUSEUM"

Biblical Beersheba is identified with Tell es-Seba', a ruin located some 2.5 miles east of the modern Israeli city of Beersheba. In the Bible the name, "Beersheba," is traced back to two aetiologies associated with the Ancestors, Abraham and Isaac (see Gen. 21: 28–31; 26: 33). The name is usually understood to mean "well of seven" or "well of oath." However, there are no known Semitic cognates of the word *sheva'* with the meaning "to swear" or "to oath." Furthermore, there is no obvious connection between "oath" and "seven."

Figure 11 Iron Age Beersheba – gate and store rooms.

The Bible and Beersheba

In the Bible, Beersheba is mentioned several times in connection with the stories of Abraham, Isaac, and Jacob (see Gen. 21: 32, 33; 22: 19; 26: 23, 33; 28: 10; 46: 1, 5). However, the archaeological history of this site (see below) and contemporary critical scholarship would suggest that these biblical stories were created long after any supposedly "ancestral" period in Israel's history.

The expression, "from **Dan** to Beersheba," to describe the territorial limits of Israel, also occurs several times in various parts of the Bible (Judg. 29: 1; 1 Sam. 3: 20; 8: 2; 2 Sam. 3: 10; 17: 11; 24: 2, 15; 1 Kgs. 4: 25). In Chronicles, for some reason, the order of the names is reversed. There the expression reads: "from Beersheba to Dan" (1 Chron. 21: 2; 2 Chron. 30: 5). According to a tradition in Joshua (15: 20ff.), Beersheba belonged to the tribe of Judah (see 1 Kgs. 19: 3) but another text specifically allots the town to Simeon (Josh. 19: 2) which was part of greater Judah. Beersheba is also mentioned in the prophetic book of Amos (8: 5, 14). Interestingly, the prophet condemns Beersheba, along with the cities of Dan, Gilgal, and **Samaria**, for having its own patron deities. After the Exile (post 539 BCE), the author of Nehemiah (11: 27, 30) claims that some Judeans lived ("camped" in v. 30) in Beersheba. Two other curious notes about the place appear in the Bible: according to traditions preserved in the Book of 2 Kings, the mother of Jehoash, king of Judah, came from Beersheba (2 Kgs. 12: 1); and Josiah, king of Judah during the last half of the seventh century BCE, claims to have defiled the "high place" of Beersheba (2 Kgs. 23: 8).

Archaeology and Beersheba

Iron Age I (twelfth–tenth centuries BCE)

The archaeological excavations of Beersheba began in 1969 under the direction of Yohanan Aharoni of the Tel Aviv University. He conducted seven seasons of excavations through 1975. After his death in 1976, the dig directorship was passed to Ze'ev Herzog who completed an eighth season in the same year. Herzog returned to the site in 1990 to renew the excavations in conjunction with Israel's National Parks Authority, which is seeking to preserve the site.

In all, the excavators identified nine strata of occupation. The earliest four strata (IX–VI) were dated to Iron Age I, and Strata V–II to Iron Age II (end of the eighth century BCE). The final stratum (I), dated to the early seventh century, represents an unsuccessful attempt to revitalize the city of Stratum II. Indeed, the major contribution of this excavation has been the horizontal exposure of much of an Iron Age II "official" town in the northern Negev (see Figure 11, p. 46).

The Beersheba valley was home to a major Chalcolithic culture of the fourth millennium BCE and some Chalcolithic material was recovered at Tell Beersheba. However, only in the beginning of the Iron Age is there evidence for human habitation, mainly in the form of pits dug into the bed rock of the site. Some of the pits were interpreted as storage facilities while others are believed to have been used for human dwelling. It has been estimated that the human population at Beersheba during this time would have been no more than 120–200 people.

Following the destruction of the Stratum IX settlement, the first houses were built. They appear to be prototypes of the famous "four-room" houses that are ubiquitous in later Israel. This phase of the site's history did not last long. The site was abandoned at the end of the eleventh century, to be replaced by the town's first "enclosed settlement," (Str. VII). This was created by the back, outside walls of the houses being joined to form a "wall" around the perimeter of the area. Aharoni thought this occurred during the time of Saul to provide some defensive measures against the Amalekites. Also, the sons of Samuel, Joel, and Abijah, are said to have served as "judges over Israel . . . in Beersheba" (1 Sam. 8: 1–2). However, archaeologically this claim cannot be verified. Dating also to this period is a rich assortment of clay vessels, iron tools, and jewelry. During the first half of the tenth century BCE, changes were made to the earlier town. Some of the houses from the previous stratum were subdivided into smaller rooms while others were dismantled altogether. Apparently, this phase of occupation (Str. VI) was very short-lived, coming to an end by the middle of the tenth century.

One of the more famous discoveries from the Iron Age I history of Beersheba is the "well." Dug into the slope of the site, this well is so deep that the bottom could not be reached for safety reasons. (There is also confusion in the publications, however, on exactly how much of the fill was removed – the number varies from 66 to 226 feet!) Since the bottom has not been excavated, the precise date of its origin cannot be determined archaeologically, although the excavators believed it originated during Iron Age I.

Assuming the Iron Age I date is accurate, it is most unlikely that any "Ancestor" had anything to do with this structure. Even if one gives some historicity to the Ancestor stories (and many scholars would give very little, if any), the date(s) of their activity is still disputed. The most popular suggestion seems to be during the first half of the Middle Bronze Age (eighteenth century BCE). If this is the case, the "Ancestors" were some seven hundred years too early to have had anything to do with this well! Finally, even if it could be shown *archaeologically* that the well in fact was first dug during the Middle Bronze Age, that alone could not "prove" some link with characters in biblical stories. This kind of argument gets very circular very quickly. It is precisely the lack of Middle Bronze and Late Bronze Age material at the site that has led some authorities to suggest that Tell es-Seba' is not the site of biblical Beersheba. But this argument seems to presuppose the historicity of the Genesis stories. The biblical stories cannot be used to identify the well, and then the well used to verify the biblical stories! (Well, they could, but not very convincingly.)

However, the now-known archaeological history of the Iron Age I site is important for helping to understand the northern Negev culture during this period, For example, a lot of cattle bones were recovered from Beersheba as well as other Iron Age I sites in the region, such as Tel Masos. This material points to a growing agriculturally based economy at this time. Herzog has pointed out that during the eleventh century BCE, the Beersheba valley was more densely populated than at any other time in its pre-modern history.

Iron Age II (tenth–eighth centuries BCE; Str. V–II)

It is the Beersheba of Iron Age II from which comes the best archaeological evidence for a well-planned administrative town in southern Judah (see Figure 11, p. 46). The site obtained its largest area of habitation, around 2.8 acres, during this period. But despite its small size, the town was well planned. It was also during Iron Age II that the site was fortified with its own wall, first a solid one (Str. V–IV), and later a casemate wall (Str. III–II). Both were entered and exited through a four-chamber gate system. All of the occupational strata of this period were destroyed, especially Strata V and II. Stratum V is thought to have been destroyed by Shishak of Egypt in his campaign in the region at the end of the tenth century BCE. The agent of the destruction of Stratum II has been controversial. The excavators have argued for a date at the end of the eighth century BCE and credited Sennacherib, the Assyrian king. Others have suggested a later date in the seventh century. Whatever the case, the destruction of Stratum II was massive, reflected in collapsed buildings and large amounts of clay vessels found in the debris.

The Iron Age II town in its prime had well-laid-out streets, public buildings identified as storehouses, in which were found large amounts of vessels mentioned above, and a large plaza (*c.*40 × 66 feet). In addition, what has been identified as the "governor's house" near the gate was uncovered, as well as a building (called the "basement house") on the western side of the site. This latter building is believed to have been constructed on the site where a temple once stood. The evidence for this claim is the stones of a large horned altar found incorporated into the walls of the storehouses. When reconstructed, the altar was a cube of some 5.2 feet on each side. In 1990, Herzog discovered on the north-east side of the tell a massive water system also dated to Iron Age II. It consisted of a vertical square some 50 feet deep which led to a tunnel that led in turn to a series of cisterns for catching and storing rain water.

While there is archaeological evidence for activity on the site following the Iron Age II destruction (whatever the exact date turns out to be), the town never achieved its former importance as an administrative center. Maybe it is appropriate then, that following the Early Arab period of occupation, the site became a graveyard for local bedouin.

Further reading

Aharoni, Yohanan, ed., *Beersheba I: Excavations at Tel Beersheba, 1969–1971 Seasons.* Publications of the Institute of Archaeology, 2. Tel Aviv: Institute of Archaeology, Tel Aviv University, 1973.

—— "Excavations at Tel Beersheba. Preliminary Report of the Fourth Season, 1972." *TA* 1 (1974): 34–42.

—— "The Horned Altar of Beersheba." *BA* 37 (1974): 2–6.

—— "Excavations at Tel Beersheba. Preliminary Report of the Fifth and Sixth Seasons, 1973–1974." *TA* 2 (1975): 146–168.

Fowler, Mervyn. "The Excavation of Tell Beersheba and the Biblical Record." *PEQ* 114 (1982): 7–11.

Herzog, Ze'ev. "Israelite City Planning in Light of the Beersheba and Arad Excavations." *Expedition* 20 (1978): 38–43.

—— ed. *Beersheba II. The Early Iron Age Settlements.* Publications of the Institute of Archaeology, 7. Tel Aviv: Tel Aviv University and Ramot Publishing, 1984.

—— Anson F. Rainey, and S. Moshkovitz. "The Stratigraphy at Beersheba and the Location of the Sanctuary." *BASOR* 225 (1977): 49–58.

—— M. Aharoni, Anson F. Rainey, and S. Moshkovitz. "The Israelite Fortress at Arad." *BASOR* 254 (1984): 1–34.

Rainey, Anson F. "Hezekiah's Reform and the Altars at Beersheba and Arad." In *Scripture and Artifacts. Essays on the Bible and Archaeology in Honor of Philip J. King*. Michael D. Coogan, J. Cheryl Exum, and Lawrence E. Stager, eds. Louisville: Westminster John Knox Press, 1994: 333–354.

—— "No Bama at Beersheba." *BAR* 3.3 (1977): 18–21, 56.

Shanks, Herschel. "Yigael Yadin Finds a Bama at Beer-Sheba." *BAR* 3.1 (1976): 3–12.

Yadin, Yigael. "Beersheba: The High Place Destroyed by King Josiah." *BASOR* 222 (1976): 5–17.

BETHEL (TELL BEITIN)
NO GOLDEN CALF: YET

Tell Beitin is located about nine miles north of **Jerusalem** (see Figure 12). In biblical times it was in the tribal territory of Benjamin. In 1838 Edward Robinson (1794–1863), an American biblical scholar and explorer, identified Tell Beitin with the biblical place of Bethel. For the most part, Robinson's identification has been upheld by later authorities (but see Livingston, 1989). This identification was re-confirmed recently by Anson F. Rainy in a paper given at the 2004 meeting of the American School of Oriental Research in San Antonio, Texas (Rainy, 2004). Except for Jerusalem, Bethel ("house of El" (or God)) is the most often mentioned town in the Hebrew Bible (some 70 times). Throughout its history, the site seems to have

Figure 12 Bethel from the air.

been associated with a cult shrine of some sort, serving first the religious needs of the local Canaanites then the later Israelites. However, the biblical writers considered it to be an apostate site, at least from the time of Jeroboam I (late tenth–early ninth century BCE) who is accused of setting up the "golden calf" here (1 Kgs. 12: 29–33). The tradition in 2 Kings (23) claims that the sanctuary was finally destroyed by King Josiah during the last half of the seventh century BCE. Whether this is history remembered or idealized stories created by the later Deuteronomic Historian cannot be determined by the archaeological data alone.

In the stories of the Ancestors, Bethel is presented in a positive light. In fact, according to the Bible, the site obtained its name, "Bethel," from a divine revelation that occurred here to Jacob (Gen. 28: 10–22; but see Gen. 35: 15). According to one tradition, the Canaanite name of the site was "Luz"; Gen. 28: 19). However, some authorities question this identification and such texts as Joshua 16: 2 imply that Bethel and Luz were two separate places. The Bible also claims that Joshua destroyed the site during the "conquest" (Josh. 8: 17; Judg. 1: 22–28; see below for the archaeology of the site). If so, it was re-occupied fairly quickly because Bethel is inhabited in the Bible during the time of the "Judges" (4: 5; 20: 18 ff.). We are told that Samuel included Bethel on his circuit (1 Sam. 7: 16) and the site is mentioned in the exploits of Saul (1 Sam. 10: 3; 13: 2).

Bethel came under the harsh judgment of the eighth century BCE prophets, Amos and Hosea (Amos 3: 14; 5: 5–6; 7: 10, 13; Hos. 10: 15; 12: 4). Finally, the post-exilic writings of Ezra (2: 28) and Nehemiah (7: 32; 11: 31) indicate that Bethel was still occupied during the fifth–fourth centuries BCE. Both the literary and archaeological evidence indicate that the site was occupied from the Hellenistic through the Byzantine periods.

For such an important role given Bethel in the Hebrew Bible, one would have hoped that the archaeological exposure of the site would have shed invaluable light on the historical contexts of the biblical traditions (assuming the identity of Bethel with Tell Beitin) that only the material realia can do. Unfortunately, such is not the case. Tell Beitin was first excavated under the direction of W. F. Albright (1891–1971) in 1934. James Kelso, Albright's assistant, directed three more seasons at the site in 1954, 1957, and 1960. Except for relatively short reports, particularly in volumes of *BASOR*, the only final report was authored by Kelso and published by ASOR in 1968 under the title *The Excavation of Bethel (1934–1960)*.

As critics have pointed out (especially W. G. Dever; see bibliography), while one can obtain a general outline of the archaeological history of the site from Kelso's publication, precise historical reconstruction of strata is very difficult, if not altogether impossible. In Dever's own words:

> Bethel was probably one of the more prominent Bronze-Iron Age towns in central Palestine, and it is also significant in biblical history. Yet the excavations as carried out and published allow us to do no more than sketch the archaeological history of the site, and even that with little precision or confidence in any single detail. The exposure was inadequate, the results of the various seasons are poorly coordinated (there were no stratum numbers), and the description of the successive phases is minimal and sparsely illustrated. Still more serious is the lack of any research design, save the apparent notion of "illuminating the Bible" in some way or another. Albright's early work in 1934 may have been adequate for the time, but the later excavations (and the final publication) are marred by transparent biases, as well as by an embarrassing naivete. Fact and interpretation are so entangled throughout the final report that few data emerge for the archaeologist, historian, or biblical scholar.
>
> (1992: 651–652)

Perhaps a new excavation at Tell Beitin can help resolve some of these difficulties. Until such time, it is virtually impossible to correlate anything in the archaeological material record with biblical data.

Further reading

Dever, W. G. "Beitin, Tell." *ABD* 1. David Noel Freedman, ed., NY: Doubleday, 1992: 651–652.

Kelso, James L. "Excavations at Bethel." *BA* 19.1 (1956): 37–43.

Livingston, David. "One Last Word on Bethel and 'Ai – Fairness Requires No More." *BAR* 15.1 (1989): 11.

Rainy, Anson F. "The Location of Bethel." Paper read at the Annual Meeting of the American Schools of Oriental Research, San Antonio, Texas, November, 2004.

BETHLEHEM

WAS JESUS REALLY BORN HERE?

The modern-day village of Bethlehem ("house of bread") is located some four–five miles south of **Jerusalem**. The site is revered out of all proportion to its size because of the biblical associations of the place with David in the Hebrew Bible, and with Jesus in the New Testament.

Bethlehem in the Bible

Including the handful of references to Bethlehem in the New Testament (Matt. 2: 1ff; Luke 2: 4; John 7: 42), the site is mentioned nearly fifty times in the Bible. It is first mentioned in the Hebrew

Figure 13 Bethlehem: "shepherds field."

Bible in conjunction with a story about the death of Rachel, one of the wives of Jacob (Gen. 35: 19; 48: 7). Already by the time of the final editing of Genesis, Bethlehem had been identified with "Ephrath/ah" (see the Genesis references above and Ruth 1: 2; 4: 11; Micah 5: 2. Elsewhere, Ephrathah is the wife of Caleb as in 1 Chr. 2: 19). In 1 Chronicles, Bethlehem is confusingly identified as a son of both Salma and of Hur (1 Chr. 2: 51, and 54 for the former; and 4: 4 for the latter).

In the Masoretic Text of Joshua (19: 15), Bethlehem is mentioned only once in the context of the inheritance of the tribe of Zebulun. In the Septuagint (Greek Bible), however, Bethlehem is said to have belonged to the towns of Judah (Josh. 15). The town is referred to in Judges only in connection with the stories of two Levite priests. In Judges 17, the Levite is from Bethlehem but leaves home to find his fortune. He ends up in private employ of a certain "Micah" (Jud. 17: 8), only to be "kidnapped" by the passing Danites and made to serve as their priest. Judges 18: 30 implies that this Levite was named Jonathan, and was the grandson of Moses. His claim to fame is that he initiated an idolatrous cult at **Dan** which lasted until the Assyrian destruction of Israel during the last half of the eighth century BCE (Jud. 18: 30).

Not content with telling one story of a faithless Levite associated with Bethlehem, the biblical author(s) add another, even more horrific tale. This time the Levite is not from Bethlehem but his concubine is (Jud. 19–21). After going to retrieve her from her father's house, to which she had fled after a family quarrel, the happy couple end up spending the night in Gibeah, a town in the tribal territory of Benjamin. The tale of her subsequent rape by the men of Gibeah, her murder (by whom is not clear), and her bodily dismemberment (by her husband) makes for a sordid story indeed.

The story of Ruth begins (Ruth 1: 1) and ends in Bethlehem (4: 11) and is probably best understood as a late apologetic for the mixed ancestry of David, who is introduced into the story at the end. David is associated with Bethlehem in several texts in Samuel (1 Sam. 16: 4; 17: 12, 15; 20: 6, 28; 2 Sam. 23: 14–16). Bethlehem is his boyhood home and it is there that he is anointed king by Samuel. Asahel, a brother of Joab, the nephew of David, is said to have been buried at Bethlehem (2 Sam. 2: 32). According to the tradition in 2 Samuel 23, the Philistines were able to establish a garrison here and the town is described as fortified with a "gate" and having a "well."

Oddly, Bethlehem is never mentioned in the Books of Kings. But the Chronicler repeats the story of the Philistine garrison located here and the tale of Three Warriors who broke into the place to get water from the "well," for David (1 Chr. 11: 16–18; see 2 Sam. 23: 14ff.). The Chronicler also claims that Rehoboam "built up Bethlehem" and other Judean towns for defensive purposes (2 Chr. 11: 6).

Bethlehem is mentioned in only two prophets, Micah and Jeremiah. Micah (5: 2) prophesies that a future ruler of Israel will come from Bethlehem, and in Jeremiah (41: 17) a group of people fleeing to Egypt in the aftermath of the Babylonian debacle are said to have encamped near the town. Following the Exile, Ezra reports that 123 returnees went to live in Bethlehem and another 46 went to Netephah (2: 2). In Nehemiah, however, the total number for both Bethlehem and Netephah is 188 (7: 26).

While there may be some historical basis for the stories about Bethlehem in the Hebrew Bible, the same cannot be said for the birth legends of Jesus in the New Testament. Though the stories found in Matthew (2: 1ff.) and Luke (2: 4ff.) differ in many respects, they both have Jesus born in Bethlehem. In Luke, his birth is even accompanied by angels appearing to shepherds (2: 8–20; see Figure 13, p. 55). For all of the religious (sentimental?) use made of these marvelous stories throughout the world for centuries by Christians, the critical conclusion is that they are fiction. That the birth accounts have profound theological meaning need not be denied, but such concerns are far beyond the purpose of this brief description of the biblical village. The only other reference to Bethlehem in the New Testament is in the Gospel of John (7: 42) where the author apparently had never heard of the birth legend. Beyond the stories in the Bible, Bethlehem is mentioned by early Christian writers such as Jerome and Justine. Due to Roman influence there seems to have been a cult to Adonis established there, but Bethlehem officially became a Christina shrine in the time of Constantine (fourth century).

The archaeology of Bethlehem

The area that would become Bethlehem was visited by humans as early as the Stone Age and while there is some archaeological evidence of activity here during the Late Bronze and Iron Ages, there is no evidence to support the biblical claim of a fortified settlement containing a special "well." This doesn't necessarily mean the biblical descriptions of these things are false, only that there is currently no archaeological support for such descriptions. The most famous, and written about, construction in Bethlehem is, of course, the Church of the Nativity. First built by Constantine (306–337 CE) in 326, it was rebuilt by Justinian (527–565) after its damage during the Samaritan revolt in 529. It is this structure, with repairs during the years, that is seen today by visitors to the site.

Further reading

Crossan, John Dominic. *Jesus: A Revolutionary Biography*. San Francisco: HarperCollins, 1994: 18–21.

Gunman, S. And A. Berman. "Bethlehem." *RB* 77 (1970): 583–585.

Salma, Sylvester, J. "Iron Age remains from the Site of a New School at Bethlehem." *Stadium Biblicum Franciscanum / Liber Annuus* 18 (1968): 153–180.

Stockman, Eugene. "The Stone Age of Bethlehem." *Liber Annuus* 17 (1967): 129–148.

Tsafir, Yoram. "Ancient Churches in the Holy Land." *BAR* 19.5 (1993): 26–39.

BETHSAIDA

FROM THE LOST AND FOUND DEPARTMENT: AN IRON AGE CITY REAPPEARS

The archaeological ruin now identified with ancient BethSaida lies about one and a half miles north of the Sea of Galilee (see Figure 14). Mentioned only seven times in the New Testament (but often enough to make it the third most mentioned New Testament city after **Jerusalem** and **Capernaum**; the site is not mentioned by this name in the Hebrew Bible), its location/identification has been something of a controversy. The New Testament texts seem to locate the town close to the shore of the sea (i.e. Mark 6: 45). Thus, some authorities have suggested other possible locations such as el-Araj or Mesadiyye, both of which are much closer to the current shore line. However, recent probes at these two sites revealed no remains

Figure 14 Tell BethSaida.

predating the Byzantine period. Thus, et-Tell (literally "the ruin" which is the modern name of the current site under investigation (not to be confused with the et-Tell identified as ancient **'Ai**)) is believed by the current excavators to be the only real possibility for ancient BethSaida.

According to the New Testament, much of Jesus' Galilean activities took place at or near the town. Also, three of the disciples, Andrew, Peter, and Philip, are said to have lived here (John 1: 44; 12: 21). Luke records the feeding of the five thousand here (9: 10–17) and Mark says it was here where Jesus cured a blind man (8: 22–25) and walked on the water (6: 45–51). Despite these positive references to the place, however, BethSaida is also listed among the towns/cities condemned by Jesus for lack of repentance (Matt. 1: 20–23). Josephus claims that Herod Philip, one of the sons of Herod the Great who ruled as a tetrarch from 4 BCE to 33/4 CE, rebuilt BethSaida around 30 CE and elevated it to the status of a "city." Philip is also said to have renamed the place "Julia," in honor of Augustus' daughter.

While there were some efforts in the nineteenth century to locate ancient BethSaida, the site was ignored for the most part until the last decade of the twentieth century when a major excavation project was begun here. Beginning in 1987, the University of Haifa sponsored an archaeological project in the region. Based on the results of this work, a major excavation was started at et-Tell in 1991 under the sponsorship of the University of Nebraska at Omaha and directed by Rami Arav. That this site has only recently begun to be excavated accounts for the fact that no separate entry for BethSaida is included in *NEAEHL*.

The remains of Early Bronze Ages I and II (3100–2650 BCE) occupational periods were uncovered. However, after this time BethSaida was abandoned until the end of the Iron Age I (eleventh century BCE; 'Ai suffered a similar fate). But the biggest archaeological surprise was the evidence for a well-fortified Iron Age II city dating to the ninth century BCE. This city was surrounded by a thick wall (25 feet) which had been built above a rampart made of dirt and crushed limestones. A four-chambered gate with two guard towers was also discovered. This complex, measuring some 57 × 115 feet, and preserved to a height of ten feet, has been described by the excavator as "the largest and best preserved example of a four-chambered gate ever discovered in Israel" (Arav *et al.*, 1995: 48).

Inside the city, a large building identified as a palace in the *bit-hilani* style was discovered. It has been suggested that at this time the city was part of the empire of the Geshurites mentioned in the Hebrew

Bible (Josh. 13: 13; 2 Sam. 13: 37; 2 Sam. 3: 3). While this period of occupation is clearly ninth century (based upon ceramic analysis), the excavators believed there may be an earlier phase of occupation preserved beneath it. If the stories in the Bible relating David and Absalom (2 Sam. 3: 3; 13: 37) to this site have any historical basis that is an obvious conclusion (given the traditional tenth-century date for these two). An interesting small-find from this period is a faience (made from clay mixed with sand) figurine of the Egyptian dwarf god, Pataikos.

Another important find is an ostracon (an inscribed pot-sherd) with the name "Akiba" written on it. This is the Aramaic equivalent of the Hebrew "Jacob" and is the earliest epigraphical evidence for the famous leader of the Second Jewish revolt against the Romans (132–135 CE). From the earlier Hellenistic period (332–337 BCE) comes a clay seal showing two figures casting a net from a boat. This has now become the logo for the BethSaida Excavation Project.

However, were it not for the literary references to BethSaida in the New Testament and Josephus, there would be little to report relevant to the first-century CE town. Few remains have been discovered that can be dated with confidence to this century. As of this writing, no domestic structures have been recovered. Perhaps more first-century CE remains will be discovered in future seasons. Until then, little can be said about the archaeological history of first-century CE BethSaida. Apparently, the place was abandoned for good in the third century CE.

Further reading

Arav, Rami. *BethSaida: A City by the North Shore of the Sea of Galilee.* Kirksville, MO: Thomas Jefferson University, 1995.

—— "BethSaida 1996–1998." *IEJ* 49.1–2 (1999): 128–136.

—— and Monika Bernett. "The *bi hilani* at BethSaida: Its Place in Aramaean/Neo-Hittite and Israelite Architecture in the Iron Age II." *IEJ* 50.1 (2000): 47–81.

——, Richard A. Freund, and John F. Shroder, Jr. "BethSaida Rediscovered." BAR 26.1 (2000): 44–56.

Khun, Heinz and Rami Arav. "The BethSaida Excavations: Historical Archaeological Approaches." In *The Future of Early Christianity.* Minneapolis: Fortress Press, 1991: 77–106.

Pixner, Bargil. "Searching for the New Testament Site of BethSaida." *BA* 48 Dec. (1985): 207–216.

BETH-SHEAN

WHY IS THERE A "CIGAR-SHAPED" COFFIN IN THIS PLACE?

Beth-Shean (also spelled "Beth-Shan," see 1 Sam. 31: 10, 12; 2 Sam. 21: 12) means "house/temple" of "Shan" and most likely refers to an otherwise unknown deity after whom the biblical city was named. Known today as Tell el-Husn, the ancient ruin is located on the eastern end of the Jezreel Valley some two-and-a-half to three miles west of the Jordan River (see Figure 15). It is about 18 miles south of the Sea of Galilee. Its modern Arabic name, Beisan, reflects the original Beth-Shean. However, during the Hellenistic, Roman, and Byzantine periods the name of the site was Nysa Scythopolis.

Figure 15 Beth-Shean from the air. Roman–Byzantine remains are located at foot of the tell. Theater is in right-hand corner, partially covered by shadows.

Beth–Shean in literature

The few references (six times as "Beth-shean": Josh. 17: 11, 16; Judg. 1: 27; 1 Kgs. 4: 12; 1 Chron. 7: 29; and three times as "Beth-shan"; see above) to this city in the Hebrew Bible seem to belie its importance in antiquity as now known from archaeological data. According to biblical tradition, Beth-Shean was given to Manasseh after the "conquest" (Josh. 17: 11, 16), but this tribe was unable to secure it because the Canaanites who lived there had "chariots of iron" (Josh. 17: 16; see Judg. 1: 27). According to a tradition preserved in 1 Kgs. 4: 12, Beth-Shean was part of the fifth district resulting from the reorganization of the state under Solomon. Finally, it is on the walls of Beth-Shean that the corpses of Saul and Jonathan were displayed by the Philistines (1 Sam. 31: 10, 12; see 2 Sam. 21: 12). Outside of the Hebrew Bible, the site is briefly mentioned in the context of the political machinations that went on in Palestine during the Maccabean period (second century BCE; 1 Macc. 5: 52; 12: 40–41).

Beth-Shean appears several times in Egyptian texts, the earliest from the time of Thutmose III who re-asserted Egyptian hegemony over the area during the first half of the fifteenth century BCE. Stelae found during the excavations also mention Seti I (c.1318–1301) and Ramses II (c.1301–1234). Such inscriptions would seem to imply that Beth-Shean was of considerable importance to the Egyptians at this time (1550–1200 BCE). However, the archaeological evidence suggests otherwise (Amihai Mazar, 2001).

The archaeological history of Beth-Shean

The first expedition to this city took place between 1921 and 1932 and was sponsored by the University of Pennsylvania. During these years the excavation had a succession of directors: C. Fisher, A. Rowe, and G. M. FitzGerald. This team identified 18 strata of occupation stretching from the Neolithic period (sixth millennium BCE) to the early Arab (seventh-eighth centuries CE). Unfortunately, like other excavations following World War I, the Beth-Shean team used what today would be considered outdated excavation methods. To try to solve some of the problems created by this early attempt, Amihai Mazar, an Israeli archaeologist, directed new excavations here from 1989 to 1996 (prior to Mazar's work, a single three-week season was conducted on the mound in 1983 by S. Geva and the late Y. Yadin, but with unsatisfactory results).

Early Bronze Age (fourth–third millennium BCE)

Mazar was able to confirm that an impressive Early Bronze Age city did exist at the site. In addition to architectural remains, he recovered a considerable amount of so-called "Khirbet Kerak"-ware. This ware has a very distinctive color and fabric and is believed to have been introduced into this region by people who migrated here from the north. Its name derives from the site (Khirbet Kerak: ancient Beth Yerah) located on the SW shore of the Sea of Galilee where it was first discovered. This Early Bronze culture ended abruptly toward the end of the third millennium, and like other sites known from this time, was followed by a much poorer period of occupation (Early Bronze Age IV). However, many shaft tombs with rich pottery assemblages were found dating to this period.

Middle Bronze Age (2000–1550 BCE)

Following an occupational gap, the tell was once more inhabited beginning in the eighteenth century (Middle Bronze Age II). However, Mazar was not able to discover any defensive structures that could be dated to this time. This is something of a mystery given Beth-Shean's strategic location and the fact that huge rampart fortifications are known from a variety of other sites dating to the same period (i.e. **Dan, Hazor,** and **Jericho**).

Late Bronze Age (1550–1200 BCE)

In any case, during the Late Bronze Age, Beth-Shean came under Egyptian influence. A rich assortment of archaeological data has been recovered from this period. This includes temple remains, many stelae, carved orthostats, jewelry, and rich tomb deposits, many with anthropoid coffins (see Figure 16, p. 65) which were clearly influenced by Egyptian burial practices. Close parallels to the latter can be seen from the famous cemetery at Deir el-Balah. Based on these discoveries, the excavator estimated that the sacred area at Beth-Shean was probably used for at least 500 years. However, as impressive as these remains are in themselves, Mazar concluded that the size of the town, from the Middle Bronze Age through the Iron Ages, was only about three-and-a-half acres. In his words: "it appears that Bronze Age and Iron Age Beth-Shean had never been a major city of central importance" (2001: 292).

Figure 16 Anthropomorphic clay coffin: Beth-Shean.

Iron Age (*c*.1150–586 BCE)

Two strata dated to Iron Age I (twelfth–eleventh centuries) had already been identified by the American excavators and this conclusion was confirmed by Mazar. During this period Beth-Shean was still very much under Egyptian influence (Twentieth Dynasty), reflected in, among other finds, the distinctive anthropomorphic coffins associated with them (see Figure 16, p. 65). However, this seems to have ended with a violent destruction around the middle of the twelfth century BCE. Who or what caused this destruction is not clear.

Following this destruction, Beth-Shean may have been occupied by a combination of Canaanites and Philistines. This seems to be the only time into which the biblical story of Saul and Jonathan could possibly fit, assuming its historicity. This Iron Age I city was also violently destroyed, but Mazar's suggestion that this destruction was brought about by King David has not been confirmed.

The following Iron Age II period (tenth–eighth centuries) is confusing partly due to the primitive excavation techniques of the Americans, and partly due to the complication of the remains themselves. What seems clear is that in the second half of the eighth century, Beth-Shean was once more destroyed, this time by the Assyrians.

During the Hellenistic, Roman, and Byzantine periods, the city changed its name to "Nysa Scythopolis" and the area around the mound was developed (see Figure 15, p. 62). It is estimated that by the Byzantine period, the city incorporated over 320 acres. Today, thanks to the restoration efforts that have been going on since the 1960s, a visitor to the site can experience a lot of what the place must have looked like during this time. Included in the restoration is a Roman theater which is connected to the ancient tell by a colonnaded street nearly 600 feet long and over 33 feet wide.

Further reading

Foerster, Gideon. "The Excavations at Beth-Shean (Nysa-Scythopolis)." *BAT 90*: 147–152.

Mazar, Amihai. "The Excavations at Tel bet-Shean in 1989–1990." *BAT 90*: 606–619.

—— "The Excavations at Tel Beth-Shean During the Years 1989–94." In *The Archaeology of Israel: Constructing the Past, Interpreting the Present.* Neil Asher Silberman and David Small, eds. JSOT Supplemental Series 237. Sheffield: Sheffield Academic Press, 1997: 144–164.

—— "Four Thousand Years of History at Tel Beth-Shean: An Account of the Renewed Excavations." *BA* 60.2 (1997): 62–76.

—— "Beth-Shean During the Iron Age II: Stratigraphy, Chronology and Hebrew Ostraca." *SAIA*. Amihai Mazar, ed., Sheffield: Sheffield Academic Press, 2001: 289–309.

Mazar, Gaby and Rachel Bar Nathan. "The Bet Shean Excavation Project – 1992–1994: Antiquities Authority Expedition." *Excavations and Surveys in Israel*. Vol. 17. Jerusalem: Israel Antiquities Authority, 1998: 1–38.

BETH-SHEMESH
OF MICE AND (PHILISTINE) MEN

The tell identified as biblical Beth-Shemesh (see Figure 17) is located about 15 miles south-southwest of **Jerusalem**. The name means "house of the sun" and may reflect the existence of a Canaanite solar cult, though no archaeological evidence of such an institution has been found. The name of the place is preserved in the nearby Arab village, 'Ain Shems ("spring of the sun"). Rising some 800 feet above sea level, the site is about seven acres in size. It was first identified with the biblical town, as were so many others, by Edward Robinson in 1838.

Figure 17 Beth-Shemesh.

Beth-Shemesh and the Bible

Mentioned 22 times in the Hebrew Bible (the city is not mentioned in any known ancient non-biblical text), the town plays an important role in the story of Samuel (see 1 Sam. 6) and may have been a significant border military/administrative center during most of the eighth century BCE (see 2 Kgs. 14: 11, 13; 2 Chron. 25: 21, 23). In the Book of Joshua (19: 41, where the site is called Ir-shemesh, "city of the sun"), Beth-Shemesh is allotted to the tribe of **Dan**. But in another text (Josh. 15: 10), it is listed as part of the northern boundary of Judah. It is also listed among the cities given to the Levite priests (Josh. 21: 15; see 1 Sam. 6: 15; 1 Chron. 6: 59). These somewhat confusing lists may reflect the later realities of the book's editor(s).

The longest biblical story about the town occurs in 1 Samuel 6. After capturing the Ark and taking it to **Ashdod**, the Philistines are afflicted with "tumors" (1 Sam. 5.1 ff). Told by their own priests to send the ark back after placing "five gold tumors" and "five gold mice" (a plague?) in it, the Philistines send it off towards Beth-Shemesh (1 Sam. 6: 1–16).

Beth-Shemesh is also among Solomon's administrative districts (1 Kgs. 4: 9), and was the scene of a battle between Amaziah, King of Judah, and Jehoash, King of Israel, at the end of the ninth, beginning of the eighth century BCE (2 Kgs. 14: 11, 13, with parallels in 2 Chron. 25: 21, 23). Although the archaeological evidence suggests that by the time of Hezekiah (last quarter of the eighth century BCE), Beth-Shemesh was back in control of Judah, a tradition preserved only in 1 Chronicles 28 (v. 18) claims that during the time of Ahaz, Hezekiah's father, Beth-Shemesh was controlled by the Philistines. After this reference to the time of Ahaz, the Bible is silent on the later history of the town.

Beth-Shemesh and archaeology

As noted above, the location of the biblical site has been known for a long time. However, no archaeological work took place here until the early twentieth century. In fact, there have been three different excavations of the site, the last of which is still in progress. The first was during 1911–1912, led by Duncan Mackenzie from Scotland. Working without the benefit of modern excavation methods, Mackenzie did find a defensive system that included a gate and what he labeled as a "strong wall." He dated these to his "Canaanite" period, but this date has been revised by the current excavators.

From 1923 to 1928 Elihu Grant, of Haverford College (Pennsylvania), directed here. The major publication of the final report was prepared by G. Ernest Wright (1939), one of the best-known students of the famed W. F. Albright.

The most recent excavation was begun in 1990 and is directed by Shlomo Bunimovitz and Zvi Lederman, under the auspices of Bar Ilan University, Israel. While the excavation is not yet completed, the current excavators have clarified the stratigraphy which may be simplified in the following outline:

Stratum VI – Early Bronze Age IV–Middle Bronze Age II A (*c*. twenty-second–eighteenth centuries BCE). Represented by pottery sherds only.

Stratum V – Middle Bronze Age II–III (*c*.1700–1550 BCE). Was fortified; architectural remains identified as a "patrician house"; tombs; end of Middle Bronze Age not too clear, but perhaps caused by the Egyptians *c*.1550 BCE.

Stratum IVa–IVb – Late Bronze Age (*c*.1550–1200 BCE). Evidence of a relatively prosperous Canaanite town with significant architectural remains, rock-cut cistern and copper-smelting furnace. Tombs, gold jewelry, and a "proto-Canaanite" ostracon also discovered from this period. The excavators thought the Late Bronze Age city was destroyed around 1200 BCE, but the agent of destruction is unknown.

Stratum III – Iron Age I (*c*.1200–1000 BCE). There seems to have been a thriving village here during this period, though the identity of its inhabitants is unknown. Based on the almost total absence of pig bones in the remains, some have suggested they were "Israelites." However, the presence of the Philistine bichrome pottery as well as architectural remains in continuity with the preceding Canaanite occupation, make such an identity ambiguous at best.

The most remarkable discovery dated to this period, however, is an incredible rock-hewn water reservoir. Discovered in 1994, this structure, which is shaped like a cross, has been described by the excavator as ". . . one of the finest examples of water engineering and management in the kingdom of Judah" (Bunimovitz and Lederman, 1997: 76). Designed to catch rain-water runoff, the facility has a capacity of some 7,500 cubic feet. Whether this project required outside skilled laborers is still an unanswered question. In any case, the reservoir is believed to have been in use for centuries until blocked by the Philistines sometime during the seventh century BCE.

Another significant discovery from the tenth century is a double-sided game board with the name "Hanan" inscribed on its narrow side. This name has also been found from a tenth-century bowl from the nearby site of Tel Batash/**Timnah**. Elihu Grant also found this same name on a twelfth-century BCE "proto-Canaanite" ostracon during his excavation at Beth-Shemesh. The family of Hana seems then to have been an important one in the region for several generations.

Stratum IIb (c.950–701 BCE). Archaeologically, this was a significant period in the history of the town. Toward the end of the ninth, or beginning of the eighth century BCE, Beth-Shemesh was re-fortified, including a new gate system on the northern side of the site. This activity has been associated with King Amaziah of Judah who fought a battle here against King Jehoash of Israel (according to 2 Kgs. 14). It is possible, though, that it was Amaziah's son, Uzziah, who renovated Beth-Shemesh for the latter's political pursuits (see 2 Chron. 26: 6). What does seem clear is that during the eighth century Beth-Shemesh was a thriving town with an olive oil and/or wine industry (industrial complex). Furthermore, since the excavation of the site began in the early twentieth century, dozens of the so-called "*lmlk*" ("to (for) the king") stamped jar handles, as well as several "royal" stamped handles have been discovered. These handles have been associated with the rule of King Hezekiah of Judah (c.727–698 BCE; see now Na'aman, 1979 and 1986). Thus Beth-Shemesh seems to have been one of Hezekiah's military/administrative centers during the last quarter of the eighth century. All of this was brought to a fatal end with the invasion of Sennacherib, king of Assyria, in 701 BCE.

Stratum IIc (701–586 BCE). Based primarily on ceramic evidence, there does appear to have been a small occupation of the site after the Assyrian assault. The inhabitants are believed to have lived mainly in the vicinity of the water reservoir. However, this was a meager settlement compared to previous generations of inhabitants. The current excavators have concluded that perhaps the Philistines blocked the reservoir sometime during the first half of the seventh century BCE, insuring the site's total abandonment.

Stratum I – Hellenistic-Medieval. Following the Babylonian attack of 587/586 the site lay in ruins for hundreds of years. Based on some pottery finds, coins, and a few architectural remains, the excavators were able to conclude that some activity took place on the site during the Hellenistic, Roman, Byzantine, and Medieval periods. All of this activity was assigned to Stratum I.

Conclusion

During biblical times, Beth-Shemesh served as a defensive post on the northern border of Judah. It reached its major role in this respect at the end of the eighth century BCE in its futile resistance against the onslaught of the Assyrian forces. Its history is also important for shedding light on the political/social interactions between "Philistines" and "Israelites," which seem more complex than a cursory reading of the Bible would suggest.

Further reading

Barkay, Gabriel. "'Your Poor Brother': a Note on an Inscribed bowl from Beth Shemesh." *IEJ* 41/4 (1991): 239–241.

Bunimovitz, Shlomo and Zvi Lederman. "Beth-Shemesh Cultural Conflict on Judah's Frontier." *BAR* 3.1 (1997): 42–49; 75–77.

—— and Zvi Lederman. "Tel Beth-Shemesh, 1997–2000." *IEJ* 50.3–4 (2000): 254–258.

—— and —— "The Iron Age Fortifications of Tel Beth-Shemesh: a 1990–2000 Perspective." *IEJ* 51.2 (2001): 121–147.

Hillers, Delbert R. "A Reading in the Beth-Shemesh Tablet." *BASOR* 199 (1970): 66.

Na'aman, Nadav. "Sennacherib's Campaign to Judah and the Date of the *LMLK* Stamps." *VT* 29 (1979): 61–86.

—— "Hezekiah's Fortified Cities and the *LMLK* Stamps." *BASOR* 261 (1986): 5–21.

Sass, Benjamin. "The Beth-Shemesh Tablet and the early History of the Proto-Canaanite, Cuneiform and South Semitic Alphabets." *Ugarit-Forschungen* 23 (1992): 315–326.

BETH-ZUR

A FORGOTTEN OUTPOST
OF JUDAH?

Mentioned only four times in the Hebrew Bible, the ruin of Beth-Zur is identified with modern Khirbet et-Tubeiqa, a mound located about 18 miles south of Jerusalem and some three-and-a-half miles north of **Hebron**. This tell is over 3,300 feet above sea level, making Beth-Zur one of the highest settlements in all of ancient Israel (for comparison, nearby Hebron is 3,050 feet above sea level and **Jerusalem** averages about 2,407 feet).

Beth-Zur in literary sources

While seldom mentioned in the Bible, Beth-Zur is frequently referred to in the Apocryphal books of 1 and 2 Maccabees and in Josephus's *Antiquities*. According to the tradition in Joshua (15: 58), Beth-Zur, along with other cities, was given to Judah after the "conquest" of Canaan by the Israelites. However, many authorities believe that this list is much later than the assumed time of Joshua. 1 Chronicles 2: 45 traces the ancestry of the place back to the Calebites, and according to 2 Chronicles 11: 7, Rehoboam, the son of Solomon, rebuilt Beth-Zur. The first claim may or may not have any historical credibility, but the later is without any archaeological support (see below) if Khirbet et-Tubeiqa is, indeed, the location of the ancient city. The same problem exists for the last biblical reference to the place: Nehemiah 3: 16. Here the town is thought important enough to list as a "district" from which men came to help re-build Jerusalem. The archaeological evidence suggests that the site was sparsely occupied during this time.

The references in the books of Maccabees and Josephus deal primarily with the struggle that ensued in the late third and first half of the second centuries BCE between the Ptolemies and the Seleucids for control of the site. It was during this time that Beth-Zur achieved its economic zenith.

Excavations of Beth-Zur

Two excavation seasons have been conducted here: the first in 1931 and the second in 1957. Both seasons were under the direction of O. R. Sellers. The 1931 campaign was sponsored by McCormick Theological Seminary (Chicago), and by the American School of Oriental Research. While pottery sherds indicated that some human activity took place here during the Early Bronze Age, the first real settlement was not constructed before the Middle Bronze Age II (seventeenth–sixteenth centuries BCE). Even then, only in the latter part of this period was the city fortified with a wall some eight feet thick. It was estimated that the wall enclosed some 2–4 acres (it was not completely traced around the city). This phase of the occupation was brought to a violent end around 1550 BCE, perhaps by Thutmose III.

Following this destruction, the site experienced something of a hiatus during the Late Bronze Age (1550–1200 BCE). There is little evidence of any occupation during this 350-year period. In the eleventh century (Iron Age I, Str. III), the site was re-inhabited, but its occupational area was reduced from that of the previous Middle Bronze Age. The new-comers were identified as "Israelites" by the excavators, but this ethnic identity comes from the Bible not the archaeological remains. Whoever the people were, their time here was short-lived. Towards the end of the century, the town was once more violently destroyed, though by whom or what is not clear.

Interestingly enough, following the end of the Iron Age I occupation, there was another 300-year gap in the site's history. This lack of remains during this time raises serious historical questions concerning the biblical claim that Rehoboam rebuilt the city (2 Chron. 11: 7). The discovery of a dozen or so *lmlk* jar handles indicates that there may have been at least a military garrison here during the reign of Hezekiah (*c.*727–698 BCE). There is little evidence, however, for any Assyrian destruction at the end of the eighth century. Furthermore, even though the excavators claimed, during the 1931 season, to have recovered evidence of a sixth-century BCE Babylonian destruction, this was not corroborated in the 1957 excavation.

Following the Exile, there is some evidence of a Persian presence here but the next significant occupation came during the second century BCE. Now called "Bethsura," the archaeological and literary sources indicate that the town prospered during this time though it was something of a political football tossed around between the

Ptolemies and the Seleucids. Around 164 BCE, the Seleucid general, Lysias, took control of it (1 Macc. 4: 28–34; Josephus *Antiquities* 12.7.5). The discovery of 29 Rhodian wine-jar handles attest to some 20 years of Seleucid occupation. But towards the end of the second century BCE, Simeon, a Hasmonean, gained control of Beth-Zur and by 100 BCE the tell was abandoned for the last time.

Further reading

Funk, Robert W. "The 1957 Campaign at Beth-Zur." *BASOR* 150 (1958): 8–20.

Sellers, Ovid R. *The Citadel of Beth-Zur.* Philadelphia: Westminster Press, 1933.

—— "The 1957 Excavations at Beth-Zur". *AASOR 38.* Cambridge, MA: American School of Oriental Research, 1968.

CAESAREA MARITIMA
HEROD'S CITY BY THE SEA

Caesarea (called "Maritima" in modern times to distinguish it from Caesarea Philippi), is located on the Mediterranean coast between Tel Aviv to the south and Haifa to the north (see Figure 18). In antiquity the city was called a variety of names including "Qisri," and "Qisrin" (mainly in rabbinic sources). It was Herod the Great who named the place "Caesarea," to honor Augustus. This name survives today in the modern Arabic, "Qaisariya." In Greek and Latin sources, the site was referred to as "Caesarea of Straton," "Caesarea of Palestine," and "Caesarea near Sabastos." "Sabastos" is the Greek equivalent of "Augustus."

Figure 18 Caesarea Maritima excavations with view to Mediterranean Sea.

Caesarea Maritima is never mentioned (by any name) in the Hebrew Bible. It is, however, referred to simply as "Caesarea" in the New Testament, with all references coming from the Book of Acts (8: 40; 9: 30; 10: 1, 24; 11: 11; 12: 19; 18: 22; 21: 8, 16; 23: 23, 33; 25: 1). Jesus is never said to have visited the place.

While some exploration of this site occurred as early as the eighteenth century CE, systematic excavations did not begin until 1959 by an Italian team under the direction of A. Frova. Shortly thereafter (1960) A. Negev, from the Israel National Parks Authority, began to excavate the Crusader moat and other ruins including the so-called high-level aqueduct. In 1971, R. Bull (Drew University) began what is called "The Joint Expedition to Maritime Caesarea." This massive endeavor involved nearly two-dozen colleges and universities from the US as well as Canada and lasted for 12 seasons. To the above land-based excavations must be added the underwater exploration of Caesarea's harbor beginning also in 1960. Called the "Caesarea Ancient Harbor Excavation Project" (CAHEP), this effort lasted for years and was successful in recovering much of the past history of this ancient engineering marvel.

The role of Caesarea in the spread of the early Christian church is well documented. According to the Book of Acts (chap. 10), Christianity took root here quite early and by the middle of the third century, the city was a center of Christian activity due to the efforts of the brilliant Egyptian scholar, Origin of Alexandria. The town continued to thrive as a Christian center up until the sixth century. Another famous Christian resident of the place was Eusebius, the Bishop of Caesarea around 315–339. One of his lasting contributions to ancient historical knowledge is his *Onomasticon*.

At the same time that Christianity was flourishing here, so was Judaism. There is some evidence of a rabbinic academy in the third century, and a learned rabbi, Abbahu, was a contemporary of Eusebius. However, during the first quarter of the sixth century, positive relations with the non-Christians of Caesarea began to turn sour and by the middle of the seventh century (634) the city was controlled by the Arabs. The city fell back into Christian hands, briefly, during the time of the Crusades (c.1100–1265). But in 1291 Caesarea was destroyed by the Arabs and never recovered.

While there was a thriving Byzantine city here (the largest city ever to exist here), as well as other periods of occupation (especially Crusader), as the above brief summary shows, a great deal of the archaeological effort expended has been to recover as much as possible of what by all accounts (literary as well as archaeological) must have been a magnificently beautiful city from the time of Herod the Great. The basic literary source for Herod's accomplishments at Caesarea comes from the first-century Jewish historian, Flavius Josephus:

> Now, upon his [Herod's] observations of a place near the sea, which was very proper for containing a city, and was before called Strato's tower, he set about getting a plan for a magnificent city there, and erected many edifices with great diligence all over it, and this of white stone. He also adorned it with the most sumptuous palaces and large edifices for containing the people; and what was the greatest and most laborious of all, he adorned it with a harbor, that was always free from the waves of the sea. Its size was not less than the Piraeus (in Greece) had, toward the city, landing places and secondary anchorages inside for the ships. It was of excellent workmanship; and this was the more remarkable for its being built in a place that of itself was not suitable for such noble structures, but was to be brought to perfection by materials from other places, and at very great expenses.
>
> (*Antiquities* 15: 331–332; see 15: 333–337;
> *JW I*, 408–414)

In addition to the harbor and palaces, Josephus also claimed that Herod built a theater, amphitheater, and a market-place; a temple to Caesar accompanied by a colossal statue of the emperor, and a temple to Roma, the official goddess of Rome. For the most part, archaeological excavations have confirmed in dramatic fashion the lavish description given the city by Josephus.

Remains identified as the theater (see Figure 19, p. 79) were uncovered by the Italians. They showed that the facility, with modifications, of course, was used up to the third–fourth centuries. In fact, a reused stone (a step) from this latter period was discovered in 1962. On it was a Latin inscription mentioning Pontius Pilate. How many local residents could have read Latin when the inscription was up for public notice is not clear. What is clear is that Herod's buildings, statues, and harbor, as well as the later inscription, were all reminders that during this time Rome controlled not only Caesarea but the entire country (Crossan and Reed, 2001: 54–62).

As mentioned above, one of Herod's most astonishing achievements is the harbor he had built here. The full extent of this structure did not begin to come to light until the 1960s when underwater

Figure 19 The remains of the theater of Herod the Great.

explorations were undertaken. Several groups were involved including the Underwater Exploration Society of Israel and the Center for Maritime Civilizations at the University of Haifa. Since 1979, annual excavations were conducted under the auspices of the Center for Maritime Studies, directed by A. Raban. The excavations have shown that exaggerations and inaccuracies occur in Josephus's description of this structure. This is especially true of the submerged parts which Josephus probably could not have seen very well. Nevertheless, the underwater teams have shown that the harbor was built of three basins, one inside the other. The outer basin required further construction of two breakwaters. This construction required engineering techniques called the "first of its kind in history" (A. Raban, *NEAEHL* 1: 290).

To what extent the harbor was used in later periods is not totally clear. By the Late Roman period (third–fourth centuries), the original Herodian breakwaters had apparently submerged into the sea, creating a dangerous situation for later ships that tried to use the facility. How dangerous is clearly reflected in the "seventeen concentrations of broken amphorae and ballast stones" found from ships that wrecked while trying to sail over the tops of the sunken structures (Raban, *NEAEHL* 1: 290). Though the town continued to be occupied, reaching its greatest size in the Byzantine period, the fate of the harbor was the reverse.

Further reading

There are many publications on Caesarea dealing with various aspects of its history and archaeology. The entries in both the *NEAEHL* and the *OEANE* contain their own bibliographies. For a popular, though dated, book on Caesarea see: Kenneth G. Holum, Robert L. Hohlfelder, Robert J. Bull and Avner Raban. *King Herod's Dream: Caesarea on the Sea*. New York: WW Norton, 1988.

For the underwater excavations, see now: Raban, Avner, *et al. The Harbours of Caesarea Maritima: Results of the Caesarea Ancient Harbour Excavation Project, 1980–1985*, Vol. 1, *The Site and Excavations*. John Peter Olson, ed. British Archaeological Reports, International Series, no. 41. Oxford, 1989.

See also, Robert L. Hohlfelder, "The 1984 Explorations of the Ancient Harbors of Caesarea Maritima, Israel." *Preliminary Reports of ASOR – Sponsored Excavations 1982–85. BASOR Supplement No. 25*. Walter E. Rast, ed. Baltimore: The Johns Hopkins University Press, 1988: 1–12.

Crossan, John Dominic and Jonathan L. Reed. *Evacuating Jesus Beneath the Stones, Behind the Texts*. San Francisco: HarperSanFrancisco, 2001.

CAESAREA PHILIPPI (BANIAS)

THE MAGNIFICENT PALACE OF AGRIPPA II

The magnificent remains of Caesarea Philippi (see Figure 20) are located about 24 miles north of the Sea of Galilee. Lying at the south-western base of the Mt. Hermon range, it is very close to the modern borders of Lebanon and Syria. From this site comes one of the three sources of the River Jordan. The original name of the place was "Panion" which refers to the cave sanctuary located here that was dedicated to the Greek god, Pan. This sanctuary is believed to have been established during the third–second centuries BCE. Nearly 2,000 years ago, Josephus, the first-century Jewish historian, gave a graphic description of this cave:

Figure 20 Aerial view of Caesarea Philippi (Banias).

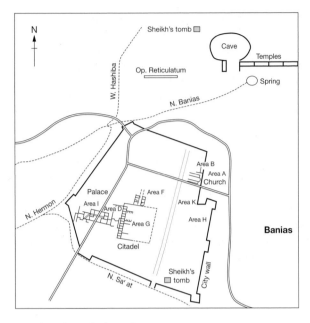

Figure 21 Archaeological plan of site.

"This is a very fine cave in a mountain, under which is a great
cavity in the earth, and the cavern is abrupt, and prodigiously
deep, and full of still water; over it hangs a vast mountain, and
under the caverns arise the springs of the river Jordan."

(*Ant.* 15.10.3)

Later sources refer to the site as "Paneas," "Panias," and "Panium."
The name by which the site is known today, "Banias," is the Arabic
version of the Greek name.

Agrippa II (53–93 CE), around the middle of the first century CE,
named the city "Neronias," in honor of Nero, the Roman emperor
(Josephus, *Ant.* 20.9.4). However, this name never seems to have
caught on. The city built here in 3 BCE by Herod Philip (4 BCE–34
or 40 CE), the son of Herod the Great, was called "Caesarea Philippi"
(Josephus, *Ant.* 18.2.1). It is this name by which the site is known
in the New Testament (see Matt. 16: 13; Mark 8: 27). Also, according
to Josephus, Herod the Great built a temple of white marble here in
honor of Augustus sometime after 20 BCE (*JW*, 1.21.3).

Prior to the establishment of the cult of Pan, it is not clear what
activities, if any, took place on the site. Some scholars have suggested

that cultic practices associated with the names "Baal-gad" (see Josh. 11: 17; 12: 7; 13: 5) and "Baal-hermon" (see Judg. 3: 3; I Chron. 5: 23) may have occurred here (Wilson, 2004: 1–2) It was the establishment of the cults devoted to Pan and other deities that prevailed here during the Hellenistic and Roman periods. According to literary, inscriptional, and numismatic sources, the Pan cult was still thriving in the first century CE when Banias became a large Roman city (Wilson, pp. 2ff.). It was this city which is now beginning to come to light thanks to recent archaeological excavations.

Another interesting tradition associated with this site concerns the story of the woman healed of a hemorrhage by Christ (Matt. 9: 20). According to Eusebius, a fourth-century church historian, the woman was from this place and erected statues both of herself and of Christ to commemorate the event. Eusebius claimed to have seen these statues, as well as paintings of "Peter and Paul, and of Christ himself" (*Ecclesiastical History*, 7.18).

Even though Banias has long been known to biblical historians and geographers, systematic excavations of the ruins did not begin here until the mid 1980s. One of the digs has centered around the Pan sanctuary, both inside and outside the cave. This work has been under the direction of the district archaeologist of the Golan, Zvi Maoz, of the Israel Antiquities Authority (Maoz, "Banias" 1993). The other excavation was centered in the city itself and was conducted by a consortium of American colleges and universities under the direction of Dr. Vassilios Tzaferis, formerly of the Israel Antiquities Authority. Unfortunately, due to the current political situation in Israel, the excavation was closed down after the 2000 season.

The ancient Roman city of Caesarea Philippi covered many acres and while much has been discovered during the previous seasons, much is yet to be found. A major problem here, as on many antiquity sites, is that much of the ancient remains have been robbed out, reused and/or otherwise destroyed or lost. Thus caution is in order in trying to reconstruct the archaeological history of the site. Also, modern roads have been built on the site, thus limiting in some cases where excavation can occur. However, enough has been found to allow the conclusion that during the Early Roman period (basically the last half of the first century CE), Banias was a large city containing many magnificent monumental buildings.

Among these is an incredible complex that came to light during the 1993 season. Constructed of large, dressed, limestone blocks, this structure has been identified as the royal place of Agrippa II (see Figure 23, p. 84). The palace was constructed in a mirror-like fashion

Figure 22 Cave of Pan with spring. The water originally emerged from within the cave.

Figure 23 Remains from the Palace of Agrippa II.

so that the western half is exactly matched by its eastern half (see Figure 24). Measuring over 400 feet wide, from east to west, the palace contained covered passageways, courtyards, a basilica, a fountain and pool, and huge semi-circular guard towers. Evidence of the use of imported marble to decorate the buildings was found in both the debris and in fragments still fastened to the walls with iron nails. On the eastern side of this complex, 12 vaulted rooms, extending more than the length of a football field, were exposed. Each room is approximately 25 feet high, 30 feet long and 20 feet wide. These rooms are thought originally to have belonged to an upper story of the palace complex. Elsewhere, the upper floors had been robbed out over the years to provide material for later constructions. But enough has been recovered to vividly illustrate the engineering skills and wealth it took to build such a huge complex. Datable coins from the remains indicate that this monumental mansion was built during the latter half of the first century CE.

Leading to the city's center was a wide (30 feet) main street called a 'cardo' (see Figure 24). The street ran in a north–south direction and originally was lined with large columns, remains of which were found reused in later walls. Because of disturbances, both ancient and modern, it is not known exactly where this street ended. But it probably led to the heart of the city which was composed of monumental buildings that included temples, a nymphaeum (a fancy water fountain), and other public structures. The archaeological evidence for this conclusion can still be seen in scattered architectural remains

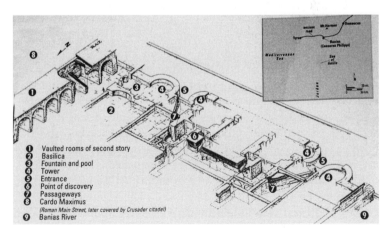

① Vaulted rooms of second story
② Basilica
③ Fountain and pool
④ Tower
⑤ Entrance
⑥ Point of discovery
⑦ Passageways
⑧ Cardo Maximus
   (Roman Main Street, later covered by Crusader citadel)
⑨ Banias River

Figure 24 Plan of palace.

from this time that include large column drums measuring over four feet in diameter as well as beautifully sculptured heart-shaped column bases. Other remains include intricately decorated friezes, mosaic floor fragments, elaborate water pipe systems and pieces of different colored frescos. All of these remains witness to a monumental Roman city that once existed here. The full extent of this part of the city may never be known since a considerable part of the area has been converted to a modern parking lot for visitors.

According to Josephus (*JW*, 3.9.7), the Roman generals, Vespasian and Titus, visited the city, along with their troops. Vespasian was invited by Agrippa himself (Wilson, 2004: 32–34). Josephus reports that Titus "stayed there a considerable time, and exhibited all sorts of shows there; and a great number of the captives were destroyed, some being thrown to wild beasts, and others in multitudes forced to kill one another, as if they were enemies" (*JW* 7.2.1). In all, Josephus claims that over 2,500 Jews were killed at Banias. Even allowing for some exaggeration, these references to large numbers of people visiting Banias for extended periods of time and entertaining themselves with "all sorts of shows" imply facilities large enough to accommodate such activities. But its elaborateness is well attested archaeologically, indicating that Agrippa spared no expense in its construction.

By the end of the first century, however, this Roman city came to an end. Over the palace remains in Area D a massive bathhouse was built that existed through two phases. The first phase dates to the Late Roman period (second–fourth centuries CE). The second phase is from the Byzantine period of the fourth–fifth centuries. Remains of hypocausts and the furnaces that supplied the heat to the cauldarium (hot room) were found scattered over a wide area. In Area B, next to the modern parking lot, a late fourth–early fifth century basilica was found which may have functioned as a Christian church (see Figure 25, p. 87). If so, this is one of the earliest churches found in Israel. For reasons which are not clear, this part of the city (Area B) was abandoned, probably during the fifth century, until the arrival of the Crusaders. The remains of the latter's massive structures – walls, defensive towers, and other projects – can still be seen today. These building activities, however, destroyed much of the earlier remains, making the full recovery of the first-century city of Caesarea Philippi almost impossible.

One of the last chapters of the past history of Banias was written by a group of people called the "Mamluks." The Mamluks (thirteenth century and later) were originally slave children from Turkey taken to Egypt to serve in high-ranking homes. They became a military elite group and eventually came to control Egypt. From there they

Figure 25 Area B, showing ruins from the Early Roman through the Crusader periods. The basilica (church) apse can be seen to the left of top-centre.

spread throughout the Near East and remained powerful into the early part of the nineteenth century. At Banias evidence of their presence can be seen in their ceramic remains, architecture, and even coins. A beautiful stone courtyard with an accompanying fountain, benches, and arches dates to this period. However, a detailed description of their activity at Banias is hampered due to disturbances caused by latter Ottoman as well as modern construction in the area.

Like many ancient sites in this part of the world, Banias witnessed many centuries of struggle for existence. The names of many gods and goddesses were no doubt invoked here. Perhaps, then, it is most fitting that tradition has located in this vicinity the great confession of Peter: "You are the Christ" (Mark 8: 29).

Further reading

Maoz, Zvi. "Banias." *NEAEHL* 1. Ephraim Stern, ed., Jerusalem: Simon & Schuster, 1993: 136–143.

Wilson, John Francis. *Caesarea Philippi: Banias, The Lost City of Pan*. London: I. B. Tauris, 2004.

——— and Vassilios Tzaferis. "Banias Dig Reveals King's Palace." *BAR* 24.1 (1998): 54–61; 85.

CAPERNAUM
OF FISHERMEN AND
GOLD COINS

The Gospels locate the center of Jesus' Galilean ministry in and around Capernaum, the remains of which are located on the north-western shore of the Sea of Galilee. Known as "Tel (or Tal) Hum" in Arabic (the "Hill of Hum"), and "Kefar Nahum" in Hebrew (the "Village of Nahum"), Capernaum existed for more than a thousand years, from the first through the tenth–eleventh centuries CE. During this long period of time the town experienced periods of prosperity when magnificent public buildings were built, such as the beautiful synagogue of the fourth–fifth centuries (see Figure 27, p. 89), as well as periods of decline and destruction. From around 1000 CE up to

Figure 26 Capernaum: general view. The Franciscan property with the famous synagogue is hidden by the trees on the right-hand side of the photo.

the nineteenth century, the site, now known as Tal-Hum, was unoccupied, used only by Bedouins for seasonal agriculture and grazing and by local fishermen.

Though visited by many pilgrims in antiquity, the first modern researcher to survey the site was the American scholar, Edward Robinson. In June of 1838, Robinson correctly recognized the remains of the synagogue but failed to identify the site with Capernaum, which he located some two miles to the southwest, at what is now known as Khirbet Minya. There are many reasons for discounting Robinson's suggestion, the most compelling one being that Khirbet Minya has been excavated and no remains antedating the Early Arabic periods (seventh–tenth centuries) were discovered.

In 1866 a British explorer, Captain Charles Wilson, identified the ancient ruins of Tal-Hum with Capernaum. He thought he had uncovered parts of the first-century synagogue which is said in the Gospel of Luke (7: 5) to have been built by a Roman centurion for the people who lived there. Thus, from the middle of the nineteenth century, a tradition was established which became the main cause of the sacredness of the place and its attraction to Christian pilgrims.

In 1894, the ruins of the synagogue (later to be dated correctly to the fourth–fifth centuries) and the western part of the site were acquired by the Franciscan Custody of the Holy Land, while some years later the Greek Orthodox Church of Jerusalem acquired the

Figure 27 Capernaum synagogue.

northeastern section. Slowly Capernaum began to arise from the abyss in which it had been buried both by man and by nature.

The first real archaeological excavation of the site was conducted by German excavators at the beginning of the twentieth century. Very soon, however, the Franciscans, well aware of the tremendous archaeological and religious value of their property, proceeded on their own. In 1905, they began an excavation of the site, which has continued to the present day, with many interruptions.

On the other hand, the Greek Orthodox section, comprising an area over 200,000 square feet, had a different history. Until 1930 the site was totally neglected, the only visible remains being those of poorly constructed huts which were used for seasonal fishing. In 1931 a small church and winter residence were built here by the Greek Patriarch of Jerusalem. The buildings were used for only a few years and then abandoned. In 1948 the property fell between Syrian and Israeli borders becoming a "no man's land" and was neglected once again. After the Six Day War, in 1967, the section was returned to the Greek Church and beginning in 1978 archaeologists were allowed for the first time to work on this side of the ancient site. The excavations ran through 1987. Thus two separate and totally independent excavations have been conducted here. But it must be emphasized that the story of ancient Capernaum is one, and the results of both excavations need to be consulted.

In all, four areas on the Greek side of the property were excavated (called simply Areas A, B, C, D), the results of which have shed a great deal of light on the settlement of the site from the first–eleventh centuries. During this long period, Capernaum survived through a thriving fishing industry, agriculture products, and trade. The town was located on the main trade route leading to Syria from the port cities of Acco-Ptolemais and Caesarea and was a border town between the Golan and the Galilee.

Evidence of the fishing industry consists not only of fishhooks and lead sinkers but also in the remains of a building in the southeast corner of the site containing what is believed to be an ancient fish pond or holding tank. This structure, measuring some 6.5 × 16 feet was water proofed with a thick plaster coating. Similar structures have been found at other ancient sites located on the shore of the lake. An ancient sea wall and port were also discovered several feet to the south of this holding tank. The wall seems to have run the entire length of the town and probably functioned as a retaining wall to hold back the sea (see Figure 28, p. 91). These structures are believed to date to the Byzantine period (fifth–sixth centuries).

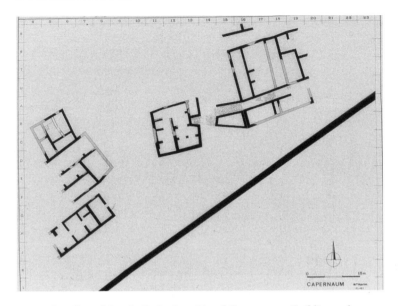

Figure 28 Plan of Greek Orthodox side of Capernaum. Building at bottom left is the Roman bathhouse.

Throughout the excavated areas, the evidence of the Arab presence at Capernaum, which began in the seventh century, could easily be seen. Earlier public buildings were divided by secondary walls into domestic dwellings and a great amount of the common glazed ware, as well as the so-called "Kirbet Mefjer Ware," were discovered. These ceramic types all belong to the Umayyad Period of the seventh–eighth centuries. But the most unexpected discovery from this period occurred in June of 1982. Underneath a stone slab in one of the paved courtyards in Area A, a hoard of 282 Umayyad gold dinars was found (see Figure 29, p. 92). These coins are 22-carat gold and are about the size of an American quarter. They were minted between 696/697 CE and 743/744 CE. Except for the dates of the coins, they all bear the same inscriptions except one. These inscriptions are abridgements of longer Islamic sentiments found on the Dome of the Rock in Jerusalem and are particularly directed against Christian beliefs. While other such hoards have been found, both in and outside of Israel, the Capernaum hoard is extremely important because it was discovered under controlled archaeological conditions. Thus these coins provide a unique look into the cultural, political, and religious world at the point where Islamic and Byzantine cultures intersect.

Figure 29 Umayyad Gold Hoard on day discovered.

Another unexpected discovery in Area A was the occupational history of this part of the site. It was the hope of the excavators to find here remains from the Early Roman period which might shed some light on the history of the town from the first century CE. However, no architectural remains were found earlier than the late sixth–early seventh centuries.

But discoveries from the earlier periods were waiting in the south-west corner of the site (Area B) next to the lake. Here a continuous sequence of occupation from Early Roman through the Early Arab periods (first–tenth centuries) was discovered. The excavation of this part of the site was begun in 1984.

One of the first public buildings to be found was a Roman bath-house of the second–third centuries (see Figure 28, p. 91). Although the western end of the building disappears under the wall separating the Greek and Franciscan properties, many elements of a typical Roman bath were recovered. Its early date and plan, a single row of rooms, may indicate that it was built to serve a Roman clientele rather than Jewish. A very similar bathhouse, dating to the first century, has been found at Ein Gedi, where it too served the needs of a Roman garrison stationed there.

Underneath the bathhouse was found an earlier building dating to the first century. In general, the lines of the plan of this building are similar to the bathhouse above it. If this earlier structure served the same purpose, then this discovery may confirm the existence at Capernaum of a Roman centurion and of a Roman garrison referred to in Matthew 8: 5ff (see Luke 7: 1–10; John 4: 46–53).

The remains of other large public buildings, also dating to the second–third centuries, were found in close proximity to the bathhouse. However, the exact functions of these buildings are still not known. But the archaeological evidence clearly indicates that during the Late Roman period, Capernaum was a well-organized and prosperous little town, with several large and well-constructed public buildings lining the water front.

However, the extent of the town during the first century is not as clear. The archaeological evidence for this period consists mainly of wall fragments and isolated remains of a few buildings. Thus it should be emphasized that the Early Roman finds in both sections of Capernaum do not give a clear plan of the settlement during this period. What is known indicates a small village of limited habitation of probably no more than a thousand people. During this time the town was located on a narrow strip along the shore of the lake. The remains also indicate that the buildings were spacious and well constructed with hewn stones and a large amount of plaster. This would suggest that the first-century village flourished economically. Its location on the crossroads of important trade routes, the fertile lands surrounding it, and the rich fishing available, contributed to its economic development. It is therefore not surprising that the Gospels mention the presence here of customs officers as well as a Roman centurion.

However, not until the second–third centuries did Capernaum become a real town with well-constructed houses, public buildings, and public spaces all set within a well-organized town plan. It is at this time, too, that the town probably acquired its first organized port installations built along the shore of the lake. The mass migration of Jews from Judaea, which followed the havoc of the Jewish revolts of the first and second centuries, no doubt contributed to the town's expansion and economic growth. But in the middle of the fourth century, a major catastrophe occurred which caused a temporary abandonment of the buildings and a subsequent reorganization of the town. The evidence, rooms filled with jumbled rocks and stones, clearly indicates that the cause of the destruction was a major earthquake. Much of the area was levelled and new buildings were put up while old ones were re-organized and re-arranged to meet the needs of the population.

In the framework of this re-organization must be placed the building of the magnificent synagogue and the octagonal church, both on the Franciscan side of the property. The presence of both Jewish and Christian places of worship so close to each other from the same time period raises important questions about the population make-up of Capernaum during this period.

In summary, the archaeological excavations on both sides of the contemporary wall that divides the two properties have succeeded in reconstructing the history of Capernaum by providing concrete archaeological data. Nearly an entire town, with its houses, courts, religious and other public buildings, has emerged from obscurity. During its long history, Capernaum was plundered by men, at least three times, and an equal number of times was destroyed by earthquakes. The last one, occurring in the eleventh century, dealt a fatal blow from which the town never recovered.

Thus from a prosperous village/town of the Early Roman times, to a well-organized and flourishing town of the Late Roman/Early Byzantine periods, Capernaum declined after the Arab conquest, in the seventh century, to an insignificant village. In the ninth–tenth centuries, it passed into obscurity and finally, during the Middle Ages, became an unknown seasonal fishing village until it was totally abandoned and forgotten, never to be occupied again.

Jesus' prophecy of doom: "And you Capernaum, which is exalted unto heaven shall be brought to hell" (Matt. 11: 23), was thus fulfilled, even though it took a thousand years.

Further reading

Carbo, Virgilio. *The House of St. Peter at Capharnaum: A Preliminary Report of the First Two Campaigns of Excavations, April 16–June 19/September 12–November 26, 1968.* Jerusalem: Studium Biblicum Franciscanum Collectio Minor, 5, 1972.

—— *Cafarnao, vol. 1, Gli edifici della citta.* Jerusalem: Studium Biblicum Franciscanum no. 19, 1982.

Laughlin, John C. H. "Capernaum From Jesus' Time and Afterwards." *BAR* 19.5 (1993): 54–61; 90.

Loffreda, Stanislao. *Cafarnao, vol. 2, La ceramica.* Jerusalem: Studium Biblicum Franciscanum no. 19, 1974.

—— *Recovering Capharnaum.* Jerusalem: Studium Biblicum Franciscanum Guides, 1, 1985.

Spijkerman, Augusto. *Cafarnao, vol. 3, Catalogo delle monete della citta.* Jerusalem: Studium Biblicum Franciscanum no. 19, 1975.

Testa, Emmanuele. *Cafarnao*, vol. 3, *I graffiti della casa di S. Pietro*. Jerusalem: Studium Biblicum Franciscanum no. 19, 1972.

Tzaferis, Vassilios *et. al. Excavations at Capernaum Volume I 1978–1982*. Winona Lake, IN: Eisenbrauns, 1989.

CHORAZIN

DID THE CURSE REALLY WORK?

Not very far from **Capernaum** is another village associated in the Gospels with Jesus: Chorazin. Located some two-and-a-half miles north of the Sea of Galilee, the location of this village affords one a spectacular view of the Sea and the Golan Heights. The identity of the site, called Khirbet Karazeh in modern times, with Chorazin was made in the mid nineteenth century by the Dutchman, C. W. M. Vande Velde, and was confirmed by the British scholar, Charles Wilson, in 1869. Chorazin is mentioned only twice in the New Testament (Matt. 11: 21–24 with parallel in Lk. 10: 13–16) where it is condemned by Jesus, along with Capernaum and **BethSaida**. The town is also mentioned in ancient Jewish sources (Tosefta *Makot*, 3:

Figure 30 Chorazin synagogue remains.

8; Babylonian Talmud, *Menahot*, 85a) where it is described as a "medium size" town and praised for its fine wheat. Thus Chorazin is a good example of how archaeology has filled in many gaps that would not be known from the literary sources alone.

While Wilson had identified the remains of a synagogue during his nineteenth-century visit, it was not until the first decade of the twentieth century that actual excavations began. This activity was the work of two German archaeologists, Heinrich Kohl and Carl Watzinger, who worked on the site between 1905 and 1907. In 1926, the site was completely cleared by the Mandatory Department of Antiquities.

The first real scientific excavation of the site took place during the 1960s and 1980s under the direction of Zeev Yeivin. His efforts have resulted in a remarkable restoration of the town as it looked during its Byzantine (fifth–sixth centuries) phase of occupation. The center piece of the restoration is a "Galilean" type synagogue (see Figure 30, p. 96) that stands in the center of the town. It is comparable to other synagogues known in Galilee from this time (third–sixth centuries CE) such as the ones at Capernaum and Barʿam. All of the buildings at Chorazin were constructed from the ubiquitous black basalt stones native to the region. Both public and private buildings were excavated. In some cases the function(s) of the structures could be identified such as ritual baths (*mikve*), olive presses, and water cisterns.

Yeivin identified three major occupational phases of the town dating from the early fourth through the seventh–eighth centuries CE. Of considerable interest is the fact that he did not discover any archaeological remains that could be dated securely to the first half of the first century, the time of Jesus.

Nevertheless, both for architectural as well as cultural/historical reasons, pride of place in the discoveries at Chorazin is the synagogue. Hundreds of architectural elements were found scattered about the site. Included in these elements is the so-called "Seat (Cathedra) of Moses" which was found in the 1920s in the ruins south of the synagogue. The main hall of the synagogue measures some 65 feet long and 45 feet wide. The excavator concluded that it was originally built at the end of the third century or beginning of the fourth century CE. Thanks to the restoration efforts carried out here, today's visitor to the site can readily see what it must have looked like centuries ago when this magnificent structure occupied a central place in the town. Inside the synagogue a large hoard of coins (2,000+) was discovered. The coins date from the fourth to the seventh centuries. Some have interpreted the coins as evidence for Christian (and maybe

Jewish) pilgrims ("tourists") who tossed their coins into the ruins when witnessing what they considered to be the fulfilment of Jesus' curse on the town.

As mentioned above, the excavator found no evidence of a first-century town or village (the oldest datable artifact is a second-century olive oil installation). Does this mean that this site is not the location of Chorazin mentioned in Matthew and Luke? Perhaps. Yeivin estimated that the size of the town during the fourth century covered over 80 acres, of which only a small portion has actually been excavated. Adding to this the very real possibility that the first-century village may have been much smaller than the later town, it is easily conceivable that these remains have so far gone undetected. If future, more extensive, excavations still turn up no such remains then the suggestion that this site is not that of ancient Chorazin will have to be seriously considered.

Further reading

Yeivin, Zeev. "Ancient Chorazin Comes Back to Life." *BAR* 13.1 (1987): 22–36.

—— "Chorazin." *NEAEHL*, 1. Ephraim Stern, ed., Jerusalem: Simon & Schuster, 1993: 301–304.

DAMASCUS

A VERY OLD CITY WHERE PAUL ALMOST GOT HIMSELF KILLED

Damascus, the capital of modern-day Syria, is located about 130 miles northeast of **Jerusalem** and 80 miles inland from the Mediterranean Sea. It lies at the foot of Mount Hermon on the western edge of the Syrian desert. It is popular to refer to Damascus as the oldest continuously occupied city in the world. However, there is no archaeological evidence to support such a claim. Most of its history is known only from literary references. In the 1970s it was reported that the name, "Damascus," had been found in the Ebla tablets which had just been discovered at Tell Mardikh (Ebla) in northern Syria. If this report had been true, the literary evidence for the existence of the city would have been pushed back to at least the twenty-fourth century BCE. Unfortunately, this suggestion has not been confirmed by further studies. Thus, until some discovery to the contrary, the oldest known literary reference to Damascus is from the time of Thutmose III, a fourteenth-century BCE Egyptian pharaoh. Furthermore, the origin of the name, Damascus, is also unclear.

No doubt what attracted the area's first settlers, whatever the date, is the presence of two water sources which flow in or near the city. One is the perennial river, the Abana (or Barada), upon whose banks the city was built. The other, which is located about ten miles south of the city, is the Pharpar (Nahal el-A'waj). These are the rivers said to have been "better than all the waters of Israel," by Naaman, an Aramean who came to Elisha to be healed of a skin disease (2 Kgs. 5: 12). Throughout its ancient history, Damascus was on the major trade routes between Mecca to the south, Baghdad to the east, and the Mediterranean and Egypt to the west and southwest. This trade connection ensured the city a cultural and economic significance it might otherwise have never attained.

In the Old Testament, the site is first mentioned in connection with the stories of Abraham (Gen. 14: 15; 15: 2). Unfortunately, neither of these references aids us in establishing an early date for the existence of the city. Elsewhere, Damascus, and the Aramean empire it represented, played a significant role in the histories of both Israel and Judah (see 2 Sam. 8; 1 Kgs. 11, 15, 19, 20; 2 Kgs. 5, 8, 14, 16, 18; Isaiah 7, 8, and others). One of the most disastrous ventures happened in the eighth century BCE when Bar-Hadad, King of Syria (called Rezin in the Bible; see Isa. 7.1), led a coalition of states, that included Israel, against the Assyrians. The result was defeat for both Damascus (c.732 BCE) and Israel (722/721 BCE).

The most recent archaeological discovery relating to this period is an Aramaic inscription found at Tel Dan in 1993. This inscription, dated to the ninth century BCE, was apparently part of a victory stela set up by the king of Aram (Syria) believed to have been Ben-Hadad, or perhaps Hazael (2 Kgs. 10: 32–33; 12: 17–18). This memorial stone celebrated the victory of the Arameans over the "king of Israel," as well as the "House of David." Thus this inscription has very important historical implications. However, by the end of the ninth century, the Aramean empire began to fall apart. Its end came in 732 BCE when it, along with the capital city of Damascus, was defeated and absorbed into the Assyrian empire, mentioned above.

Due to a lack of archaeological excavations, no architectural remains of the city are known prior to the Roman period (some artifacts believed to date to earlier periods have been found in secondary contexts). If such remains exist they are most likely buried under what is known today as the Old City, although the exact location of ancient Damascus is still a moot issue. It is known, however, that beginning with the time of Pompey (64 BCE), Damascus became part of the Roman empire. Later in this period, Herod the Great, according to Josephus, the first-century CE Jewish historian, built many new buildings here, including a gymnasium and a theater (*JW* 1: 422). Another building erected during the first half of the first century CE was a temple built in honor of the Roman god, Jupiter. This building was surrounded by a large outer court, the eastern and western gates of which are still visible today. However, no remains of the temple have ever been found. Damascus is also famous for its major east–west thoroughfare, called a "Cordo Maximus." This major avenue is commonly identified as the "Street called Straight" in the Book of Acts (9: 11). However, other architectural remains associated with this street, including an arch marking a shift in the direction of the thoroughfare, indicates that it was not totally "straight." A gate on the eastern end of the street still exists, though in its present form it is thought to date no earlier than the third century CE. While the first-century Roman city was certainly experienced by Paul, the association of any of the remains known there today with the Apostle's life is speculative.

Nevertheless, the importance of this Syrian city in the New Testament lies precisely in the story of Paul's conversion to Christianity while on his way there to arrest Jewish Christians who were still worshiping in the local synagogues (Acts 9: 1–2). Very little is actually known regarding the coming of Christianity to this city. From Luke's account (Acts 9: 13–14) it would appear that most or all of the Christians living there were converted Jews. How large the Christian community might have been is also unknown. Nor is it clear how Christianity found its way to this city. It has been suggested that either Christians fled there from Galilee shortly after Jesus' crucifixion, or some church leaders from **Jerusalem** may have gone there. Perhaps a little of both events took place. In any event, by the time of Paul there must have been a sizable group of Jewish Christians living in Damascus to have attracted his attention.

The reference to "synagogues at Damascus" (Acts 9: 2) also implies a sizable Jewish population during this time. According to Josephus, 10,500 Jews (all men) were massacred by local inhabitants during the first Roman war (66–70 CE), an event which took place approximately 30 years after Paul's visit to the city. Whatever their number, Luke reported that after Paul's conversion, the Apostle so angered the Jews who heard him preach that they tried to kill him (Acts 9: 23–24). We are told that they watched the city gates "day and night" in order to catch him. That they were watching the gates may imply that Paul was able to hide himself within the city, being vulnerable to capture only when attempting to leave.

On the other hand, when Paul himself wrote about his trouble in Damascus (2 Cor. 11: 32), he did not mention any threats from the local Jews. Rather, he accused the city's political head (called an "ethnarch") of trying to seize him. This person (usually referred to as a "governor" in English translations) would have been a Nabatean. The Nabateans were an Arab kingdom who came to political prominence during the late Hellenistic and Early Roman periods (third–first centuries BCE). While their political center was located at Petra in the Transjordan, they ultimately came to control most of southern Syria (and thus Damascus) as well as the Negev and the Sinai. Their empire reached its zenith during the reign of the king, Aretas IV (9 BCE–CE 40). It is this king to whom Paul referred in his Corinthian correspondence (2 Cor. 11: 32). Why Paul would have attracted the attention of such a person as this "governor" is not stated. Perhaps the local Jewish reaction to his preaching caused him to be viewed as a trouble maker, thus the attempt to seize him and force him to leave the city (however, Paul did not explain for what purpose the governor was trying to capture him). Whatever the case, in both Luke's and Paul's accounts (Acts 9: 25; 2 Cor. 11: 33), we are told that Paul escaped the efforts to apprehend him (by whomever) by a clandestine nocturnal departure from the city "through the wall."

Perhaps some day more intensive archaeological excavations will uncover additional physical remains from the Damascus of Paul's time. Until, or unless, that happens this city that played such a pivotal role in the life and ministry of the Apostle will of necessity remain hidden from modern eyes. In the eighth century CE, the Umayyad, Caliph al-Walid, built what is now known as the "Great Mosque," considered one of the finest examples of Arab architectural construction. Not long after this, however, Damascus lost its importance as a major city.

Further reading

Creswell, K. A. C. *Early Muslim Architecture*. 2 vols. New York: Hacker Art Books, 1979.

Pitard, Wayne T. *Ancient Damascus: A Historical Study of the Syrian City-State from Earliest Times until Its Fall to the Assyrians in 732 BCE*. Winona Lake, IN: Eisenbauns, 1987.

—— "Damascus." *OEANE* 2. Eric M. Meyers, ed., NY: Oxford University Press, 1997: 103–106.

DAN (TEL)

MASSEBOT AND "HIGH PLACES": THE GODS OF DAN

A well-known biblical city is Dan, whose monumental remains have been identified with modern Tell el-Qadi ("mound of the judge"). The tell (see Figure 31) is located some 25 miles north of the Sea of Galilee and is surrounded by a rich, fertile valley. The identification of the mound with Dan was first proposed by E. Robinson in 1838 and has been confirmed by the systematic archaeological excavations carried out here beginning in the 1960s. The name, "Dan," is mentioned 55 times in the Bible, many of which are anachronistic since the name of the city during the pre-Israelite periods was "Laish" (Judg. 18: 29), or "Leshem" (Josh. 19: 47). From Israelite times (late tenth century BCE–first half of eighth century BCE), Dan was a cult

Figure 31 Tel Dan from the south.

center with the famous "golden calf" set up by Jeroboam I at the end of the tenth century BCE (see 1 Kgs. 12: 29–31; or at least Jeroboam is accused of the deed). Furthermore, the expression, "from Dan to Beersheba," is used many times in the Hebrew Bible to indicate the extent of the empire claimed to have existed under David and Solomon (Judg. 20: 1; 1 Sam. 3: 20; 2 Sam. 3: 10, 17: 11; and others).

According to biblical tradition, Dan was conquered by Ben-Hadad of **Damascus** (1 Kgs. 15: 20; see 1 Chron. 16: 4), a feat which may be celebrated in the now famous "Tel Dan Stela" discovered in 1993. During the last half of the eighth century BCE, the site was captured by the Assyrians (see Judg. 18: 30; 2 Kgs. 15: 29). Apparently the city was still inhabited when the Babylonians invaded the country during the first half of the sixth century BCE (Jer. 4: 15; 8: 16).

While a very brief archaeological probe was made on the site in 1963 by Z. Yeivin, the major excavation of Tel Dan has been the work of Avraham Biran. Beginning in 1966, Biran's excavation has continued for over 30 years, making the Dan excavation the longest continuous archaeological project ever conducted in the state of Israel. The archaeological data indicate that the site was occupied at least as early as the Pottery Neolithic period (*c.*5000 BCE) and was not abandoned until the Late Roman/Byzantine period of the fourth century CE. However, the major architectural remains belong to the Middle Bronze Age and Iron Age II.

During the Middle Bronze Age I /II (2000–1800 BCE), Dan (Laish) was a large heavily fortified city. It was protected by a rampart wall, the core of which measures over 25 feet thick. The width of the base of the rampart is over 160 feet. The rampart was built at a 40° angle and was covered with crushed limestone (called "travertine"). It is believed that the limestone was added to prevent erosion of the slopes. How high the original Middle Bronze Age wall stood is not known.

Associated with this wall is one of the most remarkable discoveries made at Dan – a mud brick gate standing probably close to its original height (see Figure 32, p. 105 and Figure 33, p. 106). Discovered on the southeastern corner of the tell (Area K), the gate was preserved to a height of 23 feet and contained 47 courses of sun-dried brick. It measures over 55 feet wide and 44 feet long. Entering the gate from the outside, a person would have walked some 34 feet before exiting the gate inside the city. During the trip, the visitor or citizen of Dan would have passed by four guard chambers. On the outside, the gate was protected by two large towers. A most unexpected discovery

Figure 32 Middle Bronze Age II mudbrick gate.

was the series of arches that formed the foundation for the gate's superstructure. One arch is at the outside entrance, one in the middle, and one where the gate opens into the city. Each arch is composed of three radial courses of sun-dried mud brick. Biran concluded that the gate system was used for only a generation or so before being incorporated into the rampart system (see the chapter on **Acco** for another Middle Bronze Age mud-brick gate incorporated into a rampart wall). It was this latter development that preserved the structure until its discovery in 1979.

The Middle Bronze Age city at Dan came to an end sometime in the late sixteenth or early fifteenth century BCE. The cause of this is not clear, but an ash layer discovered in one of the squares led the excavator to suggest that perhaps the city met a violent end, as did other contemporary Middle Bronze Age cities.

While architectural remains were found dating to the Late Bronze Age, damage to these structures was widespread due to subsequent Iron Age I activity. However, evidence for a smelting industry during this last phase of the Bronze Age was found, including furnaces, slag, and muzzles of blow pipes. Another important discovery dating to the fourteenth–thirteenth century BCE is a "Mycenaean" tomb that contained the remains of some 40 people, including men, women, and children. Hundreds of grave goods were found in connection with this tomb as well as a substantial amount of pottery. Among the

Figure 33 Middle Bronze Age gate: model.

latter were over two dozen vessels imported from the Mediterranean region, the most spectacular of which is a "Charioteer" vase painted in red and black. This is the only complete example of this ware found to date in Israel. It can be viewed and appreciated today in the Israel Museum in Jerusalem. Such tomb goods would suggest a wealthy family existed here.

The Iron Age I period at Dan is identified with Strata VI–V (twelfth–eleventh centuries BCE). Stratum VI is represented primarily by pits thought to have been used as some sort of silos. Pottery remains in the Late Bronze Age ceramic tradition were also found, including the so-called collared-rim pithoi, a pottery vessel which is more common at sites south of Dan. The second phase of Iron Age I was seen in the remains of stone structures with plastered floors and roofs. This phase was violently destroyed (c.1150 BCE). The excavator linked this destruction with the biblical story of the migration of Dan told in the book of Judges (18: 27). However, this conclusion is based more on the biblical story than on archaeology.

Nevertheless, from a biblical perspective, the most important period of Dan's existence was during the next three phases (Str. IV–II), archaeologically known as Iron Age II (tenth–sixth centuries BCE). During this time Dan reached a size of 50 acres and was protected by massive defensive walls. The discoveries from this period are too many to treat fully here, but include significant architectural remains, ceramics, small objects (many of which may have cultic significance), as well as cultic installations, including what Biran identified as a "bama" ("High Place"; see Figure 34, p. 108; see 1 Kgs. 12: 31. On the complex issue of identifying cultic remains as "bama" see now Elizabeth C. LaRocca-Pitts, 2001; pp. 127–159; especially pp. 131–133 for the case of Dan), that was used from the tenth through the eighth centuries BCE.

The Iron Age defensive system at Dan is one of the largest yet discovered in Israel. It consists of an outer and inner gate that enclosed an area of some 4,500 square feet. Associated with this gate is a podium or dais of some kind and a limestone bench. What exactly these items were used for in antiquity is unclear. It has been suggested that the podium may have been used as a seat for a visiting king, or to hold the image of a god. Most surprising are the four sets of *massebot* discovered in and around the vicinity of the gates. Two of these installations consisted of five stones each (see Figure 35, p. 108); the other two seem to have consisted of only four stone each. These discoveries, however interpreted, point to the importance of the location of religious shrines at or near city gates. Whether they were for

Figure 34 Tel Dan Bama ("high place").

Figure 35 *Massebot* (standing stones) near Iron Age II gate.

the use of the city's inhabitants ("Israelites"), or for foreign non-Israelite guests, or both, is not clear. If these shrines were used by Dan's local citizenry, they are of upmost importance in attempting to understand the popular religion of the ancient Israelites as opposed to the "official" version contained in the Bible. On the other hand, the difficulty of identifying the function(s) of such stone installations has been demonstrated recently by E. C. LaRocca-Pitts (2001: 205–228).

Another important discovery made here in 1993 is a stela fragment written in Aramaic (two other smaller pieces of the stela were found in 1994). Dated to the last half of the ninth century BCE (by the excavator), the stela celebrates a victory over Dan by **Damascus** (according to 1 Kgs. 15: 20, Ben-Hadad captured Dan during his reign). The inscription has created something of a controversy because part of it has been translated to refer to the "House of David." If this translation is correct, this is the first clear reference to "David" found outside the Bible.

While the city of Dan seems to have been captured during both the Assyrian (eighth century BCE; see Judg. 18: 30) and the Babylonian (sixth century BCE) assaults, it continued to be inhabited. However, even though some significant discoveries have been made from the later periods (a very important one being the bilingual text from the Hellenistic period that mentions "the god who is in Dan"), the site never recovered its pre-Assyrian size.

Further reading

Biran, Avraham. "Tell Dan: Five Years Late." *BA* 43 (1980): 168–192.
—— "Two Discoveries at Tel Dan." *IEJ* 30.1 (1980): 89–98.
—— "The Discovery of the Middle Bronze Age Gate at Dan," *BA* 44 (1981): 139–44.
—— "The Triple-Arched Gate of Laish at Tel Dan." *IEJ* 34.1 (1984): 1–19.
—— *Biblical Dan*. Jerusalem: Israel Exploration Society Hebrew Union College-Jewish Institute of Religion, 1994.
—— "Sacred Spaces of Standing Stones, High Places and Cult Objects at Tel Dan." *BAR* 24.5 (1998): 38–45, 70.
—— "The High Places of Biblical Dan." *SAIA*. Amihai Mazar, ed., Sheffield: Sheffield Academic Press, 2001: 148–155.
—— and J. Naveh. "An Aramaic Stela Fragment from Tel Dan." *IEJ* 43 (1993): 81–98.
—— and J. Naveh. "The Tel Dan Inscription: A New Fragment." *IEJ* 45 (1995): 1–18.
—— with D. Ilan and R. Greenberg. *Dan I: A Chronicle of the Excavations, the Pottery Neolithic, the Early Bronze Age and the Middle Bronze Age Tombs.*

Jerusalem: Nelson Glueck School of Biblical Archaeology Hebrew Union College-Jewish Institute of Religion, 1996.

LaRocca-Pitts, Elizabeth C. "*Of Wood and Stone*": *The Significance of Israelite Cultic Items in the Bible and Its Early Interpreters*. Winona Lake, IN: Eisenbrauns, 2001.

Laughlin, John C. H. "The Remarkable Discoveries at Tel Dan." *BAR* 7.5 (1981): 20–37.

EKRON/TEL MIQNE

PHILISTINE CAPITAL OF THE
OLIVE OIL INDUSTRY

Ekron, identified in the Bible as one of the five cities of the Philistine
Pentapolis (Josh. 13: 3), lies in the Shephelah 21 miles or so south
of **Jerusalem**. The site was not identified as the biblical city until a
1957 survey of Khirbet el-Muqanna, the modern Arabic name of the
place. In 1964, the consonants of the Arabic name, *muqan*na, were
transliterated into Hebrew resulting in the now familiar *Miqne*.

Ekron in the Bible

The city is mentioned 25 times in the Bible, over 50 percent of
which are located in Joshua (five times) and 1 Samuel (eight times).

Figure 36 Ekron/Tel Miqne excavations.

111

In Joshua 15: 46, Ekron and its territory are said to belong to Judah, while elsewhere (Josh. 19: 43) the city is said to have been given to the tribe of Dan. Judah's claim to the place may be reinforced by a tradition in Judges 1: 18 which claims that Judah took Ekron along with Gaza and **Ashkelon**. However, in the Greek Bible (Septuagint), Judges 1: 18 states that Judah did *not* take Ekron. This may have been an attempt by the translator to harmonize the Hebrew text which claims that Judah could not drive out the inhabitants of the plain because they had chariots of iron (Judg. 1: 19).

In 1 Samuel, Ekron is very much part of the story of the abduction of the Ark of YHWH (1 Sam. 5; 6). This object is taken to Ekron (1 Sam. 5: 10) where the five "lords" of the Philistines (1 Sam. 6: 16ff) also gathered. Following the story of the defeat of Goliath by David (1 Sam. 17; but see 2 Sam. 21: 19), we are told that there was a rout of the Philistines who fled to **Gath** and Ekron.

Another interesting biblical story involving the town is recounted in 2 Kings 1. Ahaziah, the king of Israel, was injured in a fall, we are told, and appealed to the god of Ekron, Baal-zebub ("Lord of the Flies," which is most likely a deliberate corruption on the part of the biblical writers of "Baal Zebul") for help. His reliance upon Baal-zebub and not YHWH was considered apostasy by the prophet, Elijah, who subsequently pronounced a death sentence upon the king.

Ekron is also mentioned in four prophetic books: Amos (1: 8); Jeremiah (25: 20); Zephaniah (2: 4); and Zechariah (9: 5, 7). One of the most interesting of these is the last one in which the prophet suggests that the Philistines of Ekron will become like the Jebusites (Jewish converts?).

Ekron in extra-biblical texts

Unlike Ashkelon, which is mentioned in the Execration Texts of the early second millennium BCE, Ekron is not named in a non-biblical text until the late eighth–early seventh century BCE Assyrian inscriptions. Texts assigned to the reigns of Sennacherib (704–681 BCE), Esarhaddon (680–669), and Ashurbanipal (668–633) all list Ekron among their vanquished cities/territories/kings. One of the more insightful references is found in Sennacherib's claim that he took Ekron with its "officials, the patricians and the (common) people," (*ANET*, 1969: 287), hinting at a very distinctive social stratification that existed in the city during this time.

A reference to Ekron may also occur in a late-seventh-century BCE Aramaic papyrus known as "The Adon Letter." The text identifies an "Adon" as a king who appealed to Egypt for help against the Babylonians. In a new study of this text, B. Porten (1981) has argued that "Adon" is the king of Ekron. In any event, whether the king of Ekron or not, Adon's appeal went unanswered as Ekron was destroyed by the Babylonians in 603 BCE.

The city of Ekron is also mentioned in several places by Josephus (*Antiquities*) but most of them come in his paraphrasing the biblical stories summarized above. The latest non-biblical references to Ekron are found in Eusebius, the fourth-century CE Christian historian (*Onomasticon* 11: 6–7; 11: 9–10). Here the author locates Ekron in reference to a place called "Accaron."

The archaeology of Ekron

The first, and only, systematic excavation of Ekron/Tel Miqne (see Figure 36, p. 111) began in 1981 under the direction of Trude Dothan of Hebrew University and Seymour Gitin, the Director of the Albright Institute of Archaeological Research (AIAR), Jerusalem. While some Chalcolithic (fifth–fourth millennium BCE) material was discovered, the excavators have identified 11 strata of occupation of the tell dating from the Middle Bronze Age (Str. XI) down to the end of the seventh century BCE (Str. I). At its pinnacle, Ekron was one of the largest Iron Age cities yet discovered in Israel, measuring over 60 acres in size. While the site was continuously occupied from the Middle Bronze Age to Iron Age II, the excavators have shown that there were several expansions and contractions of the city. Only on the acropolis (Field I), located on the northern end of the tell, and comprising only two-and-a-half acres, was there material evidence of occupation for all of the archaeological periods catalogued. There was a 400-year gap, for example, in the lower city (some 40 acres in size) between the end of the Middle Bronze Age and its resettlement at the beginning of the Iron Age I (*c*.1200 BCE). Following the end of Iron Age I (*c*.1000 BCE), the same phenomenon occurred in the lower city again, this time for 250 years before being re-occupied at the end of the eighth century BCE. Both Iron Age I and Iron Age II cities were carefully designed and contained industrial zones, an "elite" zone, and fortifications.

The first Philistine city built here dates to the Iron Age I period (1200–1000). A large amount of distinctive Philistine pottery (e.g. bichrome decoration of white slip) came from this period as well as a rich assortment of other discoveries. Among the latter are some 25 pebbled hearths, an iron knife with an ivory handle (altogether four such handles were found), conical-shaped stamp seals, and a bull-shaped zoomorphic vessel. The remains of a very distinctive building were also uncovered. Identified as a "megaron," it is one of only two such buildings yet discovered in Israel. The other was found in Qasile, also a Philistine city. A "megaron" is a rectangular shaped building often containing a pillared porch and a large central hearth (see Figure 37). While common in the Mycenaean world, they are rare in Israel. The Philistine city of Stratum IV was destroyed around 1000 BCE, according to the excavators. This destruction has been credited to David of biblical fame. However, this conclusion is based on the Bible, not archaeological evidence.

During the first 300 years of the Iron Age II period (1000–700 BCE) only the ten-acre upper city was occupied. However, with the coming of the Assyrians, Ekron became a very prosperous city once again. During this time it became the largest olive oil production center known from the ancient world. Some 115 olive presses have so far been discovered. In addition, in the lower city (Field 14) the remains of eight courtyard-type buildings were uncovered. Among the more impressive small finds are decorated vessels, 14 Hebrew inscriptions, and dozens of pieces of silver jewelry. In fact, five caches of silver jewelry were found, making this the largest assemblage of silver found to date in Israel.

After centuries of Philistine occupation, Ekron was destroyed by Nebuchadnezzar in 603 BCE. Thousands of whole clay vessels were found beneath the destruction debris left by the devastation. Following this Babylonian destruction Ekron was abandoned until a small Roman settlement was built on the northern edge of the site. This in turn was followed by small Byzantine and Arab occupations, after which Ekron was abandoned for good.

Figure 37 Drawing of Philistine hearth discovered at Ekron.

Further reading

Dothan, Trude. "Ekron of the Philistines, Part I: Where They Came From, How They Settled Down and the Place They Worshipped In." *BAR* 16.1 (1990): 26–36.

—— "Bronze Wheels from Tel Miqne-Ekron." *Eretz-Israel* 23 (1992): 148–154.

—— "Tel Miqne Ekron: The Aegean Affinities of the Sea Peoples' (Philistines') Settlement in Canaan in the Iron Age I." *REI.* S. Gitin and W. G. Dever, eds. Winona Lake, Indiana: Eisenbrauns, 1994: 41–59.

—— and Alexander Zukerman. "A Preliminary Study of the Mycenaean IIIC:1 Pottery Assemblages from Tel Miqne-Ekron and Ashdod." *BASOR* 333 (2004): 1–54.

Eitam, David and A. Shomroni. "Research of the Oil Industry during the Iron Age at Tel Miqne." In *Olive Oil in Antiquity*. M. Heltzer and D. Eitam, eds. Haifa, 1987: 37–56.

Gitin, Seymour. "Seventh-Century BCE Cultic Elements at Ekron." In *BAT 90*: 248–258.

—— "Tel Miqne-Ekron in the Seventh century BCE: City Plan Development," in *Olive Oil in Antiquity*. M. Heltzer and D. Eitam, eds. Haifa: The Culture and Art Division, Ministry of Education and Culture, 1987: 81–97.

—— "Incense Altars from Ekron, Israel, and Judah; Context and Typology." *Eretz-Israel* 20 (1989): 52–67.

—— "Ekron of the Philistines, Part II: Olive Oil Suppliers to the World." *BAR* 16.2 (1990): 34–42, 59.

—— "The Impact of Urbanization on a Philistine City: Tel Miqne-Ekron in the Iron Age II Period." In *Proceedings of the Tenth World Congress of Jewish Studies, Jerusalem 1989*, Jerusalem: World Union of Jewish Studies, 1990: 277–284.

—— "New incense Altars from Ekron: Context, Typology, and Function." *Eretz-Israel* 23 (1992): 43–49.

—— "Tel Miqne-Ekron in the Seventh-Century BCE: The Impact of Economic Innovation and Foreign Cultural Influences on a Neo-Assyrian Vassal City State." *REI.* S. Gitin and W. G. Dever, eds. Winona Lake, Indiana: Eisenbrauns, 1994: 61–79.

—— "Tel Miqne: A Type-Site for the Inner Coastal Plain in the Iron Age II Period," in *REI.* S. Gitin and W. G. Dever, eds. Winona Lake, Indiana: Eisenbrauns, 1994: 23–58.

—— and Trude Dothan. "The Rise and Fall of Ekron of the Philistines: Recent Excavations at an Urban Border Site." *BA* 50 (1987): 197–222.

Gittlen, Barry. "The Late Bronze Age 'City' at Tel Miqne-ekron." *Eretz-Israel* 23 (1992): 50–53.

Gunneweg, Ian *et al.* "On the Origin of Pottery from Tel Miqne-Ekron." *BASOR* 264 (1986): 3–16.

Hesse, Brian. "Animal Care at Tel Miqne-Ekron in the Bronze Age and Iron Age." *BASOR* 264 (1986): 17–27.

Porten, B. "The Identity of King Adon," *BA* 44 (1981): 36–52.

FAR'AH, TELL EL- (NORTH)
– BIBLICAL TIRZAH?
IS THERE A WALL OF
"SEPARATION"?

The antiquity site identified with biblical Tirzah is located some six miles northeast of the modern village of Nablus and eight-and-a-half miles east of the tell of **Samaria** (see Figure 38). Tell el-Far'ah means "mound (ruin) of the elevated" and is to be distinguished from another site known as **Tell el-Far'ah South** (see next entry). Various suggestions were made many years ago for the biblical identification of this 25-acre site. In 1931, W. F. Albright argued that it was the biblical city of Tirzah (see 1 Kgs. 16: 23). Today his identification generally seems to be accepted by other authorities, though the archaeological evidence alone does not support unconditionedly Albright's conclusion.

Figure 38 Tell el-Far'ah (North), with what is called the "dividing wall."

The excavation of this site was conducted on behalf of the Ecole Biblique et Archeologique Francaise in Jerusalem by the late R. de Vaux. De Vaux directed nine seasons of excavation here between 1946 and 1960. Unfortunately, de Vaux died (1971) before final reports were published. Furthermore, his field methods (fairly common at the time) were heavily weighed towards architectural exposure and not stratigraphical analysis, as is emphasized today. Consequently, some of his major conclusions have been challenged. Regardless of these problems, de Vaux's work is very important for understanding the ancient history of Canaan.

Few topics are probably less exciting to a general reader of archaeological discussions than stratigraphy. But the understanding of the stratigraphical history (how a site developed over time, enabling an archaeologist to locate discoveries to a particular period of occupation) is very important for accurate interpretation. De Vaux divided the history of Tell el-Far'ah into seven major periods, some of which were sub-divided into "strata." Some of his interpretations have been revised by later scrutiny. His major periods are as follows:

I   The Pre-Pottery Neolithic (seventh–sixth millennia BCE)
II   Chalcolithic (mid-fifth–fourth millennium BCE)
III Early Bronze I (c.3300–3000 BCE)
IV   Early Bronze II (c.3000–2650 BCE)
V   Middle Bronze Age II A–C (2000–1550 BCE (note: de Vaux's Middle Bronze Age II A is called "Middle Bronze Age I" by other authorities))
VI   Late Bronze Age (1550–1200 BCE)
VII Iron Age (twelfth–fifth centuries BCE (this period was sub-divided into five distinct sub-periods labeled VIIa–VIIe)).

While evidence of the earliest occupation is that of the PPN, the best preserved remains date to the Chalcolithic, Early Bronze I and II and Iron Ages I and II. Very important tombs from the Chalcolithic period were discovered which contained what the excavator called "the most important and most complete collection of vases and objects from the Upper Chalcolithic which has yet been found" (*AOTS*, 1967: 372). While five phases from the Early Bronze Age were identified, none dated later than Early Bronze Age II (c.2700–2600 BCE). Among the remains from this time (Early Bronze Age II) is one of the earliest updraft pottery kilns ever discovered in Israel. Other important material remains, such as fortifications, also date to Early Bronze Age II. The site was abandoned after this period and was not re-occupied for some 600 years in what is now commonly called Middle Bronze Age I. The reason for the site's desertion is unclear. De Vaux suggested that malaria may have been partly responsible. Yet some close-by sites, such as Mitham Wadi Far'ah and Khirbet el-Makhruq, prospered during the Early Bronze Age III period.

The mound was re-inhabited at the beginning of the second millennium BCE, but did not become a true fortified city until Middle Bronze Age II (eighteenth century BCE). In fact, a city gate built at this time is believed to have continued in use (with repairs and changes) throughout the Iron Age. De Vaux also discovered from this period what he described as an "underground sanctuary" believed to have been connected with a Middle Bronze Age temple. Due to the poor stage of preservation of the remains, however, it is difficult to draw hard and fast conclusions concerning the details.

Period VI, dated to the Late Bronze Age, was poorly preserved and the evidence for activity during this time is unclear. A small statute of the goddess, Hathor, made of bronze and covered with silver leaf was found in what the excavator believed was a sanctuary. Others have suggested the building in which the object was found was nothing more than a private house dating from the Iron Age, not the Late Bronze Age. The end of the Late Bronze Age at Far'ah (N) is also a matter of dispute. De Vaux credited it to an "Israelite" attack while others have argued for the site's abandonment under unclear circumstances during the thirteenth century BCE. Although, in fairness to de Vaux, it should be pointed out that in a general essay on the site published in 1967, he admitted that the only evidence for an Israelite destruction was based on the assumption that biblical Tirzah was in fact located at Tell el-Far'ah. Even if this assumption proves to be true, it still does not mean that the biblical story (Josh. 12: 24) can or should be taken at face value.

The archaeological period that has generated the most discussion is the last one (Str. VII) in which were discovered the material remains from Iron Age I and II (roughly the twelfth–sixth centuries BCE). If Tell el-Far'ah (N) was biblical Tirzah, then this is a very important Iron Age site because of the role this city is said to have played in Israelite politics, especially during the time of Omri in the ninth century BCE. According to the biblical story, Omri began his reign as king with Tirzah as his capital and then quickly moved it to Samaria where he built an enormous palace complex. De Vaux argued that an "incomplete" building from Stratum VII C (ninth century) was evidence of the haste with which Omri moved from Tirzah to Samaria. The excavator also interpreted building remains from the eighth century (see Figure 38, p. 116) as evidence of a socioeconomic gap between "rich" and "poor" people condemned by prophets such as Amos (5: 11) and Hosea (8: 14). In a review of a publication on the Iron Age material, T. L. McClellan has seriously challenged these conclusions (McClellan, 1987). In his words: "there is no reliable evidence for an unfinished palace that might be attributed to Omri, nor is there evidence for a widening socioeconomic gap between rich and poor at Tell el-Far'ah (N)" (1987: 86). Perhaps future renewed excavations of the site can settle some of these disputes. What does seem clear is that the site, whether biblical Tirzah or not, was destroyed by the Assyrians during the last third of the seventh century BCE (c.732). While some finds indicate activity here during the Hellenistic–Roman periods, for all intent and purposes, the site was abandoned for good by the end of the seventh century BCE.

Further reading

McClellan, Thomas L. "Review of Alain Chambon. *Tell el-Far'ah I: L'age du fer.*" In *BASOR* 267 (1987): 84–86.

Vaux, Roland de. "The Excavations at Tell el-Far'ah and the Site of Ancient Tirzah." *PEQ* (1956): 125–140.

—— "Tirzah." In *AOTS*: 371–383.

FAR'AH, TELL EL- (SOUTH)

AN IMPORTANT CITY, BUT PROBABLY NOT SHARUHEN

The problem with identifying antiquity sites with biblical place names is clearly illustrated with Tell el-Far'ah (S), a mound located about 15 miles south of Gaza and 18 miles west of **Beersheba** (see Figure 39). While the archaeological remains indicate that there was an important town here during the Middle Bronze Age–Late Bronze Age periods (important, at least to the Egyptians), the site's identification with any known ancient place is controversial. The excavator, Sir Flinders Petrie (1853–1942), who excavated the site in 1928 and 1929, identified it with Beth-Pelet (see Josh. 15: 27). On the other hand,

Figure 39 Tell el-Far'ah (South).

W. F. Albright's equation of the ruin with biblical Sharuhen ("their fields"), which is mentioned only once in the Bible (Josh. 19: 6), was accepted by many authorities. However, other suggestions for the location of ancient Sharuhen have been made. The most popular of which today seems to be Tell el-'Ajjul. A major strength of this suggestion is that Sharuhen seems to be close to the coast (*ANET*, 1969: 333) and Tell el-'Ajjul is much closer to the Mediterranean than is Tell el-Far'ah (S). If this proves to be the case, Tell el-Far'ah (S) is a major archaeological site whose ancient identity is unknown. But because of the discoveries here and their implications for under-standing the wider context of the social/political/economic world out of which the Bible came, a brief discussion of the archaeological history of this site is justified.

The mound is over 300 feet above sea level and is about 16 acres in size. It contains layers of occupational debris nearly 50 feet deep. Archaeologically, what can be said is that during the Middle Bronze Age II B (1750–1550 BCE), a well-fortified town existed here. In fact, the three-entryway gate from this period is very similar to other gates known from such sites as **Gezer**, **Hazor**, **Shechem**, and **Tell Beit Mirsim**. From the Late Bronze Age (1550–1200 BCE), a large building (called "the residency") measuring some 82 by 72 feet was uncovered. It contained a central courtyard, bedrooms and a "bath-room." In one storeroom, 45 jars were found, some sealed with conical clay stoppers sporting the figure of a "god" riding upon a lion. The remains of a small charred wooden box with Egyptian hunting scenes and dancing girls was also recovered.

Petrie also discovered material evidence of an Iron Age I occupa-tion (1200–1000) including a city wall. Since most Iron Age I sites in Israel were unfortified, this is a significant discovery. The material from Iron Age II (*c.*1000–586 BCE) is not clear, though there does seem to have been some inhabitation during the tenth century BCE. However, the evidence, especially from the famous cemeteries, points to an occupational gap between the ninth and seventh centuries. Following the Exile (post 539 BCE) there does not seem to be another significant occupation until the Roman period of the first century CE.

Over 350 tombs are known from the cemeteries surrounding the site. These include rectangular shaft tombs from both the Middle Bronze Age and the Late Bronze Age which had been dug into the slope of the Middle Bronze Age ramparts, which apparently were no longer in use. In one tomb from the Late Bronze Age were found several Mycenean vessels, indicative of trade connections with the

Mediterranean world. Perhaps the most interesting tombs are those of the Iron Age I period which contained large amounts of Philistine ware. In addition, two cigar-shaped anthropoid clay coffins were found which are similar to coffins known from other sites such as **Beth-Shean** and Deir el-Balah. The human face on these coffins is usually depicted on the lid with a narrow elongated beard and arms emerging from beneath (behind?) the ears, joining underneath the beard. While tombs from the early part of Iron Age II (tenth–early ninth century) were also discovered, no burials were found dating from the eighth–seventh centuries. This is taken by some scholars to indicate a gap in the occupation of the site. There is some evidence of activity during the Persian period and several coin hoards date to the Roman period of occupation.

Further reading

Kempinski, Aharon. "Tell el-'Ajjul – Beth Aglayim or Sharuhen?" *IEJ* 24.3–4 (1974): 145–152.

Oren, Eliezer D. "'Governor's Residencies' in Canaan under the New Kingdom: A Case Study of Egyptian Administration." *Journal of the Society for the Study of Egyptian Antiquities* 14 (1984): 37–56.

Price-Williams, David. *The Tombs of the Middle Bronze Age II Period from the "500" Cemetery at Tell Fara (south)*. London: University of London, Institute of Archaeology, Occasional Publications, No. 1, 1977.

Rainey, Anson F. "Sharhan/Sharuhen – The Problem of Identification." *Eretz-Israel* 24 (1993): 178*–187*.

GATH (TELL ES-SAFI)
"TELL IT NOT IN GATH"

The Bible mentions the "five lords (rulers) of the Philistines" (Josh. 13: 3) and assigns to each one a city: **Ashdod**, **Ashkelon**, Gaza, **Gath** and **Ekron**. The locations of the first three have long been known, and in the cases of Ashdod, Ashkelon and Ekron/Tel Miqne major excavations have taken place. While Gaza's location is almost certain, the modern town located here has restricted archaeological work considerably. The identification of Ekron with Tel Miqne, while long suspected, was confirmed rather dramatically in 1996 with the discovery of a monumental inscription bearing the name "Ekron" (see Gitin *et al.*, 1997; Demsky, 1998; see Chapter 23).

Figure 40 Gath.

The precise location of Gath, however, has had a lengthy controversy surrounding it, with various authorities suggesting one of several antiquity sites (for where the discussion stood in the mid 1960s see G. E. Wright, 1966). However, with renewed excavations at Tell es-Safi beginning in 1997 (see Figure 40, p. 123), the controversy may be about over (Maier and Ehrlich, 2001; Schniedewind, 1998). Prior to the current excavation of the tell, the site was briefly explored by Frederick J. Bliss (1859–1937) and R. A. S. Macalister (1870–1950) in 1899. Nothing else archaeologically was undertaken on the site until a 1996 survey which revealed a ruin much larger than expected (over 100 acres). In 1997, Aren Maeir of Bar-Illan University began systematic excavations which are still in progress as of 2005.

Tell es-Safi is located roughly five miles south of Ekron on the eastern edge of the so-called "Philistine Coastal Plain." It is on an important intersection between the Via Maris, a major ancient road that runs from Egypt to Syria, and a local road that runs east-northeast through the Shephelah to Jerusalem, which is some 22 miles to the northeast.

The earliest material discovered so far dates to the Early Bronze Age II–III period (c.2900–2250 BCE), though little is known of this settlement. A Late Bronze Age II Canaanite city (c.1300–1200 BCE) showed evidence of wide destruction at the end of this period. This destruction has been interpreted by the excavators as evidence of a possible Philistine assault whose presence is well-attested at the site from the late Iron Age I (eleventh century BCE) to early Iron Age II (ninth century BCE). The archaeological evidence also points to a late ninth–early eighth century BCE destruction. The excavators have suggested that this destruction may have been the result of the invasion of the area by the king of Aram (Syria), Hazael, as recorded in the Bible (2 Kgs. 12: 17–18). If Tell es-Safi was ancient Gath, it had some form of occupation late in the eighth century when Sargon II, the Assyrian king, took the city (*ANET*, 1969: 287). This is the last significant historical reference to ancient Gath.

An interesting discovery, dated to the ninth–eighth century BCE, is a huge ditch stretching about one-and-a-half miles on three sides of the tell. This installation is 25 feet wide at the top, 20 feet deep, and 13 feet wide at the bottom. It has been interpreted as an offensive siege construction designed by the attackers to ensure that the city's inhabitants did not escape. It is a unique discovery in Israel.

While the identity of the mound with ancient Gath has not been "proven" absolutely, its location, its size, its geography, the amount of Philistine pottery, and archaeological history, all count as evidence in that direction. If it is not Gath, a very large, otherwise unknown, Philistine site has been discovered.

Based on biblical connections alone, Gath would appear to be the most important Philistine city during this time. It is mentioned more often (37 times) then any of the other Philistine cites, and was home to the only Philistine king or ruler mentioned by name (Achish) in the Bible (1 Sam. 21: 10). In addition, Gath was the home-place of Goliath, the Philistine giant (1 Sam. 17), as well as the legendary giants called the "Anakim" (Josh. 11: 22; see 1 Chron. 20: 68). Even David is said to have lived here for a while (1 Sam. 21: 10; 27: 2–4) and according to one tradition, 600 hundred "Gittites" from Gath followed David when he fled from his son, Absalom (2 Sam. 15: 18). However, the Bible also implies that the fortunes of the city frequently changed political hands. It is claimed that both David (see 2 Sam. 21: 20; 1 Chron. 18: 1) and the Judean King, Uzziah (2 Chron. 26: 6) conquered it. This latter story has no parallel in the Book of Kings and raises questions of its historicity. The archaeological evidence for such an attack is nonexistent at present.

Nevertheless, Gath may still have been inhabited during the eighth century BCE, indicated by two references from prophets usually dated to this time, Amos and Micah (Amos 6: 2; Micah 1: 10). Also the annals dating to the time of Sargon II, mentioned above, would indicate that the city was inhabited at least up to the end of the eighth century. Curiously, Gath is also mentioned in the title of Psalm 56, and related to David's run-in with the Philistines. On the other hand, Gath is not mentioned in some biblical texts where the names of other Philistine cities are listed (see Amos 1: 6–8; Jer. 25: 20; Zeph. 2: 4).

Taking into consideration both the archaeological evidence from Tell es-Safi and the biblical traditions about the city of Gath, Meir and his associates have good reasons for suggesting Tell es-Safi as the location of ancient Gath. Perhaps in the near future, the excavators will discover even more compelling evidence.

Further reading

Demsky, Aaron. "Discovering a Goddess – A New Look at the Ekron Inscription Identifies a Mysterious Deity." *BAR* 24.5 (1998): 53–58.

Gitin, Seymour, Trude Dothan, and Joseph Naveh. "A Royal Dedicatory Inscription from Ekron," *IEJ* (1997): 1–16.

Halpern, Baruch. *David's Secret Demons: Messiah, Murderer, Traitor, King.* Grand Rapids, MI: William B. Eerdmans Publishing, 2001.

Maeir, Aren and Carl S. Ehrlich. "Excavating Philistine Gath. Have we Found Goliath's Hometown?" *BAR* 27.6 (2001): 21–31.

Schniedewind, William M. "The Geopolitical History of Gath." *BASOR* 309 (1998): 69–77.

Stern, Ephraim. "Tel Zafit." *NEAEHL* 4. Ephraim Stern, ed., Jerusalem: Simon & Schuster, 1993: 1522–1524.

Wright, G. E. "Fresh Evidence for the Philistine Story." *BA* 29 (1966): 70–85.

GEZER

DID SOLOMON BUILD A
CITY GATE HERE?

The large site (33 acres) of Gezer is located 20 miles northwest of **Jerusalem** and is situated on a crossroads with the famous Via Maris ("Way of the Sea"). The site's modern name is Tell el-Jezer and was first identified with ancient Gezer in 1871 by the Frenchman, Charles Clermont-Ganneau (1836–1923). His identification has been supported both by subsequent archaeological data as well as by boundary inscriptions from the Herodian period reading "boundary of Gezer."

The site was first excavated between 1902 and 1909 by R. A. S. Macalister (1870–1950), a native of Ireland. However, due to the lack of a proper stratigraphical method on his part as well as a strange

Figure 41 Gezer: Middle Bronze Age stone installation can clearly be seen in center of picture.

chronological proclivity, many of his conclusions have proven to be of little use. In fact, he was able to identify only eight of what are now known to be 26 strata comprising the tell. In 1934, another short excavation was conducted here by A. Rowe. Not until 1964 was a genuinely modern excavation of the site undertaken. This excavation continued until 1974 and was variously directed, first by the late G. Ernst Wright of Harvard, followed by W. G. Dever of the University of Arizona, and finally by Joe Seger of the University of Mississippi. This excavation was undertaken on behalf of the Nelson Glueck School of Biblical Archaeology which is located in the Hebrew Union College-Jewish Institute of Religion in Jerusalem. Dever also conducted two more seasons at the site, one in 1984 and the other in 1990. A major innovation of the modern Gezer project was the introduction of student volunteers (mostly from America) to do the daily digging chores. This practice is now quite common in digs taking place in Israel today.

Textual references to Gezer

The oldest known historical reference to Gezer is in an inscription of conquered sites on the temple at Karnak from the time of Thutmose III (fifteenth century BCE; *ANET*, 1969: 242). In the Hebrew Bible, the city is mentioned some 14 times. Most of these come primarily from two periods: the "Conquest" (Josh. 10: 33; 12: 12; 16: 3, 10; 21: 21; Judg. 1: 29), and the time of David and Solomon (2 Sam. 5: 25; 1 Kgs. 9: 15–17). In the Amarna correspondence of the first half of the fourteenth century BCE, there are ten letters in which the name occurs (*ANET*, 1969: 486, 487, and so forth). Perhaps the most famous extra-biblical occurrence is on the so-called "Merneptah Stela" dating to the end of the thirteenth century BCE. Gezer is also thought to be listed in a cuneiform relief from the eighth century BCE palace of Tiglath-Pileser at Nimrud.

Archaeological history of Gezer

Based on the modern excavations of 1964–1974, 1984, and 1990, 26 strata of occupation are now known from Gezer stretching from the late Chalcolithic period (*c.*3500 BCE) to Roman times (late first century BCE–first century CE). The archaeological evidence indicates that only during two or three of these periods was there a thriving city here. Because the discussion of strata can become tedious and complicated, the major periods and finds associated with them are summarized as follows:

Strata	Time period	Major finds
XXVI	Late Chalcolithic (3500–3300 BCE)	Ceramics; campsites
XXV	Early Bronze Age I (3300–3100 BCE)	Cave deposits
XXIV–XXIII	Early Bronze Age II (3100–2600 BCE)	Unfortified; some domestic remains; followed by occupational gap
XXII	Middle Bronze Age I (c.1900 BCE)	Unfortified domestic remains; rock-hewn cisterns; tombs; infant burials
XXI–XX	Middle Bronze Age II A (1750–1650 BCE)	Unfortified; evidence of some city development
XIX–XVIII	Middle Bronze Age II B–Middle Bronze Age III (1650–1468 BCE)	Major fortified Canaanite city; "high place"; violently destroyed
XVII	Late Bronze Age I B (late fifteenth century BCE)	Sparse occupation; cave burials
XVI	Late Bronze Age II A (1400–1300)	Revitalization of site; Egyptian imports; six inch long bronze serpent; stratum badly damaged
XV–XIV	Late Bronze Age II B (1300–1200)	City in decline; destruction level (Merneptah?); imports cease; occupational gap
XIII–XI	Iron Age I (c.1200–1000)	Philistine presence; large granary (two phases); private houses
X–IX	Iron Age I (late eleventh–early tenth century)	"Pre-Solomonic"; pottery with distinctive streaky red wash; violent destruction (Siamun of Egypt?)
VIII	Iron Age II (c.950–920)	"Solomonic"; four-entryway gate; casemate wall; administration center; limestone altar with stick figure; "Gezer calendar"
VII	Iron Age II (ninth century)	Sparse occupation? Three-entryway gate; "Palace 10000"? Site in decline
VI	Iron Age II (eighth century)	Two-entryway gate; some domestic structures; violent destruction most likely by Tiglath Pilezer c.733 BCE
V	Iron Age II (late eighth–early seventh centuries)	Unimpressive remains; two neo-Assyrian tablets; royal stamped jar handles; destroyed by Babylonians – 598–587 BCE
IV	Persian (sixth–fourth centuries BCE)	Few remains; some tombs; small limestone altars
III	Hellenistic (late fourth–third centuries)	Few remains
II	Maccabean (second century)	Evidence of some town revival; new defenses; domestic structures; iron tools; Rhodian stamped jar handles; lead weights; destroyed; last gasp of the public town
I	Roman (late first century BCE–first century CE)	Boundary inscriptions; Gezer becomes a personal estate

Following the Roman period there were insignificant periods of activity during the Byzantine, Persian (seventh century CE; mostly coins), and Mamluk periods (thirteenth century CE; coins, pottery).

The above brief stratigraphical profile indicates that a major Canaanite city existed here during the Middle Bronze Age II period. It boasted a massive fortification system that included an estimated 25 guard towers, nine of which have been discovered: eight by Macalister and one by Rowe. The tower discovered on the west side of the city gate (called "Tower 5017" in the report) measured over 50 feet in width and has been described by the excavators as the "largest single-phase defensive work known in the country," (Dever, "Gezer," *NEAEHL* 2: 501).

To this period also belongs the famous "High Place," first discovered by Macalister. Located in the north-central area of the mound, the construction consists of ten monoliths (*massebot?*) placed in a north–south line. Some of the stones are ten feet high and the contiguous surface is plastered and surrounded by a low stone curb wall. While its construction date is fixed to the Middle Bronze Age period, its function is not clearly understood. Macalister's suggestion of a cultic site for conducting child sacrifice has generally been discarded in favor of a cultic place for some sort of covenant renewal ceremony as reflected in biblical texts such as Exodus 24: 1–11. However, without contemporary texts, what the Canaanites actually did here may never be known.

Following this period, which represents the zenith of Canaanite culture at Gezer, there is evidence of material decline until the fourteenth century BCE (Late Bronze Age II A) when some resurgence of city life seems to have occurred. The Tell el-Amarna letters which mention Gezer (there are ten of them) would indicate ties with Egypt during this time, as do the Egyptian imports that date to the same period. In addition, major tomb discoveries belong to this phase of occupation. Of particular interest are the remains of 68 people discovered in Cave I. 10A, located outside the "Inner Wall." These remains were dated between 1450 and 1300 BCE.

Following this relatively short spurt of renewed city life, another period of general decline set in until the middle of the tenth century BCE. The material dated to this period has significance beyond a historical/cultural understanding of just the city of Gezer. There is currently a major debate between biblical historians and archaeologists over the existence and extent of a "Solomonic" empire. If, in fact, the material evidence from Gezer correlates legitimately with the biblical note in 1 Kings 9: 15–17, as Dever has argued, a strong case could be made for some sort of "Solomonic" era of whatever proportions or importance. While Gezer survived on into Iron Age II and beyond, it never achieved any real important political position again except for its destruction portrayed on the relief found at Nimrud. As a "town" of any significance, its history ended following a brief revival during the second century BCE.

A noteworthy discovery by Macalister in 1908, the "Gezer Calendar," is also dated to the Iron Age II (c.900 BCE). It is usually identified as an early Hebrew inscription, though textual difficulties with this identification have been noted by various scholars. It is written on a small limestone plaque and refers to agricultural months.

Further reading

Dever, William G. "Gezer." *NEAEHL* 2. Ephraim Stern, ed., Jerusalem: Simon & Schuster, 1993: 496–506.

—— "Gezer." *OEANE* 2. Eric M. Meyers, ed., NY: Oxford University Press, 1997: 396–400 (with earlier publications, especially by Dever).

—— "Archaeology and the 'Age of Solomon:' A Case Study in Archaeology and Historiography." *The Age of Solomon: Scholarship at the Turn of the Millennium*. Edited by Lowell K. Handy. Leiden: Brill, 2001: 217–251.

Pardee, Dennis. "Gezer Calendar." *OEANE* 2. Eric M. Meyers, ed., NY: Oxford University Press, 1997: 400–401 (with bibliography).

GIBEAH (TELL EL-FUL?)
CONCUBINES BEWARE!

Tell el-Ful (Arabic for "mound of beans") is located about 4 miles north of the Damascus Gate, a major landmark in the Old City of **Jerusalem**. The ruin is 2,800 feet above sea level and is not a typical tell, the accumulated debris averaging no more than six feet deep (see Figure 42). While excavations were conducted on the site as early as 1864 by Charles Warren (1840–1927), a renowned British excavator, it was W. F. Albright (1891–1971) who led the major archaeological exposure of the tell. During 1922–1923 he dug for 17 months on behalf of the American Schools of Oriental Research and

Figure 42 Tell el-Ful (possibly Gibeah).

in 1933 spent another month here. While Tell el-Ful's ancient identification had already been debated, Albright's claim that it was the
place of biblical Gibeah became accepted by most other authorities.
It is still a commonly held view, though the claim has been seriously
challenged since the 1960s (see below). When the site was threatened
by modern twentieth-century construction, Paul Lapp (1930–1970)
conducted a six-week salvage excavation here in 1964, also on behalf
of the American Schools of Oriental Research. Lapp claimed his
results supported Albright's major conclusions, including the ancient
identification of the site. However, some of his conclusions also raise
serious questions concerning the details of Albright's earlier views.

Based partly on refinements in ceramic typology, Lapp identified
five major occupational periods for Tell el-Ful:

I   Iron Age I (*c.*1200–1150 BCE – called the "pre-fortress" period)
II   Late Iron Age I–Iron Age II A (*c.*1025–950 BCE)
III   Iron Age II C (mid seventh–sixth century BCE)
IV   Hellenistic (late third–second century BCE)
V   Roman (last third of first century CE).

Much of the discussion has centered on the first two periods
because of the attempt by Albright, Lapp, and others, to associate the
material remains from this time with the story of Gibeah as told in
the biblical books of Judges and 1 Samuel. Of course, if Tell el-Ful
is not the location of Gibeah, these associations are of no historical
value. What was identified as the remains of a fortress-tower were
dated to the Iron Age I (or early Iron Age II), as well as 24 rock-
hewn silos. Lapp also re-dated an occupational level Albright had
assigned to the eighth–seventh century, to the seventh–sixth century
BCE. The archaeological evidence supports the existence of a flourishing Hellenistic village from the third–second century BCE and a brief
Roman occupation in the latter half of the first century CE.

The controversy over the biblical place-name of Tell el-Ful is
another good example of the problem modern biblical historians and
archaeologists face in the attempt to identify the location of sites
mentioned in the Bible as well as other ancient texts (see the recent
discussion by O. Borowski, 1988). Also, as J. Maxwell Miller (1987)
has shown, once a site's identification with a biblical place has
achieved a scholarly consensus, the identification can continue even
when the reasons originally set forth for it are no longer considered
valid (Miller, and others, have suggested that Gibeah was located at
a site known today as "Jaba"; see Miller, 1975).

According to biblical tradition, Gibeah was an important Benjaminite town during the period of the "Judges" and was the locale for the story of the rape of the Levite's concubine (Judg. 19–20). The town also played an important role in the story of Saul as told in 1 Samuel. In fact, according to 1 Samuel 14: 16, Saul lived here. Furthermore, the prophetic books of Hosea and Isaiah seem to presuppose that Gibeah was occupied in the latter half of the eighth century BCE (Isa. 10: 29; Hosea 5: 8; 10: 9).

Some of the problems are the following: 1) the archaeological remains from Tell el-Ful dated to Iron Age I (which were thought to parallel the time of the "Judges") are now known to be meager and inconclusive. 2) The date Lapp gave to the remains of the supposed "fortress" from the time of Saul (1025–950 BCE; see Lapp, 1965) is so broad that if the latest date is accepted, Saul would have been dead before the "fortress" was constructed! 3) By re-dating the latest Iron Age II occupation from Albright's eighth–seventh century to his late seventh–sixth century, Lapp made the references to Gibeah (assuming Tell el-Ful was Gibeah, as Lapp did) in Isaiah and Hosea, both of whom are usually dated to the last half of the eighth century, extremely puzzling to say the least.

Given the uncertainty over the ancient name of Tell el-Ful vis-à-vis the location of biblical Gibeah, it seems prudent to stop identifying the site with the biblical town. Under such circumstances, Tell el-Ful is the site of an otherwise unknown Iron Age village in the land of Benjamin. Its remains are helpful in trying to understand village life during this period, but there is no archaeological justification for continuing to identify it with the biblical town, Gibeah.

Further reading

Arnold, Patrick M. *Gibeah: The Search for a Biblical City*. Sheffield: Sheffield Academic Press, 1990.

Borowski, Oded. "The Biblical Identity of Tel Halif." *BA* 51 (1988): 21–27.

Demsky, A. "Geba, Gibeah, and Gibeon – A Historico-Geographical Riddle," *BASOR* 212 (1973): 25–31.

Lapp, Paul. "Tell el-Ful." *BA* 28 (1965): 2–10.

Miller, J. Maxwell. "Geba/Gibeah of Benjamin." *VT* 25 (1975): 145–166.

—— "Old Testament and Archaeology." *BA* 50 (1987): 55–63.

GIBEON (EL-JIB)
A HUGE WATER WELL AND A DEADLY "GAME"

The archaeology of el-Jib

Located some 5.5 miles north-northwest of **Jerusalem**, the site of ancient Gibeon (modern el-Jib) lies some 2,460 feet above sea level. In biblical times it was located in the tribal territory of Benjamin. As in many other instances, the honor for the identification of the site with its biblical place name belongs to Edward Robinson who made the connection in 1838. The excavation of Gibeon was the work of James B. Pritchard, on behalf of the University Museum of

Figure 43 Pool of Gibeon: el-Jib. Notice human figures top right for scale.

135

the University of Pennsylvania. Pritchard conducted archaeological seasons here in 1956, 1957, 1959, 1960, and 1962. In 1983 and 1984, Hana Eshel, of Hebrew University, conducted a survey of nearby burial caves, most of which contained Iron Age remains.

While el-Jib showed some occupational activity during the Early Bronze Age IV period (2200–2000 BCE – Pritchard's Middle Bronze Age I), the first permanent settlement was dated to the Middle Bronze Age I (Middle Bronze Age II in the reports). Furthermore, many jar handles stamped with the word gbʿn (Gibeon) seem to confirm the biblical identity of the site. Most of the discussion about the city has centered around the periods thought to illuminate the biblical description of Gibeon. According to the famous story in Joshua (chapter 9), the "Gibeonites" tricked the Israelites into making a treaty with them. When the trick was discovered, the Israelites honored their oath but made the Gibeonites "hewers of wood and drawers of water for the house of (my) God" (9: 23; see vv. 21, 27). While there are considerable exegetical issues here (i.e. the date and function of this story in its biblical context), there is also a serious archaeological problem. If there was an Israelite "conquest," it is usually dated towards the end of the Late Bronze Age (c.1250 BCE). From Gibeon, the only remains that can be dated to this period are a few pottery sherds discovered in tombs. No architectural remains from the Late Bronze Age were ever found. It is true that there was not a lot of lateral exposure of this site and such remains of a Late Bronze Age city may lie buried elsewhere. But until such remains are found, the Joshua story remains historically suspect. This is even more so when the famous "sun standing-still" story is added to the discussion (Josh. 10: 12–13). While such stories may serve the theological purpose(s) of its author(s), one hardly expects to find archaeological evidence of such an event (I will leave aside the entire question of the scientific implications of such a story).

The focus of the excavation was on the Iron Age remains, a major discovery of which is a massive water system comparable to those at other Israelite sites such as **Hazor**, **Megiddo**, **Gezer**, and Jerusalem. This pool, sometimes called the "Great Pool,"(see Figure 43, p. 135) measures 37 feet in diameter and is 35 feet deep. It was descended/ascended by a spiral stairway that begins on the north side and goes down in a clockwise direction. At the bottom of the pool, the stairwell continues (79 steps) into a tunnel that leads to a water collection basin some 44 feet beneath the floor of the pool. It has been estimated that 3,000 tons of limestone were removed during the process of constructing this impressive system.

The inhabitants of the city also had access to a spring outside the city which could be reached through a narrow "water-gate" built into the city wall above the spring. Apparently, in order to have access to the water during siege, a cave was dug into the side of the hill for a distance of some 40 feet. The chamber mentioned above was hollowed out allowing the outside spring water to be collected here. The excavator concluded that the entrance to the cave would have been blocked during an attack and the citizens of the city would still have access to the water. This was accomplished by a tunnel 67 feet long that was dug from the city square inside the city walls to the collection pool inside the artificial cave. The tunnel itself contains 93 steps. While the absolute date of this tunnel-cave system is difficult to determine, Pritchard dated it to sometime in the Iron Age II period (c.900–600 BCE).

Another important Iron Age II discovery has been identified as an "Industrial Area," containing a total of 63 bell-shaped rock-cut cellars. Based on other finds (ceramics, including one whole jar, stamped handles, clay stoppers, etc.), the excavator interpreted this complex as a "winery." The total storage capacity for the system has been estimated to be some 25,000 gallons!

Gibeon and the Bible

The importance of Gibeon during the Iron Age II period is indicated by all of the above, including the royal-stamped jar handles dated to the time of King Hezekiah (c.715–685 BCE). If there really was a winery here during this period, Gibeon may have been a major supplier of the product to the surrounding localities. However, the Bible is mostly silent regarding this time period.

After stories relating the site to Joshua, Saul, David, and Solomon, the Bible does not mention the place again until the time of Jeremiah, who is usually dated to the late seventh–early sixth centuries BCE (Jer. 28: 1; 41: 12, 16). There has been considerable discussion concerning any connection between Gibeon and Saul (see bibliography), but without the Bible, none of the archaeological material would suggest such connections. One of the strangest stories with a setting at Gibeon is told in 2 Samuel 2: 12–30, where the men of Abner, representing Saul's forces, and the men of Joab, representing David's, engaged in a rather deadly game ("contest"; 2 Sam. 2: 14). The story relates how the men sat around the "pool," until they got up to play: twelve for Saul and twelve for David. The end result was the mutual killing of each man by his opponent (if this was supposed to be some kind of "game," the contestants got to play only once!). While the pool discovered by Pritchard certainly looks the part where this incident could have taken place, there is no way this can be proven archaeologically. However, given the size of the pool some credibility should be given the possibility (but even if the biblical pool and Pritchard's are one and the same, this would not "prove" the veracity of the biblical story). In any event, the end result was the routing of Abner's forces and the killing of Joab's brother, Asahel, by Abner. A full exegesis of this story is beyond the scope of this short summary, but there may be some historical validity to the tale, although the killing of Asahel by Abner may be more folktale than history since it serves the strategy of the biblical writer (see Halpern, 2001: 305–307; especially p. 342).

Another interesting story set in Gibeon is the slaughter of the seven sons of Saul, supposedly for a violation of an earlier treaty by Saul with the Gibeonites (2 Sam. 21: 1ff.). There is no biblical record of Saul having done such a deed, but the tradition preserved in 2 Samuel, historical or not, would certainly have served the political agenda of David who needed to rid himself of any Saulide claim to the throne (Halpern, 2001). Also, Gibeon is associated with the "Ark of Yahweh" as well as the "Tent of Meeting" (1 Chron. 21: 29; 2 Chron. 1: 3). These stories, and others, such as Solomon's sacrifice at "the principal high place" (1 Kgs. 3: 4; see 1 Chron. 16: 39; 21: 29; 2 Chron. 1: 3, 13), may indicate that an important cult shrine of some sort did in fact exist here.

However, as mentioned above, Gibeon is absent from most of the biblical discussion of the monarchial periods of Israel (c.926–722 BCE) and Judah (c.926–587 BCE). The earliest non-biblical reference to the site is from a tenth-century BCE list of the towns seen or captured by the Egyptian Pharaoh, Sheshonk (biblical Shishak; 1 Kgs. 14: 25; see *ANET*, 1969: 242). Josephus (*JW* 2.19.1) also mentions Gibeon as a camp site for the Roman General, Cestius Gallus, who stayed there in October of 66 CE on his way to Jerusalem.

Further reading

Edelman, Diana. "Gibeon and the Gibeonites Revisited." In *Judah and the Judeans in Neo-Babylonian period*. Oded Lipschits and Joseph Blenkinsopp, eds. Winona Lake, IN.: Eisenbrauns, 2003: 153–167.

Halpern, Baruch. *David's Secret Demons: Messiah, Murderer, Traitor, King.* Grand Rapids, MI: William B. Eerdmans Publishing Company, 2001.

Pritchard, James B. *Gibeon, Where the Sun Stood Still.* Princeton: Princeton University Press, 1962. A popular account of the excavations by the director.

HALIF, TELL (RIMMON?)
WHERE EXACTLY ARE WE?

Tell Halif, a three-acre site located about five miles southwest of **Tell Beit Mirsim**, is located on the northern fringe of the Negev overlooking a major road leading from Egypt and the Mediterranean to the Judean hills and Jerusalem. This location explains the town's importance in antiquity. Today, Kibbutz Lahav is situated on the tell's eastern side. While some archaeological work was conducted here in the 1950s, the major excavation was not begun until 1976. Called the "Lahav Research Project," the excavations were directed by Joe D. Seger (Mississippi State University), and consisted of three phases

Figure 44 Ziklag.

of field work beginning in 1976 and ending in 1993. In all, 17 strata of occupational history were identified dating from the Chalcolithic (fourth millennium BCE) down to the modern (nineteenth–twentieth century) Arab settlement called Khirbet Khuweilifeh (after 1937).

Remains of a well-fortified Early Bronze Age III (*c.*2600–2400 BCE) town were recovered. The evidence also indicated that a major destruction occurred here in the middle of the third millennium BCE. With the end of the Early Bronze Age III period (*c.*2300 BCE), the site was apparently abandoned until the first part of the Late Bronze Age (1550 BCE). Four phases of Late Bronze Age occupation were detected, with a major destruction following the second phase or Stratum X. The cause of this destruction, however, is not clear.

There was an Iron Age I settlement here represented in part by living surfaces upon which were recovered pottery, stone tools and other objects. Among the latter is a clay female figurine. Important among the ceramic remains are what the excavator has called "degenerate-style Philistine potsherds," (Seger, "Halif, Tell" in *NEAEHL* 2: 557). This ambiguous evidence for the relationship between Philistine culture and Tell Halif during this time (twelfth–ninth centuries BCE) is important for the biblical identification of the tell.

During the Iron Age II period (correlated with Str. VIB–VIA), the town experienced development and expansion, part of the evidence for which comes from a large cemetery from the ninth–eighth century BCE. However, this town, as did so many others in the region, suffered a major destruction at the end of the eighth century, believed to have been the work of Sennacherib, the King of Assyria. Following this destruction, the next significant occupation dates to the Persian period when the town probably served the Persians as an administrative center. A Hellenistic occupation was followed by a gap in the early Roman period. However, the area made a dramatic recovery beginning in the second century CE and especially during the following Byzantine period when the town was called "Tilla" (Arabic for "the tell"). The last 1300 years or so of Tell Halif's history belong to the Arabs. Only in the mid twentieth century, with the founding of the modern state of Israel, has the site come under control of the Israelis (Kibbutz Lahav).

For a long time, Tell Halif was identified by scholars with the biblical city of Ziklag (see Figure 44, p. 139), a place claimed in the Bible to have been given to David by the Philistines of Gath (see 1 Sam. 27: 6; for a defense of this identification by the excavator, see Seger, 1984). However, many authorities today suspect that

Rimmon, also called En-rimmon ("spring of Rimmon"), a site mentioned some five time in the Hebrew Bible, is the most likely candidate for the biblical city located here (Borowski, 1988). The Bible locates Rimmon in the territory of Judah (Josh. 15: 32) and claims it was part of the inheritance of Simeon (Josh. 19: 7; 1 Chron. 4: 32). The other two biblical references (Neh. 11: 29 and Zech. 14: 10) are post-exilic (after 539 BCE). The known Persian occupation of Tell Halif does not contradict the claim in Nehemiah that returning exiles were re-settled here. Rimmon in Zechariah 14: 10 is said to be "south of Jerusalem," and is part of the writer's apocalyptic hope for Jerusalem's future. On the other hand, Ziklag is described as a major Philistine site ("in the heartland of Philistia"; 1 Sam. 27) while Tell Halif was found to contain only a marginal Philistine presence. To some, this is archaeological evidence that Tell Halif should be identified with ancient Rimmon and not Ziklag. Still, the issue has not been resolved to everyone's satisfaction and until or unless further archaeological evidence is forthcoming, only tentative conclusions are in order.

Further reading

Borowski, Oded. "The Biblical Identity of Tel Halif." *BA* 51.1 (1988): 21–27.

Currid, John D. and Avi Navon. "Iron Age Pits and the Lahav (Tell Halif) Grain Storage Project." *BASOR* 273 February (1989): 67–78.

Kloner, Amos. "Hurvot Rimmon." *IEJ* 30 (1980): 226–228.

Seger, Joe D. "Investigations at Tell Halif, Israel, 1976–1980." *BASOR* 252 (1983/4): 1–23.

—— "The Location of Biblical Ziklag." *BA* 47.1 (1984): 47–53.

—— "Halif, Tell." *NEAEHL* 2. Ephraim Stern, ed., Jerusalem: Simon & Schuster, 1993: 553–559.

—— and Oded Borowski. "The First Two Seasons at Tell Halif." *BA* 40 (1977): 156–166.

HAZOR

THE MIGHTIEST CANAANITE
CITY OF THEM ALL

Archaeological history

The magnificent ruin of ancient Hazor lies some nine miles north of
the Sea of Galilee on the major highway linking Tiberias in the south
with Qiryat Shemona in the north (see Figure 45). At its height
(during the Middle Bronze Age II), Hazor incorporated some 200
acres, making it the largest Canaanite city yet discovered in Israel.
While the site was first identified in 1875 by J. L. Porter, little notice
was given it until 1928 when the British excavator, John Garstang,
attempted to explore the tell. The first major archaeological excavation of Hazor occurred during the 1950s when the late Yigael Yadin

Figure 45 Hazor: Iron Age II gate with casemate wall.

(1917–1984) worked here (1952–1958; 1968–1972). In 1984, Amnon Ben-Tor began a new long-term excavation with the somewhat cumbersome title of "The Hazor Excavations in Memory of Yigael Yadin." As of this writing (2005), Ben-Tor is still in the field. Students interested in his progress can get regular updates posted on the Hazor web site: http://unixware.mscc.huji.ac.il/~hatsor/.

The mound naturally divides itself into two unequal parts: an upper mound that is about 20 acres in size, and a lower city that encloses some 175 acres. While the site was first occupied during the Early Bronze Age (c.3200–2000 BCE), its most prosperous and heavily populated time was during the Middle Bronze Age (2000–1550 BCE). The material remains from this time, especially the fortifications, indicate that Hazor was a major Canaanite city. Unfortunately, some of the gate remains were badly damaged by the construction of the modern road that cut through the extreme southeast corner of the tell.

Following the Egyptian (?) destruction of the Middle Bronze Age city (c.1500 BCE), Hazor enjoyed something of a renaissance during the following Late Bronze Age (c.1500–1200 BCE). Perhaps the best-known remains from this time are of several temples (three) discovered in the lower city (see Figure 46, p. 144), especially in what was called "Area H." The excavator believed the first temple was constructed during the preceding Middle Bronze Age but was modified considerably in its third, and, apparently, last phase of use during the fourteenth century BCE. The architectural style (porch, hall, holy of holies) of the last building is thought to be very similar to the tripartite description of the temple described in 1 Kings 9, presumably built by Solomon. Associated with the temple remains are many interesting small finds. Among these are votive vessels, clay models of animal livers, altars, and a pottery kiln (apparently used to produce the vessels used in the temples).

From Area C, another Late Bronze Age temple was found containing several stelae (standing stones). Today, interested visitors can view many of these discoveries at the Hazor Museum located just north of the site on the grounds of Kibbutz Alyelet Hashahar.

The Late Bronze Age city was destroyed towards the end of the thirteenth century BCE, and is associated by some authorities with the story told in the book of Joshua. However, the problems of identifying the source(s) of destruction of Late Bronze Age Canaanite cites, including Hazor, with invading "Israelites" are well known, leading many experts to suggest other scenarios.

During the Iron Age (c.1200–586 BCE) only the upper mound seems to have been occupied, and for the first part of this period

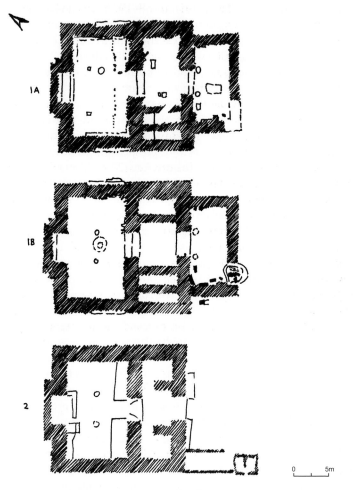

Figure 46 Three Bronze Age temples from Hazor.

(Iron Age I, twelfth–eleventh centuries), Hazor was little more than a squatters' camp. However, during the Iron Age II (tenth–sixth centuries), the upper city was rebuilt, presumably by the Israelites. A controversy has erupted between historians and archaeologists over the date of the earliest remains from this period. Some, including Ben-Tor, have dated the remains of a four-entryway gate to the tenth century BCE (see Figure 45, p. 142), and have confirmed the historicity of the biblical text that asserts that "Solomon" rebuilt Hazor along with **Megiddo** and **Gezer** (1 Kgs. 9: 15–17). Others (most notably

144

I. Finkelstein) have dated the material to the ninth century and have argued that there never was a "Solomonic" empire (at least not of biblical proportions). Perhaps Ben-Tor's efforts will further clarify this very important archaeological-historical issue.

On the other hand, most authorities do agree that from the ninth century on, to its destruction by the Assyrians around 732 BCE, Hazor regained some of its previous glory and served as a regional city for the northern kingdom of Israel. Certainly the most impressive archaeological discovery from this time is the monumental water system which was constructed in Area L on the southwest side of the Upper Mound. The system consisted of a vertical shaft 100 feet deep that was descended/ascended by five flights of steps cut into the sides of the walls. At the bottom of the shaft, a tunnel was dug that runs west/southwest for about 80 more feet to the water table. Dated to the time of Ahab (mid ninth century), this engineering feat compares quite well with the elaborate water systems known elsewhere in Israel such as those at Megiddo, **Gibeon**, **Beth-Shemesh**, and **Jerusalem**. The system was destroyed by the Assyrians and never used again. Following the late eighth century BCE destruction, Hazor entered a state of decline from which it never recovered. Its last meager remains date to the second century BCE during the so-called Maccabean period (see 1 Macc. 1: 67).

Literary history

That Hazor was an important Middle Bronze Age Canaanite city is indicated by references to it both in the Egyptian Execration Texts (*ANET*, 1969: 329) and in the Mari texts. The latter reference (along with Laish/Dan) indicates the commercial importance of Hazor during this time. The city is also mentioned in New Kingdom documents of Thutmose III (*ANET*, 1969: 242), Amenhotep II and Seti I. From the fourteenth century BCE Tel el-Amarna letters, both Hazor and its king, 'Abdi-Tirshi, are mentioned. In the Papyrus Anastasi I, believed to date from the time of Ramses II (thirteenth century BCE), Hazor is mentioned again (*ANET*, 1969: 477).

In the Hebrew Bible, Hazor is referred to 18 times, the first in Joshua (11: 1) and the last in Nehemiah (11: 33). The most controversial are the Joshua references where Hazor is said to have been burned with fire (11: 11, 13). The seeming contradiction between this story and that in Judges (4: 1ff; see 1 Sam. 12: 9) has received various explanations. Given the prevailing scholarly view concerning a "militaristic" conquest, the view that the story in Joshua is late pious fiction may be the most plausible. Hazor is also said to have been among the major cities re-fortified by Solomon, as mentioned above (1 Kgs. 9: 15). The controversy surrounding this claim has already been alluded to. After the Babylonian war of 586 BCE, Hazor continued its decline from which it never recovered. The words of Jeremiah, the prophet, became reality: "Hazor shall become a lair of jackals, an everlasting waste; no one shall live there, nor shall anyone settle in it" (49: 33).

Further reading

Ben-Tor, Amnon, ed. "*Hazor III–IV: An Account of the Third and Fourth Seasons of excavation, 1957–1958.*" Jerusalem: Israel Exploration Society, 1989.

—— "Hazor." *OEANE* 3. Eric M. Meyers, ed., NY: Oxford University Press, 1997: 1–5. See bibliography for earlier publications, especially by Y. Yadin.

—— "The Yigael Yadin Memorial Excavations at Hazor, 1990–93: 'Aims and Preliminary Results." In *The Archaeology of Israel Constructing the Past, Interpreting the Present.* Neil Asher Silberman and David Small, eds. Journal for the Study of the Old Testament Supplement Series 237. Sheffield: Sheffield Academic Press, 1997: 107–127.

Cole, Dan P. "How Water Tunnels Work." *BAR* 6.2 (1980): 8–29.

Malamat, Abraham. "Silver, Gold, and Precious Stones from Hazor in a New Mari Document." *BA* 46 (1983): 169–174.

Reich, Ronny. "The Persian Building Ayyelet ha-Shahar: The Assyrian Palace at Hazor?" *IEJ* 25 (1975): 233–237.

HEBRON

OF MYTHS AND LEGENDS: WHO'S BURIED HERE?

The remains of the city of ancient Hebron are located 18 miles south-southeast of **Jerusalem**. That this was an important place for the biblical writers is indicated by the fact that "Hebron" is mentioned over 60 times in the Hebrew Bible. Though the site was first located and identified in the 1920s by W. F. Albright and others, the first formal excavation of Hebron did not take place until the 1960s under the direction of the American, P. C. Hammond. A second excavation was carried out in the 1980s under the Israeli archaeologist, A. Ofer, on behalf of the Judean Hills Survey Expedition. The results of both digs have shown that the area was occupied from the Chalcolithic Period (fifth–fourth millennium BCE) through the Ottoman

Figure 47 Hebron: "The enclosure of Abraham."

147

Period (sixteenth–early twentieth century CE). However, due to a lack of final publications, it is difficult to be very specific concerning the archaeological discoveries.

Another factor complicating the issue is that the Hebron area is not composed of just one antiquity site. While most authorities are agreed that biblical Hebron should be identified with Jebel er-Rumeidah, there are other close-by areas that were also occupied in antiquity. Probably the most visited spot by tourists has been the Haram el-Khalil ("The Enclosure of Abraham," see Figure 47, p. 147), a site associated with a burial cave ("Machpelah") which tradition claims contains the bones of Abraham and several other notables, including Jacob, Joseph, and even Adam and Eve! The monumental architecture of the building constructed over the cave is usually credited to Herod the Great. However, for all of the published descriptions of this place, no scientific archaeological investigation of the cave and its contents has ever been allowed. Thus any conclusions made about this cave vis-à-vis the stories of the Ancestors is little more than speculation.

The modern city of Hebron is located in the Valley of Hebron nearby. Excavating here is extremely limited, but many authorities believe that the "Hebron" of the Second Temple period was located here. Another site, Haram Ramet el-Khalil, identified as ancient "Mamre," is also in the vicinity. In fact, the many names used to identify the area have only complicated the situation. In the Bible, the place is referred to as "Kiriath-arba" (literally "village of four"), "Mamre," as well as "Hebron" (see Gen. 23: 2, 19, and others).

Biblical Hebron is mentioned primarily from three different periods: the time of the founding Ancestors (the "Patriarchs"); the time of the "conquest"; and the time of David. In Genesis (13; 18; 23: 19; 35: 27; 37: 14) Abraham is portrayed as settling by the "oaks of Mamre" (was this some kind of Canaanite cult site?), buying a cave ("Machpelah" Gen. 23: 1–20) in which to bury his wife, Sarah, and in which he himself would ultimately be buried (Gen. 25: 7–10). In Joshua and Judges, Hebron is mentioned in the context of the "Israelite Conquest" of Canaan. However, there are inconsistencies in the details. According to one story (Josh. 10: 36, 39) "all Israel" took Hebron. But according to the note in Judges 1: 10, it was Judah who took the site from the Canaanites. On the other hand, Judges 1: 20 claims that the Calebites drove out the original inhabitants of the place (one of whom is identified as "Arba," who is described as "the greatest man among the Anakim," see Josh. 14: 15). As mentioned above, the absence of any significant Late Bronze Age remains points to the aetiological nature of these "conquest" stories. Hebron is also said to have become a priestly city during this time (Josh. 21: 13) as well as a place of refuge.

Hebron is mentioned only once in the story of Samson (Judg. 16: 3), but plays a major role in the time of David. Several of his sons are born here (2 Sam. 3: 2, 5) and it was David's royal residence until his move to Jerusalem (2 Sam. 3: 12, 19, 20, 22, and so forth). After being murdered by Joab, Abner was buried here (2 Sam. 3: 22). Absalom, David's son, is said to have gone to Hebron to "pay a vow" and "to worship" YHWH (2 Sam. 5: 7–8). Such a story may indicate the existence here of a local YHWH cult-shrine. Finally, it is at Hebron where David is made king of Israel by "all Israel" (2 Sam. 5: 3–5). (Interestingly enough, Solomon, who inherited David's "empire," is never said to have visited the place.)

After the story of David, Hebron is never mentioned again in the Bible except in the post-exilic Chronicler's history (1 Chron. 2: 42, 43; 3: 1, 4; 6: 2, 18, 55, 57; 11: 1, 3; 12: 23). In the non-canonical book of 1 Maccabees (5: 26), Judas is said to have destroyed Hebron, an event usually dated to around 164 BCE. Oddly, Hebron is not mentioned in any known Assyrian or Babylonian text.

Despite the role Hebron plays in the biblical stories and the two excavations that have been conducted here, there is little archaeological evidence that cen be correlated with the biblical material. Without the biblical traditions there is nothing from the archaeological record to lead one to believe famous people are buried here. Furthermore, the lack of occupational debris from the Late Bronze Age is another nail in the coffin of the now-dead "militaristic conquest" model so prominent throughout much of the twentieth century. That Hebron was an important place during the eighth century BCE is indicated by the *lmlk* jar handles found here containing the name "Hebron." Curiously enough, the Bible makes no mention of whatever role the city may have played in Judah's history during this time (late eighth century BCE).

Further reading

Hammond, Philip C. "Hebron." *OEANE* 2. Eric M. Meyers, ed., NY: Oxford University Press, 1997: 13–14, with bibliography.

HERODIAN JERICHO
WHY DID HEROD THE GREAT HAVE TO SHOW OFF SO MUCH?

The site of Herodian Jericho, known in Arabic as Tulu Abu al-'Alayiq, is located in the Jordan Valley about one mile NW of the modern town of Jericho. In the New Testament the city provides the setting for Jesus' healing of a blind man (Mark 10: 46–52; see Matt. 20: 29–34 and Luke 18: 35–43), and the story of Zacchaeus, the tax collector (Luke 19: 1–10). In 1976 and 1977, Rachel Hachlili, on behalf of the Israel Antiquities Authority, excavated a large Jewish cemetery nearby dating to the Herodian period. The size of this cemetery would indicate that a fairly sizable Jewish community existed here during Herod's (and Jesus') time. However, the only archaeological remains that have been recovered belong to the royal families of Herod and the Hasmoneans who preceded him.

Figure 48 Herodian Jericho.

Herod the Great was king of Judea from 37 to 4 BCE (he was born c.73 BCE) and constructed magnificent, monumental buildings up and down the Palestinian landscape. In Jericho, an ideal place for the winter residence of the wealthy, due to climate and abundant water sources, the Hasmonean kings, beginning with Alexander Jannaeus (103–76 BCE), had already built royal homes (palaces) before Herod came to power. What Herod accomplished here, however, dwarfed these earlier endeavors.

While the site of Herodian Jericho was first discovered in 1834 by Edward Robinson (1794–1863), the American biblical scholar and early Palestinian explorer, no real significant excavations took place here until the early 1950s. However, the major archaeological recovery of the site is due to Ehud Netzer, an Israeli archaeologist, who excavated at Herodian Jericho from 1973 to 1987, on behalf of Hebrew University, Jerusalem. Netzer discovered an enormous palace built on both sides of the Wadi Qelt by Herod (see Figure 48, p. 150). While the excavator concluded that the complex should be viewed as a single unit, he also showed that it had been constructed in three stages (thus the expression, "three winter palaces").

The first "palace," mistakenly identified as a "gymnasium" by James Pritchard in 1951, was built between 35 and 30 BCE. This structure contained a bathhouse, a ritual bath (*miqveh*), peristyle courts (surrounded by columns), a triclinium or banquet hall, and gardens. It is believed that this structure, along with the earlier Hasmonean palaces, was destroyed or damaged by an earthquake in 31 BCE. Following this earthquake, Herod expanded the first palace and built on top of the ruins of the Hasmonean buildings (Netzer suggested sometime between 30 and 25 BCE). Part of the construction consisted of combining into one what had been two separate swimming pools from the Hasmonean period. This produced a swimming pool measuring 60 × 105 feet! (Herod is accused by Josephus, the first-century CE Jewish historian, of drowning one of his sons, Aristobulus, in one of the many pools built here. See *Antiquities* XV, 50–61; *JW* I, 435–437.) In addition, a new east wing was added which was as large as the entire first palace complex. On the edge of this wing was a portico which afforded a magnificent view of the Wadi Qelt and the north end of the Dead Sea.

But few palaces in the Near Eastern world at this time could have rivaled the third stage of Herod's palace. Covering nearly seven-and-a-half acres, and built on both sides of the Wadi Qelt, it was constructed around 15 BCE. The building on the north side of the wadi was over 340 feet long and 115 feet wide, producing a palace with over 40,000 square feet of space! It contained a huge reception hall (62 × 95 feet), tile floors cut from colorful marble, much of it imported, peristyle courtyards, reception rooms, a large bathhouse, and many service rooms. On the south side of the wadi, Herod built a colossal swimming pool (138 × 295 feet) and sunken gardens. Netzer believed that the two sides were connected by a bridge that no longer exists.

In addition to this incredible palace, Herod also constructed a hippodrome at Tel es-Samarat, located some 2,000 feet south of the site of ancient Jericho, Tell es-Sultan. Netzer found monumental remains here and the place is mentioned by Josephus when he recounted the events leading up to Herod's death (*Antiquities* XVII, 175, 178, 193).

Because of Herod's ruthless, and often merciless, behavior he has often been judged as a villain, and perhaps rightly so. Nevertheless, as king of Judea he ushered in a time of relative peace and prosperity (for some) that is reflected in the monumental remains of his building program. None of these remains is any more impressive than those of his palaces at Jericho. That he achieved what he did despite his horrible domestic troubles was no mean accomplishment.

Further reading

Hachlili, Rachel. "Herodian Jericho." *OEANE* 2. Eric M. Meyers, ed., NY: Oxford University Press, 1997: 16–18, with accompanying bibliography.
—— "A Second Temple Period Jewish Necropolis in Jericho." *BA* 42 (1980): 235–240.
Netzer, Ehud. "The Hasmonean and Herodian Winter Palaces at Jericho." *IEJ* 25 (1975): 89–100.

HESHBON (TELL HESBAN)
A "LOVER'S EYES"

Heshbon and the Bible

Biblical Heshbon is identified by most experts with Tell Hesban, a site of several acres, located east of the Jordan river 15 miles southwest of Amman, the modern capital of Jordan. Heshbon is mentioned 38 times in the Hebrew Bible, most of them to identify the Ammonite king, Sihon (see Deut. 1: 4; 2: 24, 26, 30; 3: 2, 6; 4: 46; 29: 7; Josh. 9: 10; 12: 2, 5, and others). According to the tradition in Numbers 21: 21–31 the "Israelites" killed Sihon and settled in Heshbon (Num. 21: 25) at the time of the "conquest." The biblical traditions also claim that ultimately the city was given to the tribes of

Figure 49 Iron Age pools at Heshbon.

153

Reuben and Gad (Josh. 13: 8ff; but see Josh. 13: 17 and Num. 32: 37 where only Reuben is given the place; contrast Josh. 13: 27, where Gad is given the city for an "inheritance"). In Joshua 21: 38–39, Heshbon is said to have been given to the Levites from the tribe of Gad.

The story of Jephthah's confrontation with the Ammonites (Judg. 11: 19–26) asserts that Israel had lived in Heshbon and its villages for 300 years! In the prophetic books of Isaiah (15: 4; 16: 8–9) and Jeremiah (48: 2, 34–35), Heshbon is mentioned in oracles of judgment against Moab, implying that during the final editing of these books, the Moabites, not the Ammonites, controlled the city. However, Jeremiah 49: 3 implies that the Ammonites were still in control of the city, at least during the time of the prophet. The latest biblical reference to Heshbon is Nehemiah 9: 22, where the site is referred to again in the re-telling of the "conquest." An interesting poetic illusion to the place is the description of a female lover's eyes as "pools of Heshbon" in Song of Songs 7: 4 (v. 5 in the Hebrew Text; see Figure 49, p. 153). There are many post-biblical literary references to this city, the scope of which is beyond this brief summary (see Vyhmeister, 1968).

Heshbon and archaeology

Excavations at Heshbon began in 1968 under the direction of S. H. Horn, a professor at Andrews University, Michigan. He also directed the 1971 and 1972 season. The next two seasons (1974 and 1976) were directed by L. T. Geraty. In 1978, Baptist College (Pennsylvania) sponsored a sixth season primarily devoted to the excavation of a Byzantine church.

Like so many excavations before it, Heshbon was begun in the traditional "biblical archaeology" mind-set, looking for "archaeo-logical proof" that the Bible was true; in this case, the conquest story in Numbers 21: 21–32. Much to the disappointment of the first participants, no such evidence was found. In fact, no archaeo-logical remains were discovered pre-dating the twelfth century BCE. While 19 strata were identified, only four dated from the Iron Age (c.1200–500 BCE), and the best preserved of these was from the Iron Age II C phase (seventh–sixth centuries). Based upon the material remains, especially the pottery and several ostraca, the town at this time was still controlled by the Ammonites.

The lack of remains signifying a significant settlement here during the thirteenth century BCE (the usually accepted date for the "conquest") raises serious questions concerning the historical reliability of the biblical story. When the evidence, or lack of it, from Heshbon is added to that from other sites, such as **Jericho** and **'Ai**, one's suspicions only increase. Suggestions that Tell Hesban is not biblical Heshbon, or that the Late Bronze Age layer here just hasn't been found yet, or that it has disappeared over time, have not been very helpful in dealing with the known archaeological history.

On the other hand, after an occupational gap of some 300 years (c.500–200 BCE), Heshbon was re-occupied, with few gaps, from the Hellenistic to the modern period. Thus, despite the failure of the original goal to somehow "prove" the Bible true, the excavators realized they had an opportunity to understand the culture of Jordan that had existed over a long period of time. In 1982 they launched what was to become known as "The Madaba Plains Project." Included in this work has been the excavation of Tell el-'Umeiri, an 11-acre site some six miles south of Amman. Among impressive discoveries has been "one of the best preserved early Iron Age I cities in all of Palestine" (Herr, 1993: 37). The long-term multidisplinary approach of those involved in this project has become a model for contemporary archaeological work in the Middle East. In fact, in a review of the publication of the first final report (LaBianca, 1990), a leading archaeologist described the Heshbon excavation and the Madaba Plains Project in general as "one of the most sophisticated and truly interdisciplinary of all American archaeological excavations in the Middle East" (Dever, 1993: 127).

Further reading

Dever, William G. "Syro-Palestinian Archaeology 'comes of age': The Inaugural Volume of the Heshbon Series: A Review." *BASOR* May–June, 290–291 (1993): 127–130.

Geraty, Lawrence T. "Hesban." *OEANE* 3. Eric M. Meyers, ed., NY: Oxford University Press, 1997: 19–22, with bibliography.

Herr, Larry G. "The Search For Biblical Heshbon." *BAR* 19.6 (1993): 36–37; 68.

LaBianca, Øystein. *Sedentarization and Nomadization: Food System Cycles at Hesbon and Vicinity.* Berrien Springs, MI: Andrews University, 1990.

Vyhmeister, Werner. "The History of Heshbon From Literary Sources." *Andrews University Studies* 6 (1968): 158–177.

JERICHO (TELL ES-SULTAN)

A BIG NAIL IN THE COFFIN OF A "MILITARISTIC CONQUEST"

The famous tell of ancient Jericho lies on the northwest side of the modern Arab town with the same name. The site is about five-and-a-half miles west of the Jordan River. The modern name of the site, dating from the Middle Ages, Tell es-Sultan, comes from the spring located nearby, 'Ain es-Sultan ("Elisha's Fountain"). The archaeological history of "Jericho" actually involves two sites: Tell es-Sultan, identified with the Jericho mentioned in the Old Testament, and Tulul Abu el-Alayiq, a site located west of the modern town close to Wadi Qelt. This latter site is usually called "New Testament" or **"Herodian" Jericho**.

Figure 50 The mound of biblical Jericho: looking east.

156

Jericho in the Bible

The Jericho of Hebrew Bible fame is mentioned many times, with most references found in the books of Numbers, Deuteronomy, and Joshua. Jericho is best remembered because of the dramatic story of its destruction told in Joshua 6 (see below). A tradition remembered in 2 Samuel 10 (see 1 Chr. 19: 5) implies that Jericho was still occupied during the time of David (tenth century BCE). And, according to 1 Kings 16: 34, the town was rebuilt by Hiel of Bethel in the ninth century during the reign of Ahab. Part of the physical setting of the Elijah/Elisha story also takes place in Jericho (2 Kgs. 2), and near here ("in the plains of Jericho") Zedekiah, king of Judah, was captured while trying to flee from the Babylonians in the sixth century BCE (2 Kgs. 25: 5; see Jer. 39: 5; 52: 8). According to Ezra (2: 34) and Nehemiah (7: 36) 345 exiles returned to Jericho following their release from captivity by the Persians.

The archaeological history of Jericho

Jericho is over 800 feet below sea level, making it the lowest continuously inhabited place on earth. It also may have another distinction: it claims to be the oldest city in the world: at least that is what the markers, located on each end of the town, read! It does contain Mesolithic remains (ninth millennium BCE), but the first permanent settlement was not established here until the Neolithic period (c.8800–4200 BCE).

The excavations

There have been three major archaeological excavations at Jericho (see Figure 50, p. 156). The first was by the Germans, Ernst Sellin and Carl Watzinger, in 1907–1909 and again in 1911. They discovered the remains of Early Bronze Age as well as Middle Bronze Age habitation. Included in the latter was a massive rampart defensive wall (it would be learned later that this wall went through three stages or phases). However, these early archaeological pioneers originally misdated both the Early Bronze Age and Middle Bronze Age remains. The Middle Bronze Age wall was dated to Iron Age II, leading them to believe that they had found archaeological corroboration for the story in Joshua 6. Watzinger, however, corrected these mistakes a few years later. In any case, even those who today still believe that the story of the destruction of Jericho as recounted in the Bible has historical credibility do not date this destruction to Iron Age II.

157

The second major excavation was conducted between 1932 and 1936 by John Garstang of England. Garstang, assuming the historicity of the story in the Book of Joshua, did not accept the conclusions of the Germans. He, too, found evidence of collapsed walls and immediately concluded that he had discovered evidence to support the biblical story. However, his archaeological methods were primitive by modern standards, meaning that Garstang knew little about "stratigraphy." Many of his conclusions have subsequently been abandoned by most authorities.

The most scientific excavation of the tell was the achievement of the late Kathleen Kenyon. She excavated here between 1952 and 1958. All discussions of Jericho must now refer to her work. She opened three large trenches on the tell as well as excavating numerous tombs in the vicinity.

Neolithic (8600–4200 BCE)

While Kenyon found some evidence of Mesolithic activity (also called "Natufian," because this culture was first discovered, in Israel, in the wadi Natuf), which she dated *c.*9000 BCE, the first permanent settlement was during the Neolithic era. This long culture phase has been conveniently divided into four major sub phases: Pre-pottery

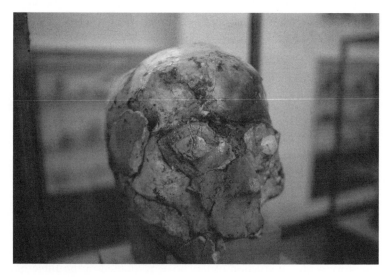

Figure 51 Plastered skull, pre-pottery Neolithic period.

Neolithic A and B (c.8500–5500) and Pottery Neolithic A and B (c.5500–4200). These periods are usually abbreviated "PPNA," "PPNB," "PNA," and "PNB" respectively.

One of Kenyon's major discoveries from the PPN phases is a stone wall and tower. The tower stands some 25 feet high and access to its top is through an inside staircase. She interpreted the tower and wall to be defensive in nature, thus qualifying this early phase of Jericho to be called a "city." However, another interpretation is that the wall and tower served more as a dam to hold back flood debris (Bar-Yosef, 1986). Another significant discovery from this pre-pottery phase is human skulls that were plastered over, perhaps to imitate live humans (see Figure 51, p. 158). In later PPN levels, the inhabitants fashioned stylized human heads from clay instead of using the actuall skulls. Kenyon interpreted these skulls (both real and clay imitations) as indicative of some sort of Neolithic religious ritual involving ancestor worship, but this is only a guess.

Beginning in the sixth millennium BCE, humans learned how to shape vessels from clay and to fire them to alter permanently their chemistry. It is now a carefully worked-out ceramic sequence that provides archaeologists the best means of deriving absolute dates for their discoveries. Following the end of the Neolithic period, the site was apparently abandoned for centuries and not re-occupied until the beginning of the Early Bronze Age, around 3300 BCE. The absence of any significant Chalcolithic material is surprising given that a major Chalcolithic culture is known to have existed in Israel.

Early Bronze Age (c.3300–2000 BCE)

In stark contrast to the non-existent Chalcolithic period, Kenyon was able to show that Jericho was inhabited during much of the long Early Bronze Age, though there was a gap of several centuries between the end of the Early Bronze Age III period (c.2650 BCE) and Early Bronze Age IV (c.2300–2000). The Early Bronze Age city was fortified and contained remains of domestic structures and storage bins (Early Bronze Age II–III). But around 2650 BCE Jericho came to a violent end, though the reason for this is unclear. What is clear is that the tell was abandoned for a period of several centuries until around 2300 (2250) BCE. Kenyon believed the new-comers were the "Amorites" of biblical fame. Whoever they were, they left pottery remains indicative of a northern origin (Syria?). A major discovery from Early Bronze Age IV is a group of rock-cut tombs which were entered through vertically cut shafts. Kenyon identified seven types of tombs based upon their contents, or in the case of one, its size, which she called "Outsize." These tombs seem to indicate that during this Early Bronze Age IV period, Jericho was a seasonal camp which attracted different groups (tribes?) of people.

Middle Bronze Age (2000–1550 BCE)

A major town existed at Jericho during the Middle Bronze period. It was protected by a massive rampart wall system that experienced at least three stages or phases of construction. However, as impressive as the wall must have been in its heyday, it was not enough to save the town it was suppose to protect. At the end of the Middle Bronze era, Jericho suffered a violent destruction by fire. Associated with this destruction are tombs in which Kenyon found entire family remains, prompting her to conclude that some sort of plague may have struck the town. From these tomb remains she reconstructed what she believed to be a typical Jericho house's furnishings.

Late Bronze Age (1550–1200 BCE)

Kenyon's discoveries (or better, lack of discoveries) from the Late Bronze Age have sparked considerable debate among biblical historians and archaeologists. The reason is simple. The almost universal date for an "Israelite conquest," if there was one at all, is the end of the Late Bronze Age period, sometime during the thirteenth century. And, of course, the most dramatic biblical story connected with this event is the destruction of Jericho told in Joshua 6. However, not only did Kenyon not find a city at Jericho at the end of this period, what she did discover indicates that Jericho was not fortified at all during the Late Bronze Age (there go the tumbling walls!). In fact, all she could date for sure to this time was an oven and a small juglet found on a house floor dating to the fourteenth century BCE. The implications of this for the Joshua story will be discussed below.

The Iron Age (1200–587/539 BCE)

Based on Kenyon's work it has generally been assumed that after Jericho's abandonment in the fourteenth century BCE, the site was not re-occupied for centuries. But recent ceramic studies have led some to believe that some activity occurred here earlier in the Iron

Age. Despite this, nothing known about the archaeological history of Jericho to date can be made to substantiate the historicity of the biblical story. Perhaps this is as good a place as any to look at that story a little more closely.

Jericho and Joshua: What most Sunday school quarterlies don't tell you

The city of Jericho is mentioned over 50 times in the Hebrew Bible. In almost 50 percent of these (26 times), the reference to the site is for geographical location/orientation. The expression: "across the Jordan from Jericho" often occurs (Num. 22: 1; 26: 3, 63; 31: 12; 33: 48, etc.). Sometimes the expression is to the "plains of Jericho," as in Jeremiah 39: 5 and 52: 8. Ten times "Jericho" appears in reference to its king: Joshua 2: 2, 3; 6: 2; 8: 2; 10: 1, 28, 30; 12: 9. To complicate matters just a little, there seems to be two different versions of the "battle" for Jericho by the "Israelites." The more famous one, with the tumbling walls, is found in Chapter 6. But there are no few curiosities to this story. After mentioning the city by name in the opening two verses of the chapter, "Jericho" is never mentioned again until verse 25. There is no mention of any king, and perhaps even more puzzling, no mention of any resistence on the part of the city's inhabitants.

The story in 24: 11, however, is a much more cryptic account that links the defeat of Jericho with that of other peoples including the "Amorites" and "Canaanites." Also in this summary passage we are specifically told that the "citizens of Jericho fought against" Israel (24: 11b). Conspicuously absent, however, is any mention of marching around, trumpet blowing, walls falling flat, harlot rescuing, or the imposing of the "ban" (6: 17). Stuck in the larger "Shechem renewal speech" by the biblical editor(s), this version of the capture/ destruction of Jericho seems to come from a very different source than that preserved in Chapter 6.

Both stories, whatever their ultimate origin, seem to be literary creations of their author(s) when the archaeological data recovered from Jericho are examined. As we have just seen, Kenyon has shown that no Late Bronze Age Jericho of biblical proportions could possibly have existed here. The efforts by some to skirt this problem by suggesting that Tell es-Sultan is not the site of Jericho, or that the Late Bronze Age city has "eroded" are not convincing and amount to what one archaeologist has called "wishful thinking." When combined with a host of other archaeological data now known about Israel at the end of the Late Bronze Age/Iron Age I horizon, a case for a historical "Conquest" of biblical proportions is no longer possible.

Persian to Byzantine (539 BCE–636 CE)

Following the Babylonian Exile (587/586–539 BCE), Tell es-Sultan, for the most part, seems to have been abandoned. References to "Jericho" in the Apocrypha and the New Testament refer to the site now known as Tulul Abu el-Alayiq ("New Testament Jericho").

Conclusion

The history of Jericho is very important for understanding the beginning stages of the rise of human "civilization." Its long, almost continuous, occupation provides us with important snapshots of changes and developments from one age to the next. It is unfortunate, in this author's opinion at least, that in the popular mind (of those who would even recognize the name at all today) "Jericho" seems only to be connected to the story in the Bible, and a fictitious one at that.

Further reading

Bar-Yosef, Ofer. "The Walls of Jericho. An Alternative Interpretation." *Current Anthropology* 27 (1986): 157–162.

Coogan, Michael David. "Archaeology and the Book of Joshua." *The Hebrew Bible and its Interpreters. Biblical and Judaic Studies* Volume 1. William Henry Propp, Baruch Halpern and David Noel Freedman, eds. Winona Lake, IN: Eisenbrauns, 1990: 19–32.

Holland, Thomas A. "Jericho." *OEANE* 3. Eric M. Meyers, ed., NY: Oxford University Press, 1997: 20–224, with earlier bibliography.

JERUSALEM
WHATEVER HAPPENED TO "DAVID" AND "SOLOMON"?

Of all the towns/cities mentioned in the Bible, none stirs the imagination like Jerusalem (the name is thought to mean something like: "the god of Salem is its foundation"). Occupied for nearly 6,000 years, this city played (and still plays) a major role in the world's three theistic faiths: Judaism, Christianity, and Islam. A walk through the Old City is an unforgettable experience: all of one's senses are stimulated with sights, sounds, smells, tastes, and the literal touching of history. In the Hebrew Bible, Jerusalem is mentioned hundreds (672) of times (the first time is in Josh. 10: 1). When other names used

Figure 52 Jerusalem from the southwest.

for the site are added to the list, such as "Zion" (153 times; see 2 Sam. 5: 7), "Mount Zion" (19 times; 2 Kgs. 19: 31, etc.), "Salem" (twice; Gen. 14: 18; Ps. 76: 2), "Jebus" (5 times; Josh. 18: 26; Judg. 19: 10, 11; 1 Chron. 11: 4, 5), and the "City of David" (40 times; 2 Sam. 5: 7, and so on), the number of references approaches 900. If the New Testament and the Apocryphal references are included, Jerusalem is referred to over 1,250 times (142 times in the New Testament and 214 times in the Apocrypha ("Mount Zion" 11 times)). By way of comparison, the second most mentioned biblical site in the Hebrew Bible is **Bethel**: only 73 times (Bethel is mentioned twice in the Apocrypha; it does not appear at all in the New Testament).

Taking all of these biblical (and apocryphal) references at face value, one gets the clear impression that Jerusalem, at least from the time of David and Solomon (traditionally dated to the Iron Age II A–tenth century BCE), was a thriving metropolis in which was centered the "Davidic Dynasty" that ruled over an empire stretching from Egypt to the far north (until the "United Monarchy" split following the death of Solomon c.926 BCE, after which time Jerusalem was the capital city of Judah until its destruction by the Babylonians in 586 BCE).

However, in recent years Jerusalem has become the center of a major controversy in discussions by archaeologists and biblical historians who have raised serious questions about the status and role of the city (or town) during the time of David and Solomon. While it is one of the most excavated cities in the world, the remains from several archaeological periods relevant to the biblical story (particularly the end of the Late Bronze Age through the early part of Iron Age II: thirteenth–tenth centuries) are meager and subject to a variety of interpretations. Hillel Geva, in her contribution to the entry on Jerusalem in *NEAEHL* (2: 801–804), listed no fewer than 126 archaeological excavations conducted somewhere in this city between 1853 and 1992. Since 1992 other major archaeological projects have been (and still are) conducted here (see the bibliography for Ronny Reich and Dan Bahat).

It is not practical to list all of the excavations that have taken place here, but four stand out:

1   Between 1961 and 1967, the late Dame Kathleen Kenyon (1906–1978) excavated in the City of David (see Kenyon, 1974). Unfortunately, Kenyon died before final reports were published. M. Steiner, from the Netherlands, is in the process of making Kenyon's field notes available to the public (see further reading).

2   A second major excavation was conducted by the late Benjamin
    Mazar (1905–1995) outside the walls of the Temple Mount from
    1968 to 1978. Most of his discoveries relate to the post-exilic
    (after 539 BCE) periods of the Hellenistic (fourth century BCE)
    through the Early Arab (tenth–eleventh centuries CE) periods.
3   Following the Six Day War in 1967, Nahmah Avigad (1905–1992)
    was able to conduct excavations in the Jewish Quarter of the
    Old City. He discovered major remains dating as early as the Iron
    Age II C (eighth–sixth centuries BCE) and as late as the Ayyubid
    period (thirteenth century CE). One of his most important finds
    is a huge wall (called the "broad wall") dating to the eighth
    century BCE, thus establishing archaeologically that Jerusalem
    expanded to the west during this time.
4   Between 1978 and 1984 the late Yigael Shiloh (1937–1987) went
    back to the City of David. Unfortunately, his premature death
    also stymied final publications. Currently, Jane Cahill, one of his
    assistants during the excavations, has taken on the responsibility
    of this task (see bibliography under Cahill).

Since the 1990s, renewed excavations near the Gihon spring
located on the southern slope of the City of David have been
conducted by Ronny Reich (University of Haifa and the IAA; see
bibliography). The results of Reich's efforts have not only confirmed
that Jerusalem was a major fortified town during the Middle Bronze
Age II (eighteenth century BCE), but also that the traditional interpretation of the so-called "Warren's Shaft" is incorrect (for the latter
see Reich and Shukron, 1999 and 2000).

The difficulties involved in trying to recover the Jerusalem of
archaeology and history are formidable. First, Jerusalem has been a
continuously occupied site for thousands of years, thus greatly
restricting archaeological access. One such restriction applies to the
Temple Mount. Home of the famous "Dome of the Rock" (see
Figure 52, p. 163), this site, believed by many authorities to be the
place were Solomon's temple stood, has been off-limits to archaeologists for centuries and will most likely stay that way.

Second, as mentioned above, Jerusalem has been excavated in one
way or another for nearly 150 years. The paper needed for all of the
literature that has been produced by all of these efforts has resulted
in the deaths of many trees. In 1988, J. D. Purvis published a
bibliography for Jerusalem that contains nearly 6,000 entries. This was
followed in 1991 with Vol. II containing 4,475 entries. Since then

numerous other publications have appeared. It is a daunting task even to know where to start one's reading.

Third, Jerusalem has been destroyed and re-built as well as expanded through the centuries. Often, stones of earlier constructions have been robbed out for later buildings (see Reich and Billig, 2002). Thus, there is often an "absence of evidence"; this is especially so for the periods relevant to the question of a "Davidic and Solomonic Jerusalem" (Cahill, 2003). All of the above conditions have impacted attempts to reconstruct the full history of this famous and important city.

For clarity, the city can be conveniently divided into three parts, archaeologically speaking:

1   The biblical city that existed during the time of David and Solomon is traditionally called the "City of David" (see 2 Sam. 5: 7). Jerusalem at this time was situated on a narrow mountain spur that is south of today's Old City walls and the Temple Mount (the Haram es-Sharif). Measuring some 720 feet wide on its northern end extending some 2,050 feet in length, the crest of the spur is about 12 acres in size; 15, when the area on the eastern slope is added. A 12- to 15-acre "city" is hardly the impression one gets from reading the heightened description of Jerusalem in the Bible. On its eastern side, the site is bounded by the Kidron Valley and on its western and southern by the Tyropoeon ("Cheesemakers") Valley. This latter valley has been filled in with debris over the centuries and is not as deep as it was in antiquity.

Another extremely important feature of this spur is a water source known as the "Gihon Spring," located at the bottom of the eastern slope of the City of David. It is the only perennial water source in the area and was no doubt a major reason for the early settlement of the region. The earliest architectural remains found here date to the Early Bronze Age I (late fourth millennium BCE), though Y. Shiloh found pottery from the late Chalcolithic period.

There is ample archaeological evidence to show that Jerusalem was a prominent town during the Middle Bronze Age II (eighteenth–seventeenth centuries BCE; for recent discoveries from the Middle Bronze Age II see Reich and Shukron 1999, 2000), and again during the last part of Iron Age II (eighth–seventh centuries BCE). The current controversy is over what Jerusalem was like during the Late Bronze Age (fourteenth–thirteenth centuries), the Iron Age I (twelfth–eleventh centuries), and the Iron Age II A (tenth century). The problem in a nutshell is that there are almost no historical references to Jerusalem from these periods (for a discussion of the importance of the fourteenth-century BCE Amarna Letters that mention Jerusalem, see Na'aman, 1996; for a critique of his views, see M. Steiner, *BAT 90* and 1998), and there is little archaeological evidence. Furthermore, the interpretation of what is known from both sources is contentiously debated (see various entries in Vaughan and Killebrew, 2003).

The most prominent architectural discovery relevant to this discussion is a huge stepped-stone structure excavated on the north-eastern side of the site (see Figure 53). The date, construction, and function(s) of this artifact are at the center of a major archaeological/historical controversy (the publications on the issues here are many and growing. A good place to start is with Vaughan and Killebrew, 2003). Furthermore, recent studies on population estimates of villages/towns during Iron Age I and II A in Judah, including Jerusalem, suggest that the Iron Age II A Jerusalem had a population of 1,200 people or less, making it more a large village than a small "city" (see the discussion by G. Lehmann in Vaughan and Killebrew: 117–162). The poor archaeological remains from the tenth-century BCE Jerusalem, as well as the sparsely inhabited villages and towns in

Figure 53 Stepped-stone structure, City of David.

Judah dating to the same period, have led some authorities to question seriously the notion a "United Monarchy" of any significance. One prominent Israeli archaeologist has declared that the idea that Jerusalem, in the days of David and Solomon, ruled over the far larger and more prosperous city-states of the north is "absurd" (I. Finkelstein, in Vaughan and Killebrew: 90; for a more positive assessment of Jerusalem during the Iron Age II A period see J. Cahill, in Vaughan and Killebrew: 13–80).

The current controversy is not likely to be resolved to the satisfaction of every interested party anytime soon. Until, or unless, other major archaeological discoveries are forthcoming, Jerusalem in the tenth century BCE and the extent of the rule of David and Solomon will remain controversial.

2   The Old City. First-time visitors to Jerusalem may be forgiven if they think the current "Old City" is the Jerusalem of the early biblical period. After all, the place *looks* like something straight out of the Bible. Actually there are parts of it that do go back at least as early as the late eighth century BCE. This is a huge wall believed by the excavator to date to the time of King Hezekiah (Avigad, 1980; see Figure 54). But the current walls that now surround the "Old City" were constructed in 1537/1538 CE by the Sultan (king) Suleiman the Magnificent. The most famous gate associated with this rebuilding is the Damascus Gate (see Figure 55, p. 169). On a busy day, entering and leaving the Old City by this gate is an experience in itself. It is very helpful for the tourist to have a trustful guide book in trying to come to terms with the complexity of Jerusalem, both within and without the Old City. A very useful guide can be found in J. Murphy-O'Connor's *The Holy Land.*

3   The third general area of excavations are in tombs, cemeteries, and other sites, especially places associated with the emergence of Christianity. Remains from building periods after the Exile (post-539 BCE) are known throughout the city. But none compares to that done during the Herodian period. Jerusalem was transformed by construction on the western hill (or Upper City), addition of defensive walls (the "second" and "third" walls; see Josephus, *War* 5.147–148), and of course, the Temple Mount. It is believed that the current Temple Mount was built by Herod towards the end of the first century BCE. The construction would challenge engineers today: some of the stones in this complex are estimated to weigh hundreds of tons.

Figure 54 Hezekiah's "Broad Wall".

Figure 55 Damascus Gate, Jerusalem.

Following the Jewish War of 63–70 CE, Jerusalem was severely destroyed and not re-built until the first half of the second century (by Hadrian). During the fourth–sixth centuries, Jerusalem experienced rapid expansion, now under Christian influence of the Byzantine period. Many churches were built, the most famous being the Church of the Holy Sepulchre by Constantine during the first half of the fourth century. Jerusalem was conquered by the Arabs in the seventh century (638). Two of the most famous buildings from this period are the Dome of the Rock, built in 691, and the nearby al-Aqsa mosque which was completed in 713. The Medieval period (as well as the post-Medieval time) has attracted considerable archaeological interest over the past several years and many excavations have been conducted to better understand Jerusalem during these times. Details for interested readers can be found in the accompanying further reading section.

Further reading

Amitai, Janet, ed. *BAT.* See relevant articles on Jerusalem.

Ariel, Donald T., ed. *Excavation at the City of David 1978–1985 Directed by Yigal Shiloh Volume V: Extramural Areas Qedem 40.* Jerusalem: Institute of Archaeology and the Israel Exploration Society, 2000.

Avigad, Nahman. *Digging Up Jerusalem.* New York: Thomas Nelson Publishers, 1980.

Bahat, Dan. "Jerusalem Down Under: Tunnelling Along Herod's Temple Mount Wall." *BAR* 26.1 (1995): 30–47.

Ben-Dov, Meir. *In The Shadow of the Temple: The Discovery of Ancient Jerusalem.* Translated by Ina Friedman, New York: HarperCollins, 1985.

Biran, Avraham and Joseph Aviram, eds. *BAT 90.* Several relevant articles.

Cahill, Jane M. "Jerusalem at the Time of the United Monarchy." In Vaughn and Kellebrew, eds, 2003: 13–80.

—— "Jerusalem in David and Solomon's Time." *BAR* 30.6 (2004): 20–31; 62–63.

—— and David Tarler, "Respondents." *BAT 90*, 625–626.

Dever, W. G. "Archaeology and the 'Age of Solomon:' A Case Study in Archaeology and Historiography." In *The Age of Solomon. Scholarship at the Turn of the Millennium.* Lowell K. Handy, ed. New York: Brill, 1997: 217–251. See this entire volume for various assessments of "Solomon."

Geva, Hillel, ed. *Ancient Jerusalem Revealed.* Jerusalem: Israel Exploration Society, 1994.

Handy, L. K., ed. *The Age of Solomon: Scholarship at the Turn of the Millennium.* Leiden: Brill, 1997.

Kenyon, Kathleen M. *Digging up Jerusalem.* New York: Praeger Publishers, 1974.

Mazar, Benjamin. "The Temple Mount." *BAT*: 463–468.

Murphy-O'Connor, Jerone. "The City of Jerusalem." In *The Holy Land: an Archaeological Guide From the Earliest Times to 1700*. New York: Oxford University Press, 1986: 9–130.

Na'aman, Nadav. "The Contribution of the Amarna Letters to the Debate on Jerusalem's Political Position in the Tenth Century BCE." *BASOR* 304 (1996): 17–27.

Purvis, J. D. *Jerusalem the Holy City: A Bibliography ATLA Bibliography Series 20*. Metuchen, N. J.: Scarecrow Press, 1988. Contains nearly 6,000 entries.

—— *Jerusalem, The Holy City, Volume II*. Metuchen, NJ: Scarecrow Press, 1991. Contains 4,475 entries, some appearing for the first time, others are updates on entries first appearing in Volume I.

Reich, Ronny and Ya'akov Billig. "Triple Play." *BAR* 28.5 (2002): 40–47.

—— and Eli Shukron. "The System of Rock-Cut Tunnels near the Gihon in Jerusalem Reconsidered." *RB* 107 (2000): 5–17.

—— "Jerusalem the Gihon Spring." *Hadashot Arkeologiyot Excavations and Surveys in Israel*. Jerusalem: IAA, 1999: 109: 77★–78.★

—— "Jerusalem and the Gihon Spring." *Hadashot Arkeologiyot Excavations and Surveys in Israel*. Jerusalem: IAA, 1999: 110: 63★–64.★

—— "Light at the End of the Tunnel." *BAR* 25.1 (1999): 22–33; 72.

Shiloh, Yigael. "The City of David: 1978–1983." *BAT*: 451–456.

—— *Excavations at the City of David I, 1978–1982: Interim Report of the First Five Seasons. Qedem 19*. Jerusalem: Israel Exploration Society, 1984.

Steiner, Margreet. "The Jebusite Ramp of Jerusalem: The Evidence from the Macalister, Kenyon and Shiloh Excavations." *BAT 90*: 585–588.

—— "David's Jerusalem: Fiction or Reality. It's Not There, Archaeology Proves It." *BAR* 24.4 (1998): 26–33; 62–63.

—— "Jerusalem in the Tenth and Seventh Centuries BCE: From Administrative Town to Commercial City." *SAIA*. Amihai, Mazar, ed. Sheffield: Sheffield Academic Press, 2001: 280–288.

Tushingham, A. D. "Revealing Biblical Jerusalem: From Charles Warren to Kathleen Kenyon." *BAT*: 440–450.

Vaughn, Andrew G. and Ann E. Killebrew, eds. *Jerusalem in Bible and Archaeology: The First Temple Period*. Atlanta: Society of Biblical Literature, 2003.

Wilkinson, John. *Jerusalem as Jesus Knew It: Archaeology as Evidence*. London: Thames and Hudson, 1978.

Yadin, Yigael, ed. *Jerusalem Revealed: Archaeology in the Holy City 1968–1974*. Jerusalem: Israel Exploration Society, 1976.

JEZREEL (TEL)

WAS OMRI JUST BOASTING?

The mound of ancient Jezreel is about eight miles east of **Megiddo** in the eastern end of the Valley of Jezreel (later to become the Esdraelon Valley – though this name is not used in the Bible; see Figure 56). This Israelite Jezreel should not be confused with another place of the same name located in Judah (Josh. 15: 56) and, according to some authorities, the town from which came one of the wives of David, Ahinoam (1 Sam. 25: 43; 27: 3; etc.). According to the tradition preserved in Joshua 19: 18, Israelite Jezreel was part of the

Figure 56 Tel Jezreel.

allotment given to the tribe of Issachar. However, most critical literary scholars date the Joshua story no earlier than the tenth century BCE. The claim in 1 Kings 4: 12, that Jezreel was in one of the districts in Solomon's time, would also be tenth century, if historically accurate. Perhaps the best-known story in the Bible associated with Jezreel is that of Naboth's dispute with Ahab, the king of Israel, over a plot of land that belonged to the former's family.

This story is actually told twice, with noticeable differences (for a detailed analysis see Williamson, 1991). According to 1 Kings 21, the dispute was over a "vineyard" (this word occurs 10 times in the story) not a "garden" and Jezebel, Ahab's wife, is accused of hatching a plot that led to Naboth's death and Ahab's receiving the "vineyard." Exactly where Jezebel and Ahab are during this incident is unclear. 1 Kings 21: 8 seems to imply that they are in Samaria, not Jezreel. Whatever the case may be, for her scheming, Jezebel is condemned by God through Elijah to be eaten by dogs "within the bounds of Jezreel" (1 Kgs. 21: 23). Also to be noted is the clear conclusion that Naboth was publically executed by stoning (v.13).

The primary concern of 2 Kings 9–10 is with the *coup* of Jehu but it includes another version of Naboth's demise. Here, however, the dispute is over the "property" of Naboth (2 Kgs. 9: 21) or the "plot of ground" belonging to Naboth (9: 26), not over a "vineyard." To further complicate matters, since Kings Joram and Ahaziah *leave* Jezreel (in chariots, no less) to meet Jehu at the "property" of Naboth (2 Kgs. 9: 21), it seems that this disputed piece of ground is not in the town of Jezreel at all. In addition, while Jezebel is condemned to be eaten by dogs ("in the territory [or "portion"] of Jezreel"; 2 Kgs. 9: 10, 36; see Williamson's comments, 1991: 80–81), her sentence is not linked with the demise of Naboth but to God's revenge for "the blood of my servants the prophets, and the blood of all the servants of the LORD" (2 Kgs. 9: 7), and for "whoredoms and sorceries" (2 Kgs. 9: 22). Another interesting twist, according to Williamson, is that in this version, the murder of Naboth takes place at night ("yesterday," 2 Kgs. 9: 26), witnessed only by God (Williamson, 1991: 84–85).

How much of this story is "history" and how much the creation of the biblical writer(s) is unclear, and a number of cautions are in order. Still many scholars would probably agree with Williamson's conclusion: "Despite these uncertainties, few would doubt that the essential narrative in these two chapters (i.e. 2 Kgs. 9–10) is based on a reliable historical source" (p. 80).

Part of the literary evidence for Williamson's confidence is the reference from the eighth century BCE prophet, Hosea (1: 4; Hosea also uses "Jezreel" as a metaphor for Israel: 1: 11 (2: 2 in the Hebrew text), 2: 22 (2: 24 in the Hebrew Text)).

Up until the 1990s no major excavation of Tel Jezreel had ever been undertaken. While Edward Robinson, in 1838, had identified the biblical site with modern Zer'in, not until 1990 was a modern excavation begun. Between 1990 and 1996, D. Ussishkin (Tel Aviv University) and J. Woodhead (British School of Archaeology, Jerusalem) conducted seven seasons of archaeological work on the tell. The ancient mound rises some 325 feet above the valley floor and is about 15 acres in size.

While evidence of occupation/activity on the tell can be traced back to the late Neolithic/early Chalcolithic periods (fifth–fourth millennium BCE), architectural material anti-dating the Omride period (ninth century BCE) is scanty and inconclusive. However, remains from the Late/Roman and Byzantine periods were recovered. Part of the problem for the earlier periods is that building activities from these later periods often destroyed and robbed out materials from earlier times. Most of the activity on the mound prior to the ninth century is indicated primarily by pottery remains (Gophna and Shlomi, 1997; Zimboni, 1997). The largest town ever to exist here was that of the Byzantine period.

The primary goals of the excavations were twofold: first, to elucidate the history of the site during the time of the Omride dynasty and, second, to recover the overall stratigraphy of the ruin. The excavators concluded that during the ninth century BCE, there was a heavily fortified settlement here. The fortifications included a casemate wall, corner defensive towers and what was probably a six-chamber gate that measured some 67 feet long and nearly 48 feet wide (Ussishkin and Woodhead, 1997: 12, fig. 5). This gate is similar to gates known from other sites such as **Hazor** and **Gezer**. However, the latter two have traditionally been dated to the tenth century BCE, not the ninth. It is believed that the fortified town of Jezreel was built by either Omri (882–871 BCE) or his son Ahab (873–852) and subsequently used by Ahab's sons, Ahaziah (852–851; see 1 Kgs. 22: 40) and Jehoram/Joram (851–842; 2 Kgs. 1: 17). Perhaps a surprising discovery was a huge moat protecting the town that measured between 20 and 50 feet wide in places. Apparently the approach to the city gate required crossing the moat, but exactly how this was accomplished is unclear.

While the evidence is sparse (nine arrowheads in the gate area), the pottery indicates that this town was brought to an end by 842 BCE. The excavators (as well as others) believe this reflects the violent destruction of the town by Jehu. Later Iron Age graves and pottery attest to activity on the site following this period but the fortifications were never rebuilt. It has been suggested that the town was built to serve the propagandistic purposes of the Omrides – to make clear to anyone who passed by who had the power and control of Israel. When Jezreel was destroyed by Jehu (if this is the case), and the Omride dynasty associated with it, no later king apparently had any reason to rebuild it.

Further reading

Gophna, R. and V. Shlomi. "Some Notes on Early Chalcolithic and Early Bronze Material from the Sites of 'En Jezreel and Tel Jezreel." *TA* 24 (1997): 73–82.

Moorhead, T. S. N. "The Late Roman, Byzantine and Umayyad Periods at Tel Jezreel." *TA* 24.1 (1997): 129–166.

Oredsson, Dag. "Jezreel – Its Contribution to Iron Age Chronology." *Scandinavian Journal of the Old Testament* 12.1 (1998): 86–101.

Ussishkin, David and John Woodhead. "Excavations at Tel Jezreel 1990–1991: Preliminary Report." *TA* 19.1 (1992): 3–56.

—— "Excavations at Tel Jezreel 1992–1993: Second Preliminary Report." *Levant* XXVI (1994): 1–48.

—— "Excavations at Tel Jezreel 1994–1996: Third Preliminary Report." *TA* 24.1 (1997): 6–72.

Williamson, H. G. M. "Jezreel In the Biblical Texts." *TA* 18 (1991): 72–92.

—— "Tel Jezreel and the Dynasty of Omri." *PEQ* 128 (1996): 41–51.

Zimboni, Ortna. "The Iron Age Pottery from Tel Jezreel – An Interim Report." *TA* 19.1 (1992): 57–70.

—— "Clues from the Enclosure-Fills: Pre-Omride Settlement at Tel Jezreel." *TA* 24.1 (1997): 83–109.

LACHISH

AT LEAST THE ASSYRIANS
WERE IMPRESSED

The impressive mound of ancient Lachish (modern Tell ed-Duweir; see Figure 57) is located in the foothills of Judah 30 miles southwest of **Jerusalem** and 15 miles west of **Hebron**. Before the 1930s the city was generally identified with Tell el-Hesi, a site in the coastal plain several miles northwest of Gaza. In 1929, W. F. Albright proposed the current identification. Albright's suggestion was dramatically confirmed in 1935 by the discovery of the "Lachish Letters" by James L. Starkey (1895–1938). Further confirmation of the correct location for Lachish comes from Eusebius, a fourth-century historian, who, in his *Onomasticon*, located Lachish seven Roman miles from Eleutheropolis (identified today with modern Beth-Govrim). Tell ed-Duweir is an imposing mound some 30 acres in size at its base narrowing to around

Figure 57 Tell Lachish.

18 acres on its summit. Based on both literary and archaeological sources, it can be said that Lachish was a very important city during the time of the Judaean monarchy (Iron Age II–*c*.1000–587 BCE).

The excavation of the ruins began in 1932 when the Welcome-Marston Expedition was organized by J. Starkey from England. Starkey was assisted by L. G. Harding and O. Tufnell. Preliminary reports on their results can be found in volumes of *PEQ* (65–69) published between 1933 and 1937. Unfortunately, the excavation came to a tragic end when Starkey was murdered on January 10, 1938, on his way to Jerusalem. Nevertheless, Starkey made some very impressive discoveries including the city gates of Level II and I (end of Iron Age II and Babylonian and Persian Periods), the so-called "Solar Shrine" (from Level I), the "Great Shaft," the Palace-Fort, and the "Fosse Temple." This latter discovery was dated to the Late Bronze Age.

Two brief seasons were conducted at the site in the summers of 1966 and 1968 by the late Y. Aharoni. He restricted his investigation to the so-called "Solar Shrine" located on the top of the mound. In 1973, David Ussishkin, of the Institute of Archaeology at Tel Aviv University, began a long-term excavation that lasted until 1987. Ussishkin's work has shown Lachish to have been a very important city during the biblical period (Iron Age II). His finds (especially the pottery) have also helped clarify chronological questions, particularly regarding the *lmlk* stamped jar handles (see Figure 58) and the Assyrian invasion of the area at the end of the eighth century BCE.

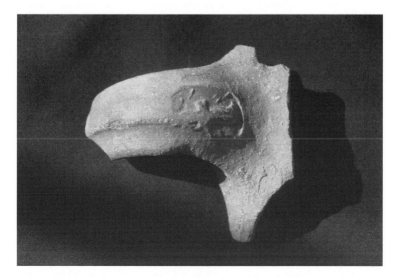

Figure 58 Lamelch stamped jar handle.

Archaeological history of Lachish

Ussishkin's work has shed considerable light on the stratigraphical history of the mound. Several periods of occupation, some with sub-divisions, were identified. The major strata dated to the Neolithic, Chalcolithic, Middle and Late Bronze, Iron Age I and II as well as Babylonian, Persian, and Hellenistic periods. The first significant occupation occurred during the Middle Bronze Age II period (eighteenth–sixteenth century BCE). During this time the site was surrounded by a huge rampart, a defensive feature seen at other Middle Bronze Age cities (**Acco, Dan, Jericho**, for examples). Palace remains were also discovered, testifying to the presence of a local ruler. It was concluded that the Middle Bronze Age II city was destroyed in a fire around 1500 BCE. Another important discovery from this period is a Canaanite inscription found on a dagger which was recovered from a tomb. Lachish did not recover from its Middle Bronze Age destruction until well into the Late Bronze Age when it became a major unfortified Canaanite city, rivaling **Hazor** in size. After the latter's city's destruction in the thirteenth century BCE, Lachish is believed to have been the largest city in the country. It is to this period that a small building found outside the city proper near the northwest corner belongs. Called the "Fosse Temple," (because it was built in a dry moat) it was originally constructed in the sixteenth or fifteenth century BCE and went through three phases before being destroyed by fire at the end of the thirteenth century (c.1225 BCE). While most authorities have accepted its identification as a temple, it has been suggested that the structure might have served the more humble function of a potter's workshop. However, other remains also identified as a temple by the excavator were found on the summit of the mound.

The political importance of Lachish is attested during the Late Bronze Age by literary references to the city. The oldest is a fifteenth-century text dated to the time of Pharaoh Amenhotep II (1427–1402 BCE). Called the Hermitage Papyrus 1116A, the inscription refers to several Canaanite cities (including Lachish) whose representatives received offerings from Egyptian officials. Dating to the fourteenth century are two letters sent from the kings of Lachish to the Egyptian pharaohs Amenhotep III and his son Akhnaten (Amenhotep IV). These letters belong to the larger corpus of the famous "Tel el-Amarna Letters" (*ANET*, 1969: 488–489). Late Bronze Lachish experienced two violent destructions during the twelfth–eleventh centuries BCE. The first is dated to around 1200 and the second to 1150–1130.

Attempts to relate these destructions, especially the last one, to the invading "Israelites" of the Bible have proven unsuccessful. Following this destruction, Lachish was not occupied as a city again for some 200 years, in the tenth century BCE.

During the Iron Age II period (*c*.1000–587 BCE; Levels V–III) Lachish became a large fortified royal city. Among the discoveries are the remains of many impressive architectural features including a massive gate system and what has been identified as a palace-fort (see Figure 59). Described by the excavator as the largest and most impressive building known from the Iron Age in Israel, this structure reached dimensions of over 250 feet in length and 118 feet in width. This palace-fort was built in the center of the city and most likely served as the residence of the local governor. First constructed in Level V (tenth century), the building was in use for several centuries until destroyed, the excavator believed, by Sennacherib in 701 BCE. Other architectural remains from Iron Age II include a huge shaft dug into the earth on the eastern side of the mound. Dubbed the "Great Shaft," and discovered first by Starkey, it measures some 72 by 82 feet and is 74 feet deep. Some have suggested it may have been intended as a water source but the excavator believed it was a stone quarry. This great Iron Age II royal city came to a violent end in 701 BCE when Judah was invaded and devastated by the Assyrians under Sennacherib.

Figure 59 Lachish: Iron Age II palace-fort.

Associated with this attack is a siege ramp built on the southwest corner of the mound. The remains of this huge structure (some 230–240 feet wide and 164–197 feet long) are still clearly visible today. Also what may be remnants of the horror of this attack are the remains of some 1,500 individuals, including men, women, and children, found in nearby caves. If these remains date to the Assyrian period, they are a grisly testimony to the massacre of the civilian population by the Assyrians. This destruction of Lachish is celebrated in the famous relief on the palace walls of Sennacherib.

Lachish and the Assyrian war are also important for understanding the ceramic history of the time. A much disputed issue prior to Ussishkin's excavation was the discussion surrounding the date and function of jars that bore a stamp with the letters "*lmlk*" (see Figure 58, p. 177) "belonging to the king." Hundreds of jar handles with these stamps were found at Lachish in datable contexts. All were made from a clay source close to the city. Some of the stamps show a four-winged symbol, others two-winged, and some handles were not stamped at all. However, it is now clear that they were all used at the same time and that they date to the time of King Hezekiah (late eighth century BCE). Apparently the storage vessels originally bearing the handles were produced in preparation for the war with the Assyrians.

Following the destruction of the city by the Assyrians, Lachish was rebuilt, but not on the scale of its predecessor. The great palace-fort of the previous centuries lay in ruins and was not reconstructed. The city became a smaller and poorer place. Yet its fate proved to be no better than its predecessors. This phase of the city's history also came to a violent end when it was destroyed by the Babylonians during the first part of the sixth century BCE.

In the Bible (Jer. 34: 7) Lachish is mention by name as one of the cities attacked by Nebuchadnezzar. From this period also date the famous "Lachish Letters." First discovered by Starkey in the ruins of one of the gate chambers, the letters are believed to be messages sent by a subordinate to a military commander at Lachish, named "Yaush." However, Y. Yadin challenged this conclusion and suggested instead that the ostraca were really "drafts" of letters composed at Lachish and not sent here. His view has not been popularly adopted by other authorities.

Following the Exile, there was some activity on the site in the Persian and Hellenistic periods. The evidence suggests that the site was finally abandoned *c.*150 BCE. The mound was used as an Israeli military camp during Israel's War of Independence in 1948.

Further reading

Aharoni, Yohanan. *Investigations at Lachish: The Sanctuary and Residency (Lachish V)*. Tel Aviv: Gateway Publishers, 1975.

Dever, William G. "Of Myths and Methods." *BASOR* 277–278 (1990): 121–130.

Ussishkin, David. "Lachish: Key to the Israelite Conquest of Canaan?" *BAR* 13.1 (1987): 18–39.

—— "Excavations at Tel Lachish, 1973–1977: Preliminary Report." *TA* 5 (1978): 1–97.

—— "Excavations at Tel Lachish, 1978–1983: Second Preliminary Report." *TA* 10 (1983): 97–175.

—— "The Assyrian Attack on Lachish: The Archaeological Evidence from the Southwest Corner of the Site." *TA* 17 (1990): 53–86.

Yadin, Yigael. "The Lachish Letters – Originals or Copies and Drafts?" In *Recent Archaeology in the Land of Israel*. Hershel Shanks, ed., Washington, DC: Biblical Archaeology Society, 1984: 179–186.

MEGIDDO

FRONT-ROW SEAT FOR WATCHING THE END OF THE WORLD

Described as ". . . the royal box in one of the great theatres of history," Megiddo was an important city during both the Bronze and Iron Ages (3000–734 BCE). Identified with modern Tell el-Mutesellim ("Mound of the Governor), the 25-acre site is located in the Jezreel Valley about 20 miles southeast of the modern city of Haifa. In antiquity the city guarded the pass through the valley and witnessed many battles. The mound was occupied almost continuously from the Neolithic (8000 BCE) through the Persian (fourth century BCE) periods.

While the archaeological evidence clearly indicates an early occupation of the site, the city is not mentioned in historical texts

Figure 60 Tell Megiddo from the air.

until its defeat at the hands of the Egyptian Pharaoh, Thutmose III, around 1468 BCE. The site is also mentioned in a Ta'anach Letter of the late fifteenth century, and in the El Amarna correspondence of the fourteenth century BCE (eight letters, six from the governor of Megiddo, Biridiya; for example, see *ANET*, 1969: 485).

Megiddo is mentioned 12 times in the Hebrew Bible (Josh. 21: 21; 17: 11; Judg. 1: 27; 5: 19; 1 Kgs. 4: 12; 9: 15; 2 Kgs. 9: 27; 23: 29, 30; 1 Chron. 7: 29; 2 Chron. 35: 22; Zech. 12: 11). We are told in these texts that the city was defeated by Joshua (Josh. 12: 21) and that Deborah was victorious over the Canaanites "by the waters of Megiddo" (Judg. 5: 19). In a much discussed text, Solomon is said to have re-fortified the city making it a very important administrative center during his reign (1 Kgs. 4: 12; 9: 15). Finally, Ahaziah, king of Israel, was killed there by Jehu (mid-ninth century BCE; 2 Kgs. 9: 27), as was Josiah (2 Kgs. 23: 29–30) in 609 BCE by the Egyptians. In fact, so many battles were fought at or near Megiddo that the apocalyptic author of Revelation made the site the location of God's final battle against the forces of evil: "Armageddon" ("the mount of Megiddo"; Rev. 16: 16).

Until recently the basic historicity of these biblical stories was defended by most biblical scholars, including the biblical insistence that Megiddo came under Israelite control during the reign of Solomon (*c*.967–926 BCE). Support for this conclusion was believed to come from archaeological discoveries that included a six-chambered gate and other architectural structures (palace, stables) that could be dated to the tenth century BCE.

However, due to the history of the excavation of the site, controversy has always been part of Megiddo's archaeological legacy. It was first excavated between 1903 and 1905 by J. Shumacher on behalf of the German Oriental Society. Between 1925 and 1939, the Oriental Institute of the University of Chicago sponsored a major excavation under the direction of C. S. Fisher, P. L. O. Guy and G. Loud. It is primarily due to this excavation with its incomplete and inadequate publications, as well as its primitive (by modern standards) archaeological methods, that much confusion over strata assignment of discoveries has occurred. In order to try to clear up some of the confusion, Y. Yadin, an Israeli archaeologist, conducted several seasons of work there between 1960 and 1972. However, his conclusions have only fueled the controversies. Thus, a new large-scale dig was begun on the site in 1992, under the direction of I. Finkelstein and D. Ussishkin, both of Tel Aviv University, and B. Halpern of Pennsylvania State University. Using newer archaeological paradigms, the excavators are attempting to understand the history of Megiddo in the broader context of city-state politics and social development. Whether their work will finally resolve much of the controversy that has surrounded this site remains to be seen.

The original excavators identified some 20 strata on the mound, some of which were subdivided, yielding a total of 25 levels of occupation. The earliest material dates to the Neolithic period of the eighth millennium BCE (mostly found in caves). There was also a small Chalcolithic settlement here (fifth–fourth millennium). At the beginning of the Early Bronze Age, a large, unfortified city was built. By the Early Bronze Age II period (c.2800 BCE), the city was defended by a wall some 13–16 feet wide. This wall reached a width of some 25 feet during the next phase of occupation (stratum XVII). Also dating to this period is what has traditionally been identified as the largest open-air altar yet discovered in Israel. Made of small stones and surrounded by a temenos (a sacred area enclosed by a wall), this construction is more than 25 feet in diameter and 5 feet high. Seven steps lead to its top. However, not all authorities are convinced that it is an altar. Herzog (1992) has argued that it served the more secular function of a granary base. In any case, the remains of temples and other structures were dated to this period as well as some of the earliest examples of local art: stone drawings of men and beasts. These discoveries have been supplemented by recent discoveries of the current excavation.

Megiddo seems to have been abandoned around 2200 BCE when the Early Bronze Age as a whole came to an end. The cause(s) of the demise of this long cultural period is still debated but decline in trade and political instability my have been chief components.

During the last two centuries of the third millennium BCE (Early Bronze Age IV), Megiddo was sparsely inhabited as evidenced by the remains of small and poorly constructed buildings. However, a number of rock-cut shaft tombs date to this time. Beginning in the second millennium BCE, a new city was built that included a mud-brick wall and the earliest gate discovered on the mound. For several centuries (2000–1150 BCE) the city thrived and was ruled by a city-state prince or king. This despite the fact that the Egyptians, under the reign of Thutmose III (1479–1425 BCE), conquered Megiddo, along with other Canaanite rebellious city-states. However, the stratigraphy during this long period has been made difficult, in part, due to a lack of clear destruction levels.

Nevertheless, Megiddo, during the Late Bronze Age (c.1500–1150 BCE) appears to have been a very prosperous city, at least for some of its inhabitants. Various treasures of gold vessels, jewelry, and carved ivories have been discovered in palace remains from Strata VIII and VII B. Also from the Late Bronze Age is a large fortified temple that went through three phases of construction by the end of Stratum VII A. A very interesting textual discovery from this period is a cuneiform fragment of the Babylonian myth called the "Epic of Gilgamesh," which contains a Babylonian version of the biblical flood narrative. Found near the tell, its origin is uncertain. However, it has been suggested that the presence of this text implies that a scribal school may have existed in the city. The last gasp of the long Bronze Age city was not without its problems. In the fourteenth century, political unrest forced the prince of Megiddo, Biridiya, to ask the Egyptian king for help to deal with marauders identified as "Apiru" (*ANET*, 1969: 485).

What happened next is a major part of the continuing controversy. Earlier authorities argued that the site was violently destroyed, possibly by the invading "Israelites" (Josh. 12: 21) or Sea Peoples, perhaps the Philistines. While there is some evidence to support some violence to the city around 1150 BCE, Megiddo was apparently quickly rebuilt and maintained its Canaanite culture (seen especially in artistic and architectural styles). This has suggested to some that its transition from a Canaanite to an Israelite city was not sudden.

But the most controversial aspect of Megiddo's history has to do with the biblical claim that the city was controlled during the tenth century by **Jerusalem** (1 Kgs. 4: 21). In fact, Megiddo is listed as one of the cities from which Solomon received provisions for his house-hold (1 Kgs. 4: 12). The biblical writers also claim that Megiddo was one of the cities fortified by Solomon after he became king (1 Kgs. 9: 15). The question posed by the archaeological record is: should (can) these biblical traditions be taken at face value? The major stratum involved is called "VA–IVB." The problem exists primarily due to the earlier Chicago expedition which succeeded in stripping away almost completely the first four strata of the mound. Thus it has long been difficult to know with confidence which remains should be assigned to which time periods. It was to try to clear up these questions that Yadin began his excavation at Megiddo in 1960. Unfortunately, his conclusions have only fueled the debate, not settled it. We can only hope that the present work will be more successful. However, there seems already to be disagreement among the directors over which, if any, material remains can be assigned with confidence to the Solomonic era. B. Halpern, in particular, has defended the biblical claim that Solomon rebuilt the city and that the six-chamber gate (see Figure 61) and certain palace remains can be assigned to this time (Solomon's reign is usually dated from *c*.967–926 BCE). Others are not as confident.

Both Finkelstein and Ussishkin have argued for a lower chronology for the stratum in question. According to them the material remains at Megiddo which traditionally have been assigned to Solomon were actually built by the Omrides of the ninth century BCE. To this later period also dates the famous water shaft and tunnel. If their revised dating is ultimately vindicated, then most of the assumed "Solomonic" presence at Megiddo disappears. The problem, as all participants in the discussion agree, is that, as of yet, there is no acceptable absolute chronology for the archaeological data in Israel that have been assigned to the early stages of the Iron Age II (basically the tenth–ninth centuries BCE). In any case, the current excavators believe that the major Iron Age city at Megiddo emerged after the time of Solomon. Furthermore, they have suggested that the first real Israelite monarchy may not have come out of Jerusalem but from Israel in the north. The role played in this political development by Megiddo is believed to have been extensive. If these new, and other theories

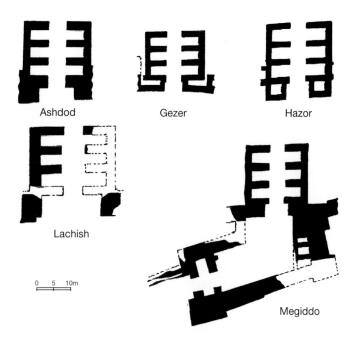

Ashdod

Gezer

Hazor

Lachish

0   5   10m

Megiddo

Figure 61 Drawing of six-chamber gates traditionally attributed to Solomon.

being proposed, can be supported by hard archaeological evidence, the biblical portrait of Solomon will have to be modified considerably. Only time will tell. What can be concluded with confidence is that even though the site continued to be occupied until around 350 BCE, the Iron Age importance of this city was brought to an end by the Assyrian onslaught during the last half of the eighth century BCE.

Further reading

Finkelstein, Israel, David Ussishkin and Baruch Halpern, eds. *Megiddo III: the 1992–1996 Seasons.* 2 volumes. Monograph Series Number 18. Tel Aviv: Tel Aviv University, 2000.

Harrison, Timothy P. "The Battleground: Who Destroyed Megiddo? Was It David or Shishak?" *BAR* 29.5 (2003): 28–35; 60, 62, 64.

Herzog, Ze'ev. "Cities." *ABD* 1 (1992): 1034.

Silberman, Neil Asher. "Armageddon, Megiddo, and the End of the World." *Archaeology* November/December (1999): 36–37.

—— Israel Finkelstein, David Ussishkin, and Baruch Halpern: "Digging at Armageddon: A New Expedition Tackles one of the Near East's Most Famous Tels – and Legends." *Archaeology* November/December (1999): 32–35, 38–39.

Ussishkin, David. "Was the 'Solomonic' City Gate at Megiddo built by King Solomon?" *BASOR* 239 Summer (1980): 1–18.

Yadin, Y. "Megiddo of the Kings of Israel." *BA* 33 (1970): 66–96.

—— "A Rejoiner." *BASOR* 239 Summer (1980): 19–23.

MIZPAH (TELL EN-NASBEH?)

WHAT'S AN "*EBENEZER*"?

Mizpah and the Bible

In the Bible, the site of Mizpah is located in the tribal territory of Benjamin (see Judg. 20: 1; 21: 8). The town plays an important role during four periods of Israel's history. The first is during the time of the so-called "Judges," when there may have been some sort of sanctuary dedicated here to YHWH, the god of Israel. We are told that the "Israelites" assembled at Mizpah "before the LORD" (Judg. 20: 1), and from there launched an attack on the Benjaminites at **Gibeah** for the rape (and murder?) of the Levite's concubine (Judg. 19: 22–30). The ultimate decimation of the Benjaminites took three attempts (despite YHWH's assurance to the Israelites that this is what he desired them to do!). To prevent the tribe of Benjamin from

Figure 62 Mizpah, offset-inset wall.

becoming extinct, the few men left are allowed to abduct virgins from the annual Shiloh festival (Judg. 21: 1–24). (As an aside, thousands of troops are said to have been killed on each side. The entire population for the north Central Hill Country during this time has been estimated at around 50,000. One suspects that the biblical writer/ editor has exaggerated the numbers for effect.)

Nothing is heard about Mizpah again until the time of Samuel (eleventh century BCE?). Once more, the place seems to be a cult site visited by Samuel on an annual basis, along with **Bethel** and Gilgal (1 Sam. 7: 16). Furthermore, the place still served as an assembly point for Israelite troops, this time before attacking the Philistines. Associated with this story, and the subsequent defeat of the Philistines, is the setting-up of the *"ebenezer"* (1 Sam. 7: 12; the "stone of help"). It is also at Mizpah where one of the "coronations" of Saul is said to have taken place (1 Sam. 10: 17ff).

Strangely enough, Mizpah is never mentioned in the Bible in relation to David and Solomon. But the site regained importance for the third time during the reign of the Judean King, Asa, who is usually dated to the first quarter of the ninth century. According to 1 Kings 15, Asa was attacked by the King of Israel, Baasha. In order to protect his northern border, Asa re-fortified Mizpah from materials that Baasha was himself using to reinforce another town, Ramah (1 Kgs. 15: 22; see 2 Chron. 16: 6).

After this story, Mizpah is not mentioned again until the aftermath of the Babylonian defeat of Judah and **Jerusalem** by Nebuchadnezzar in 587/586 BCE. A man named Gedaliah is appointed by Nebuchadnezzar to act as governor of the region (1 Kgs. 15: 23, 25). Since Jerusalem had been devastated, Gedaliah sets up his own government, such as it was, at Mizpah. However, his efforts were to be short lived. Gedaliah, along with many of his supporters, was murdered by a man named Ishmael, despite having been warned beforehand of Ishmael's planned treachery (Jer. 40–41). The last literary reference to Mizpah is from the second century BCE. Judas is said to have mustered his army there before fighting the forces of Syria (1 Macc. 46). Interestingly, this late text says Judas did this because "Israel formerly had a place of prayer at Mizpah."

Mizpah and archaeology

Mizpah is generally identified with Tell en-Nasbeh, an ancient ruin some seven-and-a-half miles north of Jerusalem, though other sites, such as Nabi Samwil and Ataroth-addar have been suggested. Tell en-Nasbeh lies over 2,500 feet above sea level and encompasses about eight acres. The site was excavated during five seasons from 1926 to 1935, by W. F. Badè who was from the Pacific School of Religion in Berkeley, California. Unfortunately, Badè died in 1936 and the major publications were done by two of his colleagues, C. C. McCown and J. C. Wampler in 1947. Due to the fact that modern stratigraphical techniques were not in place during these early years of archaeology in Israel, Badè was unable to disentangle most of the stratigraphical complexity of the site. However, thanks to the pioneering efforts of Jeffrey Zorn, currently at Cornell University (see bibliography), the various periods of activity on the site, as well as the archaeological remains belonging to these periods, are becoming clearer.

For convenience, Zorn has divided the periods into four major strata. The earliest period (Str. 4) is dated to the Late Chalcolithic–Early Bronze Age I and consisted of little more than finds from caves and tombs. What occupation there was seems to have been concentrated on the northwest corner of the site. For unknown reasons the place was abandoned at the end of Early Bronze Age I (*c*.3000 BCE) and was not again occupied for nearly 1,800 years in Iron Age I (Zorn's Str. 2). A considerable amount of pottery sherds date to this period, including those identified as "Philistine," as well as some rock-cut installations that have been identified as cisterns or silos. However, there is little known from this time that would identify Nasbeh as an important cultic site.

Stratum 3 is assigned by Zorn to Iron Age II, particularly the ninth century BCE. Much of the known architectural remains on the site are dated to this time including houses, defensive towers, and a massive wall that was uncovered for over 2,160 feet. The wall was constructed in what is called an offset-inset style (see Figure 62, p. 188) and was protected by 11 towers. The city was entered through an outer–inner gate complex, part of which was not recognized by Badè and his team. Zorn also found evidence of domestic dwellings built outside the wall. Several tombs from Iron Age II were also found, four of which contained nearly 1,600 objects. Some very interesting small finds include 87 *lmlk* stamp impressions and a seal that reads: "(belonging) to Jaazaniah servant of the king." A person with the same name is identified as a military officer during the time of Gedaliah (2 Kgs. 25: 33). A curiosity of the seal is the representation on it of a cock in a fighting stance. According to Zorn, this is one of the earliest known representations of this bird. Many other finds were dated to this period: agricultural tools such as mattocks, plow points, flint blades, mortars, and pestles. That there was still some sort of cultic activity engaged in here is indicated by dozens of female figurines and pottery remains identified as cult stands.

After the ninth century, the place seems to be devoid of activity until the sixth century BCE, following the devastating attack by the Babylonians that destroyed Jerusalem and many other Judean sites. To this time Zorn dates his Stratum 2, which he described as the most important period in the life of the town. The town plan was changed considerably from that of Iron Age II and Mizpah served as the capital city for the government, such as it was, of Gedaliah.

Stratum 1 was assigned to the Roman and Byzantine periods, even though there is some evidence of activity on the site during the preceding Persian and Hellenistic eras. However, the extent of activity during any of these earlier periods is not clear.

Further reading

Zorn, Jeffrey R. "William Frederic Badè." *BA* 51: 1 (1988): 28–35.

—— "Mizpah Newly Discovered Stratum Reveals Judah's Other Capital." *BAR* 23.5 (1997): 28–38, 66.

—— "Estimating the Population Size of Ancient Settlements: Methods, Problems, Solutions, and a Case Study." *BASOR* 295 August (1994): 31–48.

—— "An Inner and Outer gate Complex at Tell en-Nasbeh." *BASOR* 307 August (1997): 53–66.

—— "Tell en-Nasbeh and the Problem of the Material Culture of the Sixth Century." In *Judah and the Judeans in the Neo-Babylonian Period*. Oded Lipschits and Joseph Blenkinsopp, eds. Winona Lake, IN: Eisenbrauns, 2003: 413–447.

Zorn also has a web site for Tell en-Nasbeh that contains a much more extensive bibliography: www.arts.cornell.edu/jrz3/index.htm.

NAZARETH

A PEASANT VILLAGE: HOMETOWN OF JESUS

Were it not for the association of Nazareth with Jesus (or Jesus with Nazareth) in the New Testament (see Matt. 2: 23; Luke 2: 39, 51; 4: 16) there would probably not have been as much archaeological and/or historical interest as has been invested in this town. Located about 15 miles west of the Sea of Galilee, at an altitude of over 1,750 feet, Nazareth was a poor peasant village during the first century CE.

Nazareth in the Bible

Nazareth is mentioned only in the New Testament and is even then restricted to the four Gospels and the Book of Acts. Most of the 30 occurrences of the name serve to identify Jesus as having come from here (see for examples: Mark 1: 24; 10: 47; Matt. 26: 71; Luke 18: 37; 24: 19; John 18: 5, 7; Acts 2: 22; 3: 6; 4: 10; 6: 14). Luke specific-ally identifies Nazareth as the hometown of Mary and Joseph (2: 39) and other references claim that this is where Jesus grew up (Mark 1: 9; Matt. 4: 13; Luke 2: 51; 4: 16). The low status of this otherwise insignificant first-century CE Jewish village is also reflected in the Gospels (John 1: 45ff.). Beyond the New Testament insistence that Jesus grew up there, the most important story relating him to the place is found in Luke, and only in Luke: Jesus returns to Nazareth, goes to a synagogue on the Sabbath and reads from the scroll of Isaiah, after which the people become enraged and try to kill him (Luke 4: 16–30).

However, just as archaeological sites are "layered," with earlier material often mixed with later debris, texts may also be similarly "layered." The historical Jesus scholar, John Dominic Crossan, has argued that since Jesus grew up in a peasant village, it would have been most unlikely that he was "literate and learned" (Crossan and Reed, 2001: 30; for an excellent discussion of both the archaeology and the text vis-à-vis Nazareth, see the entire chapter on Nazareth). The implications of Crossan's argument for understanding Jesus, "Luke," and the formation of Luke's Gospel must be left to the interested reader. After the New Testament, there are no known literary references to Nazareth until after Christianity became the state religion of the Roman Empire (313 CE).

Nazareth and archaeology

For someone interested in the archaeological remains from the first century CE, Nazareth is something of a nightmare. For over 300 years after Jesus lived no one seems to have cared much about the village. But when Christianity became the official religion of the Empire, Christians began to build churches to commemorate the biblical stories. Thus the Church of St. Joseph is supposedly built over the location of Joseph's carpentry shop, and the Church of the Annunciation (completed in 1966) incorporates the Grotto of Mary, where the virgin supposedly received her visit from the angel Gabriel (Luke 1: 26–31). These churches, which can be seen and visited today (as well as others), were themselves built over earlier remains from both the Crusader (eleventh–twelfth centuries) and Byzantine (late fourth–seventh centuries) periods. Whether the stories about Mary

Figure 63 Nazareth: Church of the Annunciation.

and/or Joseph had anything to do with any of these locations is simply unknown and unknowable. In order to "get back" to the first century CE, 2,000 years of subsequent building and rebuilding, debris accumulation, and so forth, have to be overcome. In addition, modern Nazareth is a bustling, mostly Christian Arab, city, which severely limits archaeological exploration.

While some archaeological excavations were conducted at the end of the nineteenth and beginning of the twentieth centuries, the first large-scale modern excavation is the work of Bellarmino Bagatti carried out in 1955 (Bagatti, 1969). While the Church of the Annunciation was being rebuilt (it was first constructed in 1730 on a Crusader foundation), Bagatti was given the opportunity to excavate in and around this structure. While there is scanty evidence of some activity here as early as the Middle Bronze Age (*c.*2000–1550 BCE) and the "Israelite Period" (pottery sherds), most of the remains date to the Byzantine period or later. However, Bagatti did find locally made pottery from the first century consisting mostly of cooking pots, water jugs, and so forth. But he did not find any trace of imported vessels. There were few material remains that could be identified as houses, but what there was indicated that these structures were little more than hovels with earthen floors, sometimes incorporating caves. Bagatti found nothing that could be identified as public buildings during this time, including a "synagogue."

Based on the location of burial tombs, which would have been outside the village proper, Bagatti estimated the size of Nazareth during this period to be about ten acres with a population between 200 and 400. The remains of olive and wine presses, water cisterns, grinding stones, and other materials found scattered about, all indicate the poor, peasant nature of Nazareth during the time of Jesus. For an understanding of who Jesus was and what he was trying to do, this knowledge of the peasant character of Nazareth is far more important than trying to "mark the spot" where Joseph worked or Mary heard an angel.

Further reading

Crossan, John Dominic and Jonathan L. Reed. *Excavating Jesus: Beneath the Stones, Behind the Text.* San Francisco: HarperSanFrancisco, 2001.

Bagatti, Bellarmino. *Excavations in Nazareth, Vol. 1, From The Beginning Till the XII Century.* Jerusalem: Franciscan Printing, 1969.

——— "Nazareth." *NEAEHL* 3: 1103–1105.

Tzaferis, Vassilios. "The Crusader Church." *NEAEHL* 3: 1105.

RAMAT RACHEL (BETH-HACCHEREM)
WHY PROPHETS SOMETIMES HATED KINGS

Ramat Rachel is an important Iron Age II B, C ruin located between **Jerusalem** and **Bethlehem** (see Figure 64). In 1931 Benjamin Mazar and Moshe Stekelis excavated a burial cave on the site but the major excavation of the ruin began in 1954, when Yohanan Aharoni began four seasons of work that ended in 1962. Based upon his discoveries and the biblical textual evidence (mainly Jer. 6: 1; Neh. 3: 14; Josh. 15: 59 (in the Greek Bible)), he identified the site with ancient Beth-haccherem ("house of the vineyard"). Gabriel Barkay also excavated two trenches here in 1984 for Tel Aviv University and the

Figure 64 Ramat Rachel: excavations.

195

Palestine Exploration Society. Barkay did not think that the site was Beth-haccherem but a town known only as *mms't* on the *lmlk* jar handles (the other three towns mentioned on the handles are: **Hebron**, Ziph, and Sochoh; *mms't* has never been successfully identified).

Whatever the case may be with regard to its ancient name, Aharoni discovered the remains of a Judean Royal palace that probably dates to the last days of Judah. In fact, Aharoni believed that he had uncovered the remains of the palace of Jehoiakim, king of Judah (*c.*608–598 BCE), whose luxury was so soundly condemned by the prophet Jeremiah (Jer. 22: 13–19). In all, five major strata were identified, some with sub-divisions. The dates for these periods range from the eighth–seventh centuries BCE, for the earliest, to the seventh century CE for the latest.

Based on the dozens of *lmlk*-stamped jar handles found in constructional fills of Stratum VA, Aharoni dated Stratum VB to the end of the eighth century. The date of these handles has been fixed (especially by the evidence from **Lachish**) to the time of Hezekiah, King of Judah. They are commonly interpreted to have belonged to storage jars which were used in preparation for the confrontation with the Assyrians that occurred at the end of the eighth century BCE. However, the architectural remains from this period are sparse, though the excavator thought a casemate wall and a quarry may date to this time.

Stratum VA, dated to the seventh–early sixth century, is the major stratum of the site. At this time a double wall enclosed about two-and-a-half acres of space. Within this enclosure the remains of a large structure (measuring 184 × 236 feet) identified as a citadel were found. The architectural remains associated with this building: fine ashlar masonry, proto-Aeolic capitals, carved stone balustrades, and stone crenelation all indicate it was a royal residence. Whether or not it was one used by Jehoiakim, and later by his son, Jehoiakin, cannot be asserted for sure. Aharoni believed the site was destroyed by the Babylonians in the early sixth century BCE. Among important finds is a seal that reads: "Elyaqim steward of Yokhin." Aharoni thought the name, "Yokhin," was a reference to king Jehoiakin and consequently dated the seal to the early sixth century. Other authorities have suggested an eighth century BCE date.

Stratum IVB belongs to the late Persian/early Hellenistic period (fifth–third centuries BCE). While architectural remains are poorly represented from this time, some 270 seal impressions were found. Some of these seals bear the name of "Jerusalem," while others contain the Persian name for the country, "Yehud." Seals with private names were also found. While the absolute date for this material is difficult to determine, since the jar handles with the stamped seals were found in refuse pits, Aharoni dated most of them to the fourth century BCE.

By the Herodian period (Str. IVA), an ordinary settlement of non-royal and/or administrative peoples inhabited the site. This phase of occupation came to an end with the Roman conquest of Judea around 70 CE. Following an occupational gap of some 200 years, the Tenth Roman Legion used the site (Str. III). In addition to a Roman villa, a bathhouse was uncovered. In the remains of this structure were found tiles bearing the stamp of the Tenth Legion. Stratum II is sub-divided into two sub-phases, but both date to the Byzantine period (fifth–seventh centuries CE). The most significant building from this period is the Church of Kathisma, built around the middle of the fifth century. The name of the church, in Greek, means "seat," and comes from a tradition that Mary, the mother of Jesus, rested here on her way to Bethlehem. The final phase of occupation of the mound (Str. I) dates to the Early Arab period (seventh–eighth century CE) and is represented by poorly built architectural remains.

The importance of this site for archaeological purposes is seen in Strata VA–IVB, which correspond to Judah's history and the Persian period. There seems to be little doubt that a royal citadel and palace existed here during the first part of these periods, and a significant Persian settlement during the second. The citadel/palace remains have important architectural implications for understanding Israelite/ Phoenician influence this late in Judah's history. Furthermore, the seal impressions from the Persian/Hellenistic period add considerable epigraphic knowledge of the post-exilic period.

Further reading

Renewed exploration of Ramat Rachel has been undertaken recently by R. Reich of the University of Haifa and O. Lipschits of Tel Aviv University.

Aharoni, Yohanan. "Excavations at Ramat Rachel." *BA* 24 (1961): 98–118.

—— "Beth-Haccherem." in *AOTS*. D. Winton Thomas, ed., Oxford: Clarendon Press, 1967: 172–184.

SAMARIA

THE PRIDE OF THE OMRIDES

According to the biblical tradition (1 Kgs. 16: 21–24), Omri, King of Israel (*c.*886–875 BCE), moved the capital of Israel from Tirzah (identified by some authorities with **Tell el-Far'ah, North**) to Samaria, a prominent mound located ten miles west of Tell el-Far'ah and about 35 miles north of **Jerusalem** (see Figure 65). During the next 30–35 years, Omri and his son, Ahab (*c.*875–850 BCE) built what must have been in its day a very thriving and beautiful city. Thanks to their combined efforts, Samaria became a political and cultural center of Israel for nearly 150 years. During this time, the Assyrians referred to Israel as 'Omri-Land' (*ANET*, 1969: 284–285).

Figure 65 Samaria: general view of ruins.

The international status attained by the city can also be seen in the marriage of Ahab to Jezebel, the daughter of the king of Tyre (1 Kgs. 16: 31–33). However, this political and social attainment by the Omrides did little to impress the biblical writers who soundly condemned both kings for what were perceived to be religious and social atrocities (see 1 Kgs. 21; 22: 39; etc.). Elijah, in particular (1 Kgs. 17–22), condemned Ahab for both his religious idolatry and abuse of power (see chapter on **Jezreel**, this volume)

Following the death of Ahab by the hands of the Arameans at the battle of Ramath-Gilead (1 Kgs. 22: 29–36), Jehu was appointed by the prophet Elisha to rid Israel once and for all of the House of Omri (2 Kgs. 9: 1–10). Jehu's bloody excesses, however, earned him his own condemnation a hundred years later by the prophet Hosea (Hos. 1: 4–5).

Nevertheless, from Omri's time on, all the rest of the kings of Israel lived in, and ruled from, Samaria. The city quickly became the political center of the nation and was called by the prophet, Isaiah, the "head of Ephraim." But the city did not always have a reputation for religious idolatry and political and social exploitation (see 2 Kgs. 13: 1–9).

By the time of Amos (c.760–750 BCE), Samaria had reached its final era of greatness. Now ruled by Jeroboam II, the grandson of Jehu (2 Kgs. 13: 13; 14: 23–29), Amos attacked both the king and other wealthy and powerful people for their social, economic, and legal exploitation of the poor and powerless (Amos 2: 7; 4: 1; 8: 4–8). He also condemned their pretense at being worshipers of the God of Israel (4: 4–5; 5: 21–24). For this prophet, the end was near (see 8: 1–2). It came in 722/721 BCE when the Assyrians attacked Samaria and took many of its inhabitants into captivity.

Through the centuries that have followed since, the city continued to exist and even had its name changed to "Sebaste" (= "Augustus") by Herod the Great. In the fourth century CE, it became the seat of a bishop. Among the earlier Christians there also arose a tradition that the body and head of John the Baptist were buried here. Today the site lies in ruins, but thanks to the work of archaeologists, hints of its former glory and beauty have been discovered.

Excavations of Samaria

There have been two major excavations of Samaria in the twentieth century. The first was conducted under the auspices of Harvard University between 1908 and 1910. Directed at first by G. Shumacher, and later by C. Fisher, the excavators uncovered monumental architectural remains which were dated to the time of Omri and Ahab (ninth century BCE). The discoveries included walls, storehouses, and what was identified as a royal palace. One of the most interesting, as well as important, discoveries was a group of ostraca, which have been interpreted as tax receipts for commodities (mostly oil and wine) sent to the city.

The second major excavation took place between 1931 and 1935, and was a joint expedition sponsored by five institutions, mostly from England and Israel. This expedition was led by John W. Crowfoot and included another British archaeologist, Kathleen M. Kenyon, who went on to distinguish herself with excavations at **Jericho** and Jerusalem. In fact, it is Kenyon's publications of the results of the work at Samaria that have been the main source for understanding the history of the site during the Iron Age II period (*c*.1000–587/ 586 BCE).

However, Kenyon's conclusion that there was no usage of this site prior to the time of Omri has been challenged in recent years. It is now believed that as early as the eleventh century BCE, there were wine and oil presses cut into the rock surface. In fact, it has been argued that the price Omri is said to have paid for the site, two talents of silver (1 Kgs. 16: 24), or six thousand silver shekels, indicates that the site was not abandoned, but was probably a family or clan estate reaching back to the tribe of Issachar in the time of the Judges (Judg. 10: 1–2).

In any event, the first city to be built on the site was that of Omri's. The cosmopolitan character of the city can be seen both in the construction technique used to erect walls and buildings (using finely cut stones without mortar, thought to have been learned from the Phoenicians), as well as in the major discovery of the latter excavation: over 500 ivory fragments.

The Otraca and ivory discoveries

Certainly two of the most important archaeological discoveries at Samaria are the inscribed sherds (see Figure 66, p. 201) and ivory fragments. The absolute dates of the sherds, as well as their original function or purpose, however, are still matters of debate. The same is true of the famous ivory fragments, most of which were found in a dump. Traditionally, both discoveries have been dated to the ninth–eighth centuries BCE.

The sherds are not only important for what they reveal about ancient Hebrew writing and taxation system. They also contain information about the topography around Samaria, containing names of towns such as "Yasith," "Yashub," and "Qosoh," which are not mentioned in the Bible. Furthermore, some of the sherds contain personal names compounded with the god, Baal (i.e. "Abibaal," "Merib-baal") pointing to the religious idolatry so condemned by the prophets Amos and Hosea (Hos. 2: 16–17).

Whether these names refer to the *sender* of the goods, or to the *recipient*, is still unclear. However, the latter seems to be the most likely. If this interpretation is correct it means that some people in Samaria were receiving provisions from their country estates which may have contributed to the exploitation of the poor so condemned by Amos (see 2: 6–8) and other prophets.

That certain inhabitants of the city lived a life of luxury is indicated further by the ivory fragments which were recovered. Again, due to the circumstances of their discovery, their dates are unclear archaeologically. The excavators, based upon biblical texts, not archaeological data, dated them to the reigns of Ahab/Jeroboam II. This may be an accurate suggestion, since the final archaeo-logical disposition of material remains does not rule out an earlier usage. However, on archaeological data alone, no such date can be justified.

Figure 66 Samaria Ostraca.

Further reading

There are numerous publications on Samaria. The following, by Ron Tappy, are fundamental to any assessment of the archaeology and history of the site.

Tappy, Ron. *The Archaeology of Israelite Samaria Volume I. Early Iron Age Through the Ninth Century BCE*. Atlanta: Scholars Press, 1992.
—— *The Archaeology of Israelite Samaria Volume II The Eighth Century BCE* Winona Lakes, IN: Eisenbrauns, 2001.

SHECHEM

WHAT DO ALL THESE TREES
AND STONES MEAN?

The ancient city of Shechem ("shoulder"), located between Mount Gerizim on the south, and Mount Ebal on the north, was an important political and religious center both to the Canaanites and the Israelites. While there is evidence (mostly pottery) of human activity here as early as the Chalcolithic period (fourth millennium BCE), the first Canaanite city dates from the beginning of the second millennium BCE. The city survived, with many destructions and reconstructions, until the second century BCE, when it was destroyed for the last time by John Hyrcanus.

The earliest literary references to Shechem all come from Egyptian sources, the oldest of which is from the time of Sen-Usert III, a nineteenth-century BCE pharaoh. The city is also mentioned in the late nineteenth–early eighteenth century BCE Execration texts which were found at the site of Sakkarah (Egypt). These texts were inscribed on clay figurines and contained the names of the enemies of the pharaoh. They were broken in religious rituals with the belief that such action ensured the defeat of the city or person(s) whose names were inscribed on them. These texts have proven to be extremely important in understanding the early historical geography of ancient Canaan. Finally, in the Amarna letters of the fourteenth century BCE, the King of Shechem, Labayu, is mentioned by name. He is accused of taking other Canaanite cities by force in order to establish his own empire with Shechem at its center (*ANET*, 1969: 485, 486, 489). These references underline the political importance of this city for both the Canaanites and the Egyptians during the Middle and Late Bronze Ages.

That this city had religious and political importance to ancient Israel is clearly indicated by the numerous biblical references to it. Shechem is first mentioned in relation to Abraham (Gen. 12: 6) who is said to have stopped at the "Oak of Moreh," an expression

Figure 67 Shechem: Middle Bronze Age cyclopean wall.

referring apparently to a sacred tree or place located here. This tree also figures prominently in the story of Jacob, who is said to have buried the "foreign gods" beneath it (Genesis 35: 4). The Oak of Moreh is mentioned again in Deuteronomy 11: 30 (reading with the Greek Syriac text). There is also a tradition that Joshua set up a "large stone" (not called a *massebah*) at Shechem ". . . under the oak in the sanctuary of YHWH" (Josh. 24: 26). However, if this oak is supposed to be the same one mentioned in Genesis, it would be centuries old by traditional dating! But, it may be that the stories of the Ancestors ("patriarchs") originated much later than the dates popularly given to them (Middle Bronze Age). A "Diviner's Oak," mentioned in Judges 9: 37 in the context of the story of Abimelech, is also said to be located at Shechem. However, in this case, the biblical editor gives a negative connotation to this cult object not present in the earlier examples (for the details see LaRocca-Pitts, 2001: 58, 223), thus showing disapproval of Abimelech's actions. It would seem, then, that a tradition(s) of a sacred tree or grove at Shechem was well established and continued to function in local cultic practices for a long time (see now the discussion in Stager, 2003: 34–35).

Other stories in the Bible also reflect the religious importance of Shechem to ancient Israel. Jacob is said to have bought land from the Shechemites and built on it an altar to El-Elohe Israel ("El, the God of Israel"; Gen. 33: 18–19). A tradition of covenant making is particularly strong here. It was at Shechem that Joshua is said to have made a covenant with the people who had entered the land with him (Josh. 24). During the period of the Judges, Abimelech was made "king" of Shechem by the "Diviner's Oak," mentioned above, but later destroyed the city when the Shechemites revolted against him (Judg. 9; Stager, 2003, and below). Of particular interest in this story are the references to the temple of Baal-berith ("Lord of the covenant"); the "Tower of Shechem"; and "the stronghold of the temple of El-berith" ("God of the covenant"). As will be seen below, the archaeological excavations of Shechem may shed some light on this period of the "judges."

Interestingly enough, Shechem is portrayed as a person in Genesis 34 (the rape of Dinah), a story which, beneath the surface, indicates the less than cordial relations that sometimes existed between this Canaanite city and the biblical Ancestors of Israel. After the death of Solomon, near the end of the tenth century BCE, Rehoboam, Solomon's son, recognizing the political importance that Shechem still commanded, went there seeking to renew the support of the northern tribes. When his efforts failed, Jeroboam, who then became the first king of Israel during the period of the Divided Monarchy, rebuilt Shechem as his royal residence (1 Kgs. 12). Finally, Jeremiah implies that Shechem was still occupied at the end of the seventh, beginning of the sixth century BCE (41: 5).

It may be noteworthy that there is no biblical story relating how Shechem came to be controlled by the Israelites. In any case, the biblical traditions in Genesis, Joshua, Judges, and elsewhere, with references to a sacred tree, a sacred stone, altars, and covenant-making, all suggest that a very strong cultic tradition existed there from the earliest period through the time of the Judges and beyond.

Our knowledge of Shechem gained through a study of the literary sources has been amplified greatly by the results of the archaeological excavations of the city. The site, first identified with modern-day Tell Balatah in 1903, is a 10–12-acre mound located on the eastern end of the pass between the mountains of Ebal and Gerizim. German excavations were conducted on the site beginning in 1913 and continued, with interruptions, until 1934. But the major excavation of the site started in 1956 under the direction of the late G. Ernest Wright and the auspices of Drew University, McCormick Theological Seminary and the American Schools of Oriental Research. This excavation resulted in a much clearer understanding of both the stratification and chronology of the city.

As mentioned above, while there is evidence that the site was occupied as early as the Chalcolithic period, the first major city dates to the Middle Bronze Age I (Wright's Middle Bronze Age II A). Dating also to this early phase of the city is a large earthen podium found on the western side of the site. The function of this structure is still not known, but since religious structures were erected here in following periods, this podium may have already had some function in the Canaanite cultic practices. In fact, in a later Middle Bronze phase (eighteenth century BCE) a structure was built which subsequently went through three major reconstructions over the next century. Within the third phase of this building were found two pillar bases, the purpose of which may have been to support sacred stones (*massebot*?). Thus it has been suggested that originally the building served as a temple. If this suggestion is correct, then the cultic nature of this part of the site can be traced back at least to the eighteenth century BCE.

But one of the most astounding discoveries dates to the last phase of the Middle Bronze Age (*c.*1650–1550), during which time the northwestern part of the city was protected by a massive "cyclopean" wall (see Figure 67, p. 204). Here the excavators found the remains of what has been identified as a fortress-temple or Migdal. At the time of its discovery, it was the largest extant temple-ruin yet found in Israel (a larger Middle Bronze Age temple has been discovered at Pella, Jordan). This huge building measured some 86 by 70 feet with foundation walls over 17 feet thick. It was a tripartite building with an entrance hall (23 by 16 feet); a corridor (approximately 11 feet square) and a cella (some 44 by 36 feet). At the outer edge of the threshold, a huge boulder had been carefully dressed and provided with a circular depression measuring some 30–31 inches in diameter. Wright believed this base was for a column that once stood in the middle of the threshold. In fact, he found a fragment of such a stone that fit the base perfectly and believed this stone belonged originally to the first phase of the temple.

During the second phase of the building's use, the column was apparently removed and replaced by two other standing stones (*massebot*), each equidistant from the center of the door (cf. the two free-standing pillars of the Solomonic temple. 1 Kgs. 7: 15–22). About 30 feet from the entrance to the building another stone was found. Wright believed this latter stone was the main cultic symbol of the temple (see Figure 68, p. 208). This stone is in the shape of a slab and measures some five feet wide, one-and-a-half feet thick and five feet high (the slab is broken and its original height is unknown).

There is some confusion over what happened at Shechem at the end of the Middle Bronze Age. Wright found evidence of a major destruction of the site and concluded that the temple had also been destroyed and replaced by a similar, but smaller, temple that existed during the time of the "Judges." It is this later temple, Wright believed, which was the setting for the story of Abimelech in Judges 9. However, in a recentury review of Wright's conclusions (as well as others), L. Stager (Harvard) has argued that this Middle Bronze Age temple survived during the Late Bronze Age and on into Iron Age I. It was this building, Stager believed, into which a thousand citizens of Shechem took refuge in their futile attempt to escape the wrath of Abimelech (Stager, 2003; Judg. 9: 46–49). Stager may be correct, but his direct identification of material remains recovered on an excavation with a building mentioned in a text needs to be taken with caution. It is extremely difficult to know when material objects (even when they consist of large buildings) found by archaeologists are exactly the objects mentioned in a biblical text. Such naive identifications characterized the "Biblical Archaeology" movement from the start and have been, for the most part, discredited. Furthermore, even if the physical remains *can* be identified with the building

Figure 68 Shechem: Middle Bronze Age cultic(?) stone. Standing to the right of the stone is the late Joseph A. Callaway, who excavated at Shechem with G. E. Wright.

in the text, this in itself does not give one a good reason to take the biblical story at face value (see now the helpful observation by LaRocca-Pitts, 2001: 132–133).

In the Bible, Shechem is also the setting for a "covenant renewal" ceremony lead by Joshua (Josh. 24) after the "conquest." However, given the current understanding of the "Conquest" model in the Bible by most authorities, the historicity of the Joshua account is ambiguous at best. Furthermore, in the Septuagint (the ancient Greek translation of the Bible), the covenant renewal tradition recounted in Joshua 24 takes place at **Shiloh**, not Shechem. Shiloh was also a very important early Israelite sanctuary and this may help explain the textual confusion in Joshua 24: 1. Furthermore, Wright was very quick to use the Bible to interpret his archaeological discoveries; perhaps too quick. Nevertheless, as has been seen, a very strong cultic tradition associated with Shechem extends in the biblical traditions from the time of the Ancestors on, and the location of the covenant renewal ceremony recorded in Joshua 24 is not unexpected despite the attendant textual and historical problems.

Further reading

Campbell, Edward F. *Shechem III*. Boston: ASOR, 2002.

LaRocca-Pitts, Elizabeth C. *"Of Wood and Stone": The Significance of Israelite Cultic Items in the Bible and Its Early Interpreters*. Winona Lake, IN: Eisenbrauns, 2001.

Seger, Joe D. "Shechem." *OEANE* 5. Eric. M. Meyers, ed., NY: Oxford University Press, 1997: 19–23. With earlier bibliography.

Stager, Lawrence E. "The Shechem Temple: Where Abimelech Massacred a Thousand." *BAR* 29.4 (2003): 26–35; 66; 68–69.

Wright, G. E. *Shechem: The Biography of a Biblical City*. NY: McGraw Hill, 1965. A popular interpretation of the excavations at Shechem by the director.

—— "Shechem." *AOTS*. D. Winton Thomas, ed., Oxford: Clarendon Press, 1967: 355–370.

SHILOH

THE PLACE OF PRIESTS

At least as early as the Middle Ages, the biblical site of Shiloh has been identified with Khirbet Seilum, a small ruin of some seven acres located about 18 miles north of **Jerusalem** (see Figure 69). This tell is over 2,300 feet above sea level and is located on the northern end of a fertile valley. In Judges 21: 19 we are informed that Shiloh is located "north of **Bethel**, on the east of the highway that goes up from Bethel to **Shechem**, and south of Lebonah." Eusebius also provides additional information in his *Onomasticon* (156, 28), where he locates Shiloh about 12 miles from Shechem. The place is also shown on the famous Medeba map of the sixth century CE. However,

Figure 69 The mound of Shiloh.

this map is believed to follow Eusebius's topography. In 1838, Edward Robinson re-identified the site as he journeyed through the country on horseback.

Archaeological work on the tell began as early as 1922 and continued with a Danish expedition from 1926 to 1932, and again in a short season in 1963. However, no clear characterization of the site emerged from these efforts. The first modern/scientific excavation of the mound was conducted between 1981 and 84, under the direction of Israel Finkelstein, of Tel Aviv University. Finkelstein identified eight strata, beginning with a phase of occupation known only by pottery deposits and dated to the Middle Bronze Age II (*c*.1750–1650 BCE; Str. VIII). The first walled city was built in Middle Bronze Age III (Str. VII, *c*.1650–1550 BCE) and contained what the excavator has called a "constructural" glacis; that is, a rampart built, not for defensive purposes, but as support for the wall itself. This wall enclosed an estimated four acres and still stood in places to a height of 25 feet. The glacis was not constructed uniformly, but was built to conform to the natural contours of the mound. Along a stretch of the wall on the northern side of the site, a row of rooms was found containing the remains of numerous storage jars. Other ceramic discoveries included bowls (described as "votive"), "cultic" stands, and one bovine-shaped zoomorphic piece. Also, several silver as well as bronze objects were found. The excavators concluded that these remains are indicative of a Canaanite cult site which they believed existed on top of the tell. Notably absent from the finds were any architectural remains that could be identified as domestic or residential. A curiosity from this period is a small piece of gold jewelry shaped like a fly! This phase of the history of the site came to a violent end in the sixteenth century, perhaps brought on by the Egyptians who destroyed other cities at this time.

Stratum VI, equated with the Late Bronze Age (1550–1200 BCE), contained broken pottery vessels found in a thick deposit of ashes and bones. Many of these sherds are identified as belonging to chalices and bowls. The absence of any building remains that could be dated to this period led the excavators to suggest that during this time Shiloh was an isolated cult site.

The data associated with the Iron Age I period (Str. V, twelfth–eleventh centuries BCE) may be of more interest to biblical students. While the Late Bronze Age deposit was uncovered from only one area (D), Iron Age I remains were found in almost every area excavated. One of the most unexpected discoveries occurred on the west side of the tell in area C. In the steep glacis outside of the defensive wall from the Middle Bronze Age, remains of pillared buildings were found. These buildings had been "sunk," to use the excavator's word, into the glacis itself. From rooms in these structures came what has been described as "the richest (ceramic assemblage) ever discovered at an early Israelite site" (Finkelstein, "Seilun, Khirbet," *ABD* 5: 1072). Many of these ceramic pieces belong to what are called "collared-rim" store jars, leading to the conclusion that the buildings served the purpose of storage areas. Why they were built here and not elsewhere on the site where the construction would have been much easier is not clearly understood.

Also dating to this period are some 15 silos hewn into the solid rock surface. The silos measure about five feet in diameter and may have been used also for storage (charred wheat remains were found in two of them). Again, as in earlier periods, no architectural structures that could be identified as domestic were found. This would seem to indicate that during Iron Age I there was no typical village located here. Stratum V suffered a very violent end around 1050 BCE. Based on biblical texts alone (see below), many authorities attribute this destruction to the Philistines. After the Iron Age I activity, the site is archaeologically poor until large villages were built here during the Roman (Str. II) and Byzantine (Str. I) periods. Stratum IV (Iron Age II) and Stratum III (Hellenistic) were represented by what was called "scanty village-typed" material.

In the Bible, Shiloh plays a very important role in the history of the early "Israelites." The place is mentioned 32 times, 72 percent of which (23 times), occur in three books of Joshua, Judges, and 1 Samuel. In Joshua, Shiloh is a cultic center where the "Tent of Meeting" was set up and distribution of the land to seven of the tribes is said to have taken place (Josh. 18: 1–10). Also it was here that the Levites were given their inheritance (21: 2) as well as the place where the Cisjordan tribes gathered to prepare for war against the tribes in the Transjordan for some sort of cultic violation (Josh. 22: 12). However, many literary critics have argued that these traditions are late, part of the Deuteronomic Historian(s)'s reconstruction produced under Josianic influence during the seventh–sixth century BCE (see Halpern, "Shiloh," *ABD*).

In Judges, it is claimed that the "house of God" was here (18: 31) and some kind of virgins' ritual took place (21: 12ff.). What kind of structure the "house of God" refers to is not clear. Shiloh plays a central role in the time of Samuel (1 Sam. 1–4). It is here that Samuel is dedicated to YHWH, Israel's God (1 Sam. 1: 24), and cultic activities were conducted here, including sacrifices at a "temple (*hekal*) of YHWH." The sons of Eli are accused of treating these sacrifices with contempt (1 Sam. 2: 14). If, in fact, there was a temple built here (the Bible does not record any such story), this would seemingly contradict other biblical texts which claim that only the temple of Solomon was authorized by YHWH (see 1 Kgs. 8: 16; 1 Sam. 14: 3; 2 Sam. 7: 6–7). However, an open-air cult site would not necessarily contradict these texts. According to the tradition in 1 Samuel 4, the Philistines defeated the Israelites at **Aphek** and stole the Ark of the Covenant. The Bible does not record a destruction of Shiloh by the Philistines, but based on the archaeological record and biblical traditions, this is a popular assumption by many scholars.

Whatever happened at Shiloh must have made an indelible impression on the folk memory because centuries later, the seventh–sixth-century prophet, Jeremiah (the only prophet to mention Shiloh), used the earlier fate of the site as a warning to the inhabitants of Jerusalem (Jer. 7: 14; 26: 6, 9; see Ps. 78: 60). However, neither the prophet nor the Psalmist suggests that Shiloh suffered a violent destruction at the hands of the Philistines (in fact Ps. 78: 60 implies abandonment of the place). Furthermore, even the prophet implies some habitation of the site during his time (Jer. 41: 5).

Whether or not a "temple" was ever on the site is a moot point among scholars, and the attempt to locate the exact spot where the "Tent of Meeting" might have stood (assuming the historicity of the text) seems misguided at best. Without taking the biblical stories at face value, there is no archaeological evidence of any temple, much less a portable shrine called the Tent of Meeting. That an important Shilonite priesthood existed here during Iron Age I, and maybe during part of Iron Age II (see 1 Kgs. 12: 29; 14: 2–4; after this reference, Shiloh is never mentioned again in the Book of Kings), however, seems likely. One scholar, at least, has argued that there was a link between the Shiloh priests and the Book of Deuteronomy (Halpern, "Shiloh," *ABD*, 5: 1213).

Further reading

Finkelstein, Israel. "Excavations at Shiloh 1981–1984." *TA* 12 (1985): 123–80.

—— "Shiloh Yields Some, but not all of its Secrets." *BAR* 12.1 (1986): 22–41.

—— "Seilun, Khirbet." *ABD* 5. David Noel Freedman, ed., NY: Doubleday, 1992: 1072.

—— S. Bunimovitz, and Z. Lederman. *Shiloh: The Archaeology of a Biblical Site*. Tel Aviv: Institute of Archaeology, 1993.

Halpern, Baruch. "Shiloh." *ABD* 5. David Noel Freedman, ed., NY: Doubleday, 1992: 1213.

Watkins, Leslie. "Shiloh." *OEANE* 5. Eric. M. Meyers, ed., NY: Oxford University Press, 1997: 28–29.

TA'ANACH

HOME OF THE CULTIC PRIZE

The ruin of biblical Ta'anach is located about five miles southeast of **Megiddo** (see Figure 70). It is a relatively large site of around 11 acres. The identification of this tell with the biblical city of Ta'anach is universally accepted. In the Hebrew Bible the city is mentioned a total of seven times (Josh 12: 21; 17: 11; 21: 15; Judg. 1: 27; 5: 19; 1 Kgs. 4: 12 and 1 Chron. 7: 29 which parallels Josh 17: 11). However, there is obvious confusion in the textual traditions concerning early Israel's relationship to this town (cf. Josh. 12: 21 with Judg. 1: 27; and Judg. 21: 25 with Num. 35: 1–8 and Josh. 13: 14, 33).

Outside of the Bible Ta'anach is mentioned in Egyptian inscriptions of the fifteenth century BCE. One describes the campaign of

Figure 70 Tell Ta'anach.

Thutmose III against Megiddo (see the *ANET*, 1969: 234 ff.). According to this story, Thutmose surprised the Canaanites by taking a very narrow trail that forced his army to march in single file. The pathway opened between Megiddo and Taʿanach and allowed the king a considerable advantage over his foes. In addition, 13 cuneiform texts, all but one also dating to the fifteenth century, were discovered at Taʿanach.

History of excavations

There have been two major excavations of the site: one in the early 1900s and the other in the 1960s. The first one was under the direction of a German excavator, Ernst Sellin, who dug here between 1902 and 1904. Sellin identified four major periods ("strata") of occupation:

Stratum I: fifteenth–fourteenth centuries BCE (cuneiform archive)
Stratum II: thirteenth–ninth centuries BCE
Stratum III: eighth–sixth centuries BCE
Stratum IV: eleventh–twelfth centuries CE.

His stratification of the site was later modified by the second excavation conducted on the tell by Paul Lapp. One of Sellin's most important discoveries is a group of Akkadian tablets dating to the fifteenth century BCE. Written in cuneiform ("wedge shaped"), most of the texts are addressed to the "king" of Taʿanach, Rewashus. Since this name is Egyptian, it may indicate that at this time Taʿanach was characterized by considerable Egyptian influence. In all, over 90 names have been recovered from these texts. Of these, some 60 percent have been identified as "northwest Semitic" and 20 percent as "Indo-Aryan" or "Hurrian-Anatolian." Thus, during this period, Taʿanach seems to have been ethnically diverse (for a translation of one of these texts, see *ANET*, 1969: 490). Following Sellin's initial work, no archaeological efforts were made on the site until Paul Lapp's excavations that began in 1963.

Lapp expanded Sellin's occupational history by over a thousand years when he discovered fortification remains dating to the Early Bronze Age II–III period. Lapp concluded that there was a long gap following this Early Bronze Age occupation until the Middle Bronze Age II period (1700 BCE). A startling, and somewhat grisly, discovery from this time were human remains found beneath the floors and in the walls of Middle Bronze Age rooms. A total of 64 burials were discovered, 90 percent of which were children who had been buried in storage jars.

Figure 71 Cult stand, Taʿanach, late tenth century BCE.

Lapp also discovered modest Late Bronze Age remains which he dated to the middle of the fifteenth century BCE. Following a brief Iron Age I occupational level (1200–1000 BCE), he also discovered an important tenth-century BCE period of habitation. In fact, it is from this period that Lapp made his most famous discovery: a tenth-century BCE ceramic cult stand. This stand has evoked a great deal of controversy, especially over the question of how the scenes depicted on it should be interpreted. The vessel itself stands about 21.5 inches high, contains four panels, and is topped with a shallow basin. It is the images on the panels that have been the cause of the controversy (see Figure 71, p. 216).

The bottom image is of a nude female human figure standing between two lions. The second panel from the bottom is composed of two winged sphinxes with a hollow space between them. In a recent study of this, and other such vessels, Beck (p. 360) concluded that the two stands from Ta'anach (Sellin also found a "cult" stand) are the only ones known from Israel that contain both lion and winged sphinx images. The third panel from the bottom contains a "cosmic" or sacred tree with two animals (goats?) nibbling from either side. Enclosing this scene, again, are two standing lions. The top scene is an animal (horse? bull calf?) enclosed between two voluted columns. On the back of the animal sits a winged sun disc. This last image has been identified with YHWH, the God of Israel, although Beck identified the deity more generally as a weather god (pp. 379–381). She also concluded that while the stands were made locally they both contain Anatolian and north-Syrian influence.

In their study of this object, Stager and King (pp. 343–344) suggested that the stand should be "read" from the bottom up. The bottom register with the nude figure and lions stand outside the "temple." The second panel, sphinxes ("cherubim") with an empty space between them, guard the entrance to the temple (Stager and King do not accept a popular interpretation of the empty space as the invisible representation of YHWH). The third panel is believed to represent the main hall inside the temple. The top panel would then be the "holy of holies" where the deity, represented by the sun disc, sits enthroned upon the bull calf. Whether or not this is the best interpretation of the scenes is debatable. What is much clearer is that after the split of the monarchy upon the death of Solomon, the bull calf became an idolatrous symbol for the prophets and was condemned.

While Lapp excavated only a small part of the tell, he concluded that the site continued to be occupied throughout most of Iron Age II. There is scant evidence of Roman-Byzantine occupation, though Eusebius (fourth century CE) described the place in his *Onomasticon* as a "very large village." There is some archaeological evidence for sporadic occupation up to the early eighteenth century CE. The current village located here today dates from the nineteenth century.

Further reading

Beck, P. "The Cult-Stands from Taanach: Aspects of the Iconographic Tradition of Early Iron Age Cult Objects in Palestine." *FNM*. I. Finkelstein and N. Na'aman, eds. Jerusalem, Israel Exploration Society, 1994: 352–381.

King, Philip J. And Lawrence E. Stager. *Life in Biblical Israel*. Louisville: Westminster John Knox Press, 2001.

Lapp, P. W. "The 1963 Excavation at Taannek." *BASOR* 173 (1964): 4–44.

—— "The 1966 Excavations at Tell Taannek." *BASOR* 185 (1967): 2–39.

—— "Taanach by the Waters of Megiddo." *BA* 30 (1967): 2–27.

—— "The 1968 Excavation at Tell Taannek." *BASOR* 195 (1969): 2–49.

Rast, W. E. *Taanach I Studies in the Iron Age Pottery*. Cambridge, MA: BASOR, 1978.

TELL BEIT MIRSIM
WHAT'S IN A NAME?

For all of the archaeological work that has gone on in Israel since the late nineteenth century, site identification is still a thorny problem. Nowhere is this any better illustrated than with a ruin known as Tell Beit Mirsim (hereafter TBM). Located on the edge of the Shephelah 15 miles north-northeast of **Beersheba** and about the same distance southwest of **Hebron**, TBM was identified with biblical Debir (Kiriath-Seper; Josh 15: 15; Judg. 1: 11) in 1924 by W. F. Albright (see Figure 72). Albright conducted four archaeological campaigns here between 1926 and 1932. His work at TBM was a

Figure 72 Tell Beit Mirsim.

219

watershed in archaeological field method, especially his ceramic analysis, and his publications of his discoveries set benchmarks for all future archaeological field work in Israel. Despite his achievements, however, many of his conclusions have been challenged, and in many instances, modified or completely changed by later scholars (see Greenberg, *OEANE*). In fact, one of the most drastic modifications has been the successful challenge to Albright's identification of the site. It is generally accepted today that biblical Debir is not to be identified with TBM at all but with Khirbet Rabud, a large 15-acre site located about seven-and-a-half miles south of Hebron. If this is, in fact, the case then TBM contains the remains of major Canaanite and Israelite towns that have never been correlated with a biblical place name (although Eglon has been suggested). Because of Albright's achievement this is an important site despite its lack of biblical identity, and its inclusion in a general study of this sort is, to my mind, completely justified.

Albright identified ten major strata (J–A, with J being the first, and A, the latest stratum of occupation). He concluded that the tell had been inhabited originally around 2300 BCE (today's Early Bronze Age IV). But a closer analysis of the pottery remains by W. G. Dever and S. Richard (1977) has shown that the site was actually occupied as early as the Early Bronze Age II period (*c.*3000 BCE). However, the first major Canaanite "city" dates to the Middle Bronze Age I (Albright's Middle Bronze Age II) and belongs to Strata G–F. While there is some ambiguity surrounding the absolute dates for the Middle Bronze Age fortifications during this period, the city is believed to have been heavily fortified with a massive wall and defensive towers. Such remains indicate that the city of Stratum G was well planned.

During the late Middle Bronze Age phases (Str. E–D), the city at TBM attained its urbanized zenith. From this period comes a massive glacis and maybe a three-entryway gate. Moreover, remains identified as a "palace"were recovered. Other interesting discoveries were made inside this building including many store jars and objects made from stone, metal, and ivory. A rare discovery was a game board with a die and gaming pieces. Sometimes heralded as the most important discovery by Albright is what he identified as a "cultic stele" which he interpreted as a serpent goddess. Others have suggested a more mundane identity of a Canaanite dignitary. Other important discoveries from these remains are Hyksos scarabs and Syrian-type cylinder seals. This major Canaanite city was destroyed in the sixteenth century BCE by a fiery conflagration associated with an Egyptian invasion that brought the Middle Bronze Age in general to a close.

As is the case with many Canaanite sites, the archaeological evidence for the Late Bronze Age (Str. C) indicates a decline in urban character. In fact the site seems to have been abandoned for a considerable time following its destruction at the end of the Middle Bronze Age. However, Late Bronze Age I tombs, discovered in the 1970s, may indicate some occupation during this period. But so far no such evidence has been discovered on the mound. Whatever the nature of the Late Bronze Age phase of the site, it all came to a violent end around 1225 BCE. Albright credited this destruction to the invading "Israelites." However, this "militaristic" model for the "Conquest" has been abandoned for years by most authorities.

The Iron Age remains belong to Albright's Strata B–A and include both Iron Age I and II (c.1200–900 BCE). Stratum B, dated to Iron Age I, was divided into three sub-phases. Albright wanted to see in these remains evidence of his understanding of Israelite history. Thus he identified the poor remains of the first part of Stratum B with an "Israelite"settlement following their "conquest" of the town, and the second phase of the stratum with the Philistines (twelfth–eleventh century BCE). The final phase of Stratum B was once again assigned to "Israel" who supposedly regained control of the site in the late eleventh–early tenth century. This last phase was then destroyed by the Egyptians under Shishak when he invaded Israel around 926 BCE. This historical reconstruction by Albright has been severely challenged by other scholars.

The last period of occupation of TBM, Stratum A, is dated to Iron Age II. The remains suggest a relatively prosperous time with a well-planned constructed city that included a new gate, many pillared houses, including a very large building near the city center. Many rock-cut cisterns and installations that may have served as oil presses or "dying vats" (Albright's suggestion) indicate, perhaps, local industries. However, the destruction of this phase of occupation has stirred considerable discussion. Based on a seal impression mentioning a person named "Eliakim," who is identified as the "servant of Jehoiachin," Albright concluded that the destruction was the result of the Babylonian invasion in the sixth century BCE. However, other authorities, based on new studies of the pottery, stamped jar handles, and seals have argued for an Assyrian destruction in 701 BCE.

While many of Albright's conclusions have been modified or rejected by later studies, his pioneering efforts at TBM are commendable. His exposure of an Iron Age II Judean town has contributed greatly to understanding the local culture during this period. And his demonstration of the value of pottery analysis for differentiating between the often complex and confusing phases of a site's occupational history has had a lasting influence on subsequent generations of archaeologists.

Further reading

Albright, W. F. "Debir." *AOTS*. D. Winton Thomas, ed., Oxford: Clarendon Press, 1967: 207–220.

—— and Raphael Greenberg. "Beit Mirsim, Tell." *NEAEHL* 1. Ephraim Stern, ed., Jerusalem: Simon & Schuster, 1993: 177–180.

Dever, W. G. "Beit Mirsim, Tell." *ABD*, 1. David Noel Freedman, ed., NY: Doubleday, 1992: 648.

—— and Suzanne Richard. "New Light on the Early Iron Age at Tell Beit Mirsim J." *BASOR* 226 (1977): 1–14.

Greenberg, Raphael. "Beit Mirsim, Tell." *OEANE* 1. Eric M. Meyers, ed., NY: Oxford University Press, 1997: 295–297, with bibliography.

TIBERIAS

THE JEWEL BESIDE THE SEA
OF GALILEE

Though mentioned only once in the New Testament (John 21: 1), Tiberias was an important regional city during the time of Jesus. Located on the western side of the Sea of Galilee at the foot of Mt. Berenice (Mt. Berenice was named after the sister of Agrippa II, but this popular tradition has no known historical basis), the city was founded in 19 or 20 CE by Herod Antipas, the son of Herod the Great, and named after the Roman emperor, Tiberius. Following the death of Agrippa II in 96 CE, Tiberias came under Roman control.

Figure 73 Modern Tiberias by the Sea of Galilee.

By the third century the city had become a center for Talmudic studies and continued to prosper even after the Muslim conquest in the seventh century CE. During the Crusader period, control of the city vacillated between Christians and Muslims. In 1247 the Mamluks came into power and stayed until the British showed up early in the twentieth century.

Tiberias is another excellent example of how non-biblical sources coupled with archaeology shed considerable light on the history and importance of a site barely mentioned in the Bible. Although, in the case of Tiberias, the archaeological work has been sporadic and carried out by different people at different times. Furthermore, most of the archaeological discoveries date well after the time of Jesus. One exception is a gate discovered on the south side of the city in 1973 by Gideon Foerster, on behalf of the Israel Department of Antiquities and Museums (now called the Israel Antiquities Authority), the Hebrew University of Jerusalem, and the Israel Exploration Society. The gate was dated to the earliest period of the city (CE 20) and was apparently free-standing, serving no defensive purposes. Population estimations for Tiberias at this time range from 8,000 to 12,000 people and the size of the city has been estimated to be between 100 and 125 acres (see Crossan and Reed, 2001: 71). During the Byzantine period (fourth–sixth centuries CE), a wall was attached to the centuries-old gate for defensive purposes.

In the mid 1950s a salvage excavation uncovered part of a cardo, a bathhouse and a marketplace. Most of these constructions were dated to the Late Roman period or later. The bathhouse, dated originally to the fourth century, was still in use during the eleventh century some 700 years later! In 1964, some 250 feet northeast of this bathhouse, a large installation was found that was dubbed an "urban villa complex." More work was done here in 1993 by Y. Hirschfeld who recognized two construction phases for the complex: the first phase was dated to the fourth century CE and a second phase to the fifth–sixth centuries CE. Other significant discoveries include a two-chambered Roman tomb, found in 1976, and a Roman theater found at the foot of Mt. Berenice in 1989–1990. The seating capacity of this second–third-century CE structure is estimated to have been around 5,000 people, comparable to the theater known at **Beth-Shean**, a few miles to the south.

A Christian church, discovered on top of Mt. Berenice, has also been recovered. The site may have been picked because of the view it offers of the Sea of Galilee and its shores where Jesus reportedly spent a considerable amount of his life. The church was in use through the thirteenth century. Several synagogues have also been found, including one dating to the sixth century discovered in 1978.

Tiberias was once described by Flavius Josephus as being located "in the best region of Galilee" (*Antiq*. XVII, 36–38). While the city was not as large as such places as Scythopolis or Caesarea Maritima, during the time of Jesus, and even later, Tiberias dominated life around the lake. Its importance for understanding Jesus and his ministry is greater than the little interest shown it in the Gospels.

Further reading

Crossan, John Dominic and Jonathan L. Reed. *Excavating Jesus: Beneath the Stones, Behind the Texts*. San Francisco: HarperSanFrancisco, 2001: 62–70.

Hirschfeld, Yizhar. "Tiberias." *OEANE* 5. Eric M. Meyers, ed., NY: Oxford University Press, 1997: 203–206.

—— "Tiberias." *NEAEHL* 4. Ephraim Stern, ed., Jerusalem: Simon & Schuster, 1993: 1464–1473.

TIMNAH (TEL BATASH)
A LION, A WIFE, AND A RIDDLE

Biblical Timnah has been identified with Tel Batash, a 6-acre mound located in the northern Shephelah (see Figure 74) in the Sorek Valley. This identification seems generally accepted today by most authorities. The city is mentioned 12 times in the Bible. All but one reference come from the three books of Genesis (38: 12–14), Joshua (15: 10, 57; 19: 43) and Judges (14: 1–2, 5). The exception is in 2 Chronicles 28: 18. The story in Genesis is the very familiar one of Tamar deceiving her father-in-law, Judah, into believing she is a prostitute. Judah finds her sitting beside the road on his way to

Figure 74 Timnah.

Timnah to shear his sheep (while it is not absolutely certain that the "Timnah" in this story is the same town mentioned in the Samson narrative, the excavator concluded that it "probably" is; A. Mazar, "Batash, Tel," *OEANE*, 1: 281). From a broader historical perspective, this story raises questions of social and economic as well as political relationships between "Israel" and the people who inhabited the northern Shephelah prior to the Monarchy.

After this episode with Judah and Tamar, Timnah is not mentioned again until the time of Joshua. However, for modern identification/location purposes Joshua 15: 10–11 is very important. In this text, Timnah is said to be between **Beth-Shemesh** and **Ekron**. Tel Batash is about four miles west of Beth-Shemesh and some three miles east of Ekron. The excavators of Tel Batash have argued that this ruin is the only significant mound between the two other tells.

Probably the best known, and perhaps the most important, biblical story concerning Timnah is in Judges (14–15). We are told in this tale that it was from Timnah that the Danite hero, Samson, got his Philistine wife, though this marriage was short lived, to say the least! It was also near Timnah where Samson killed the lion (Judg. 14: 5–9). The issue here is not the historicity of these stories (which is probably very little) but the clear implication that Timnah at this time was a Philistine town. After the story of Samson, Timnah is not mentioned again until 2 Chronicles 28: 18, where the claim is made that the Philistines reclaimed Timnah, as well as other towns, during the reign of the Judean king, Ahaz (eighth century BCE). There is no archaeological evidence to confirm this claim.

Timnah and Tel Batash

Rising about 50 feet above the surrounding plain, Tel Batash (see Figure 74, p. 226) was first discovered by the French explorer, Charles Clermont-Ganneau (1846–1923) in 1871. However, the mound was neglected until the 1940s when it was mistakenly identified as Ekron. Since Ekron has now universally been identified with Tel Miqne, Tel Batash is believed to be the site of ancient Timnah.

The modern excavation of the ruin took place during 12 seasons between 1977 and 1989. The dig was co-directed by George L. Kelm, (Southwestern Baptist Theological Seminary, Texas), and Amihai Mazar of Hebrew University (Jerusalem). Twelve strata, some with sub-phases, have been identified ranging from the Middle Bronze Age II B (*c.*1700 BCE) to the Persian period in the sixth century BCE.

Strata XII–X were assigned to the Middle Bronze Age. During this period defensive ramparts were constructed that give the site its almost square shape (650 feet long on each side, at its base and some 492 feet on each side at the top). The remains of a citadel were also dated to this period. The town seems to have been partially destroyed and abandoned around 1600 BCE. The final phase of the Middle Bronze Age was poorly represented and was destroyed by fire during the sixteenth–fifteenth centuries.

The Late Bronze Age city (c.1550–1200 BCE) has been identified with Strata IX–VI. The first three phases of occupation were violently destroyed by fire indicating considerable political instability. Whether the causes of these destructions were due to local Canaanite inter-city fights or some external force is not clear. The city may have been under the control of **Gezer**, located a few miles to the north. From the fourteenth-century BCE destruction layer, the remains of what was identified as a "patrician" house were discovered. In a thick destruction level, dozens of jars were found, one of which was full of charred grain suggesting that storeroom may have been uncovered. Many of the items had been imported from such places as Cyprus and the Mycenean region. In addition to the ceramic remains, bronze arrowheads and spear points, cylinder seals and two Egyptian scarabs (one of Amenhotep II and the other of Tiy, his consort) were also recovered. More sobering was the discovery of two human skeletons giving silent testimony to the horror of war. Late Bronze Age Timnah appears to have had no well-planned fortifications, the outer walls of houses providing the only defense. However, the material remains indicate a well-to-do population, perhaps including a class of merchants. After the end of the town of Stratum VII, there was a major decline in the quality of life here as measured by the meager archaeological evidence.

While the next phase in the life of "Timnah" has received considerable discussion, due to the Samson story in the Bible, the archaeological evidence from this time (Iron Age I, c.1200–1000 BCE) is rather limited. The material remains, especially the pottery, do point to a "Philistine" presence, but there is no evidence, nor should any be expected, that can be correlated with the Samson drama. There were a few interesting isolated finds. One is a pyramidal seal with the stylized image of a lyre or harp player. Another seal contains the image of a man and animal. The excavators concluded that the Iron Age I town was founded in the second half of the twelfth century BCE and destroyed around 1000 BCE, though by whom or what is not clear (the excavators suggested David, but there is no archaeological evidence, and only oblique biblical evidence, of such an event).

Following the Samson story in the Book of Judges, Timnah is mentioned only once more in the Bible: 2 Chronicles 28: 18. In this passage, reference is made to the eighth-century BCE Judean King, Ahaz. It is assumed that the city came under Judean control during the time of the "monarchy," but there is no reference to this town in either the Books of Samuel or Kings. Nevertheless, remains dated to the tenth century BCE (the traditional date for the "United Monarchy" under David and Solomon) have been found. Identified as Stratum V, red slip hand burnished pottery, as has been found at other sites, such as **Lachish** and Beth-Shemesh, was recovered as well as an ostracon bearing the name of "Hanan." This same name was found in inscriptions from Beth-Shemesh and may indicate an important local family. In the Solomonic district list, this name appears in the phrase: "Elon Beth Hanan" (1 Kgs. 4: 9). However, the tenth-century remains do not suggest a thriving town during this time. Perhaps by now Timnah served more as an outpost for Jerusalem on its northern frontier.

All of this changed in the eighth–seventh centuries BCE when Timnah was rebuilt (Str. III–II). The city was heavily fortified, perhaps by the Judean King, Uzziah (2 Chron. 26: 6). The stamped jar handles bearing the famous *lmlk* inscription indicate that the city was still under the control of Judah at the end of the eighth century when Hezekiah made preparations to resist the Assyrians. However, no archaeological evidence has been uncovered that would substantiate the claim in 2 Chronicles 28: 18 that the Philistines re-took control of the city during the time of Hezekiah's father, Ahaz. In any case, Sennacherib conquered it around 701 BCE.

Following the Assyrian destruction, the city was rebuilt again and prospered until it was destroyed once more by the Babylonians at the end of the seventh century BCE. The excavators claimed to have exposed 12 percent of this period of occupation making Timnah ". . . one of the best known cities of the Late Iron Age in the entire country" (Kelm and Mazar, 1989: 46). Remains of well-preserved buildings date to this period as well as large numbers of restorable pottery. In addition, there was a major defensive system including double walls and an inner and outer gate. Oil presses from this period indicate the role of the olive oil industry in the local economy, as it was at other nearby sites such as Ekron, Beth-Shemesh, and Gezer. An abundance of clay loom weights gives evidence of textile production. While little was discovered that can be interpreted as "cultic" in nature, three pottery molds for making frontal nude female figurines were found. Whether they represented deities or serve some more "earthy" fertility purposes of some sort is not clear.

The ceramic remains also indicate widespread trade relations with such places as Phoenicia, the Transjordan, and even Greece, as well as Judah. Other interesting discoveries are stone weights of different shekels (1, 2, 4, 8: a shekel weighs 11.4 grams), and another weight marked with the letters "PYM." When the evidence from Tel Batash is added to that from other nearby sites, such as Ekron, not only is there clear evidence of economic prosperity during the seventh century, but also a distinct regional culture that existed during this time. Even if the city politically was under Judean control, its "ethnic" identity may have been very mixed. Perhaps there was still a considerable "Philistine" presence at Timnah. Whatever the case, this flourishing city came to a violent end around 600 BCE when it was destroyed by the Babylonians. The intensity of the destruction is seen in the hundreds of pottery vessels found on the floors of buildings. No one seems to have had time to pack up and flee with any possessions. Following this destruction, there is some evidence for a meager Persian occupation during the sixth century, but the heyday of Timnah was gone forever. After this time the site was abandoned for good.

Further reading

Kelm, George L. and Amihai Mazar. "Three Seasons of Excavations at Tel Batash-Biblical Timnah." *BASOR* 237. (1982): 1–36.

—— "Tel Batash (Timnah) Excavations, Second Preliminary Report (1981–1983)." *BASOR Supplement* 23. Walter E. Rast, ed. (1985): 93–120.

—— "Excavating in Samson Country-Philistines and Israelites at Tel Batash." *BAR* 15.1. (1989): 36–49.

—— *Timnah: A Biblical City in the Sorek Valley*. Winona Lake, IN: Eisenbrauns, 1995.

Mazar, Amihai. "Batash, Tel." *OEANE* 1. Eric M. Meyers, ed., NY: Oxford University Press, 1997: 281–283.

YOKNE'AM (TELL QEIMUM)

YOU DON'T HAVE TO BE
FAMOUS TO BE IMPORTANT

There are important archaeological sites in Israel which may not be known to a wider public. One of these may very well be Tell Qeimum (see Figure 75), identified with biblical Yokne'am (also spelled as Jokneam and Yoqne(am). The tell is a 10-acre site located in the Jezreel Valley about ten miles southwest of Nazareth. The site is included in this study primarily for two reasons: first, it was inhabited almost continuously for nearly 4,500 years, from the Early Bronze Age I (*c.*3000 BCE) through the Mamluk Period (1500 CE). Second,

Figure 75 Yokne'am: The ancient Tell is in the center of the picture.

Yokne'am was part of a regional archaeological survey undertaken in the 1970s in an attempt to try to understand how smaller villages/ hamlets were related to larger settlements such as Yokne'am. Known as the Yokne'am Regional Project, the director of this project, Amnon Ben-Tor, is also the major excavator of the tell.

Yokne'am in the literary sources

The earliest known literary reference to Yokne'am comes from the fifteenth-century BCE list of Thutmose III (*c.*1470–1425 BCE). The place is mentioned only three times in the Hebrew Bible, all from the book of Joshua. It is included in a list of conquered cities (12: 22), cited in the border description of the territory of Zebulun (19: 11), and is described as a Levitical city within Zebulun's tribal territory (31: 34). Much later references come from Eusebius's *Onomasticon* (116.21), and from the time of the Crusades. Arabic sources from this latter period refer to the site as "Qeimum," whence its modern name. After the Mamluk period (fifteenth–sixteenth centuries CE), the site is no longer acknowledged in extant sources.

Excavations at Yokne'am

Despite what should have been the obvious archaeological significance of this imposing mound, little archaeological work was carried out here prior to the 1970s. From 1977 to 1988 a major excavation was conducted by Amnon Ben-Tor on behalf of the Institute of Archaeology at the Hebrew University of Jerusalem. Ben-Tor identified some 27 strata of occupation extending from the Early Bronze Age I to the Mamluk periods. However, the occupation was sparse in some periods (i.e. Hellenistic, Roman, and Byzantine) and the first four strata (Early Bronze Age I–Middle Bronze Age I) were represented only by pottery sherds.

Middle Bronze Age (2000–1550 BCE – Strata XXIII–XXI)

During the first half of the second millennium BCE, Yokne'am was fortified by a wall some 10 feet wide which was supported in places by a glacis. Associated with this period are cave burials and in the latter part of the occupation, child burials in jars were discovered under the floor of a Middle Bronze Age II C house.

Late Bronze Age (1550–1200 BCE – Strata XXI B–XIX)

Ben-Tor did not find any evidence of destruction separating the Middle Bronze from the Late Bronze periods. The transition to the later period seems to have been more gradual than at other sites in the country. However, the Late Bronze period showed evidence of four architectural periods that spanned some 300–350 years. During this long time these settlements were unfortified, as were other Late Bronze Age towns. Perhaps they should have been fortified: the last phase of the Late Bronze Age occupation was violently destroyed sometime during the late thirteenth–early twelfth century, though by whom is not clear.

Iron Age I (c.1200–1000 BCE – Strata XVIII–XVII)

Three building phases were distinguished during this time but overall the settlements show architectural and ceramic continuity. Perhaps the most significant discovery is what was dubbed the "Oil Maker's House," which was an olive oil installation. As was the case with the preceding Late Bronze Age city, the Iron Age I phases of occupation were not fortified. Also like the preceding period, the last phases of occupation were violently destroyed. Ben-Tor's suggestion that this destruction might have been at the hands of King David and the "Israelites" is uncorroborated.

Iron Age II–III (c.950–586 BCE – Strata XVI–XI)

After a hiatus of sorts (Str. XVI), a tenth-century city protected by a casemate wall was built. This period of occupation did not last very long, however, and was followed by a rapid decline represented in the archaeological record only by pits. Following this decline, a new city was built during the eighth century which was protected by a unique double wall. The pottery from both periods of occupation reflects connections between Yokne'am and the Phoenician coast. However, the excavator did not suggest the ethnic identity of the inhabitants. Only fragmentary, poor, remains were identified from the last phase of the Iron Age.

Persian–Ottoman periods (fifth century BCE–seventeenth century CE – Strata X–I)

The last thousand years or so of occupation of the site had a checkered history. Most of the settlements were small, the only exception being the city of the Early Arab period (Str. IV – eighth–tenth centuries CE) during which time a prosperous unwalled settlement existed. The last identified occupation from the Ottoman period is represented only by pottery sherds.

Conclusions

During the Iron Age II–III, the main archaeological periods of the kingdoms of Israel and Judah, most people did not live in the large, well-known cities of the Bible, but in the surrounding towns, villages and hamlets. The regional study conducted by Ben-Tor and his team, utilizing an anthropological model called "Central Place Theory," is important for showing how small villages were related to nearby larger cites (see the biblical expression, "cities/towns and their villages"; Josh. 15: 32, 36, 41 and so forth). It is studies such as this that help students properly understand the social and economic realities of the biblical world.

Further reading

Ben-Tor, Amnon. "Jokneam." *NEAEHL* 3. Ephraim Stern, ed., Jerusalem: Simon & Schuster, 1993: 805–811.
—— "The Regional Study – A New Approach to Archaeological Investigations." *BAR* 6.2. (1980): 30–44.
—— "Yoqne'am." *OEANE* 5. Eric M. Meyers, ed., NY: Oxford University Press, 1997: 381–383. With earlier bibliography.

APPENDIX A

THE PHILISTINES

Much has been written concerning the arrival and settlement of the "Sea Peoples" in the coastal region of Israel. It is usually argued that they came in two waves, the first during the first quarter of the twelfth century. Their arrival is earmarked by the presence of a particular kind of pottery called Mycenaean IIIC:1B, which has been discovered at such sites as **Akko**, **Ashdod**, and **Tel Miqne/Ekron**. From wherever they came – the Aegean and/or Anatolian regions are usually suggested – they were stopped from invading Egypt by Ramesses III in the eight years of his reign (*c*.1175 BCE). This battle was recorded on Ramesses' temple walls at Medinet Habu in Thebes, where five different groups of Sea Peoples are identified: Philistines, Tjeker, Shekelesh, Denye (Danaoi), and the Weshesh. Of these five groups, the most famous, and the only one mentioned in the Bible, is the Philistines. However, according to the story of Wen-Amon (*ANET*, 1969: 25–29), which has been dated to *c*.1100 BCE, the Tjeker settled at Dor which is located on the northern coast of Israel. Furthermore, M. Dothan has argued (1989) that the Shardina (Sherden), also among the Sea Peoples, arrived in Israel as early as the fourteenth century BCE and occupied the city of Akko and its vicinity. Apparently the Tjeker and the Sardina were no match for the Philistines and soon were either absorbed by them or by the local Canaanite population.

The Philistines

Beginning sometime during the first half of the twelfth century BCE, the Philistines began to dominate the coastal region of Israel. For more than a hundred years they would be the military and political force to be reckoned with, as the emerging clans of "Israelites" in the Central Highlands would discover. While the ultimate origin of the Philistines is still unknown, they were part of the larger movement of Sea Peoples discussed above. There are three primary sources for reconstructing their history: Egyptian records, the Bible, and archaeological discoveries.

Textual evidence

According to the Egyptian texts at Medinet Habu, the Philistines were among the Sea Peoples defeated by Ramesses III around 1175 BCE. The reliefs on the walls have been interpreted as depicting both a land and sea battle, assuming that the Sea Peoples arrived in Canaan by both routes. After his victory, Ramesses supposedly recruited many of the survivors as mercenaries, many of whom were stationed in garrisons in Israel at such sites as **Beth-Shean** and **Tell el-Far'ah South**. This tactic by Ramesses has been viewed as the way the Egyptians exercised control over the major roadways of the time.

This traditional interpretation has recently been challenged by studies which have concluded that the Philistines, as well as other Sea Peoples, came by ship only. Furthermore, it is not clear to what extent, if any, the Philistines and others were stationed in Israel as Egyptian mercenaries. What seems more likely to have been the case was the establishment of a Philistine center of influence in southern Canaan emanating from the five Philistine city-states. Here they remained a major power until defeated by David at the beginning of the tenth century BCE. This more recent interpretation raises serious questions regarding the historical validity of the Medinet Habu wall scenes. If the Philistines, as well as other Sea Peoples, were devastated by the Egyptians as the inscriptions at Medinet Habu and elsewhere (see "Papyrus Harris I" in *ANET*, 1969: 262) indicate, how is it that in such a short period of time the Philistines became the major political power in Canaan, as both the biblical texts and the archaeological data suggest?

In the Bible, the Philistines, for the most part, are treated contemptuously. This contempt is most vividly displayed in passages that describe them as "uncircumcised" (Judg. 14: 3; 15: 18; 1 Sam. 17: 26; 18: 25), as well as in the story of Ahaziah (a son of Jezebel?) in 2 Kings 1, where the god of Ekron, Baal-zebul ("princely Lord"), is mocked as "Baal-zebub" ("lord of the flies"). But in spite of the low esteem in which the Philistines were held by the Israelites, the biblical references to these people do furnish some clues concerning Philistine culture.

Political organization

The Philistine political structure centered around the five city-states of **Ashkelon**, Ashdod, Gaza, **Gath**, and Ekron (See Josh. 13: 3; see Figure 8, p. 38). The tradition in Judges 3: 3 (see 1 Sam. 6: 4, 16) to the "five lords of the Philistines" is an apparent reference to the rulers of each of these cities. Furthermore, while the details of the procedure are not clear, according to 1 Samuel 29: 1–7, these "lords" could sit in council and override the decision of a single lord or tyrant. The word translated "lords" in the Hebrew text is the plural of the word סרנ ("seren") and is believed to be a Philistine loan word. The term is used in the Bible only in reference to the Philistines and may have in its background the Doric Greek word τυραννος ("turannos") which was applied to anyone who had made himself king by force. If this derivation is true, it would be another bit of evidence pointing to the Aegean origin of the Philistines. The lack of any substantial Philistine inscriptions may indicate the rapidity with which they began to adopt the Canaanite language as their own. This may be one of the reasons for their cultural decline.

Military organization

It is also from the Bible that clues regarding their military makeup and strength are found. According to 1 Samuel 13: 5, the Philistine army was comprised of charioteers and horsemen (however, the numbers given may be an exaggeration). Elsewhere (1 Sam. 31: 3) archers are mentioned and, of course, there would have been foot soldiers. If the description of Goliath's armor (1 Sam. 17: 5–7) was typical of others, the Philistine warriors were also well armed. According to this description (the literary nature of the story notwithstanding), all of the metal in Goliath's armor was made of bronze, except for the head of his spear which is described as weighing 600 shekels of iron, or about 15 pounds! It has been commonly held that the Philistines had a monopoly on iron work, especially in light of 1 Samuel 13: 19–22. However, recent studies have called this conclusion into question.

Religion

What is known of the Philistine cult from the material remains so far discovered will be examined below. Little information is given in the Bible. This little, however, would lead one to conclude that they quickly adopted local Canaanite cults, for all of their gods mentioned in the Bible have Semitic names. In addition, different deities seem to have been worshiped in different city-states. Dagon is said to have been worshiped at Ashdod (1 Sam. 5: 1–5) but Baal Zebub (Zebul) at Ekron (2 Kgs. 1: 1–4). However, the archaeological evidence clearly indicates that they also brought at least some of their indigenous religious practices with them.

Thus, however biased it might be in some respects, the Bible presents the Philistines as well organized politically and militarily and as a people who quickly adapted to their new homeland. This adaptation also apparently included both Canaanite religion and language. The Bible, of course, is not concerned with the cultural achievements of the Philistines but with the political and military threat which they represented with respect to the Israelites. The extent of their cultural superiority, at least during most of the Iron Age I period, is made abundantly clear by the archaeological remains.

Archaeology of the Philistines

The body of archaeological remains identified as Philistine is constantly expanding due to on-going excavations. In her 1982 study, T. Dothan identified some 40 sites in Israel known to contain Philistine remains (for a map of these sites see T. Dothan 1982: 26). Among their most distinctive cultural products is their pottery.

Philistine pottery

Clearly, one of the most distinctive material remains of these people is their pottery. It should come as no surprise, therefore, that this material has received much attention by archaeologists. This Bichrome Ware (usually black and red) contains many interesting motifs including friezes with spirals, interlocking semicircles, and checkerboards. But perhaps the most distinctive feature is birds, very often portrayed with their heads turned backwards. The ceramic repertoire includes bowls, kraters, stirrup jars, amphoriskoi, pyxes, jugs made with strainer-spouts, juglets, cylindrical bottles, and horn-shaped vessels. These pottery remains, as well as others, are attributed to the Philistines for three reasons. First, the geographical distribution of this pottery accords well with what is known of the Philistine settlement pattern. The ceramic remains are concentrated in the coastal region and on the borders of the Hill Country, but appear only sporadically in the Central Hill Country. Second, the stratigraphy of the sites associated with this pottery clearly indicates that it first appeared on the Palestinian coast during the first half of the twelfth century BCE. This date parallels the Egyptian date of Ramesses' confrontation (however much it may have been exaggerated) with the Sea Peoples. Third, a comparison of the ceramic styles that make up much of the corpus links it to the Aegean area from which the Philistines are believed to have come. At the same time, neutron activation analysis of the clay has conclusively shown that the pottery was locally made. This implies that the pottery was made by local craftsmen who knew the styles, and that it was not imported.

The ceramic corpus of the Philistines is also very eclectic, reflecting Mycenaean (Aegean), Cypriot, Egyptian, and local Canaanite influence. One of the styles attributed to local Canaanite culture is the so-called "beer jug." This vessel has a strainer or sieve built into the vessel which was thought to have served the purpose of straining out the grains used in beer manufacturing. However, it has recently been argued that these vessels were used to serve wine, not beer.

Burial practices

When burials associated with the Philistines first began to be found at such sites as Beth-Shean and Tell el-Far'ah South, it was assumed that the distinctive anthropoid clay coffins (see Figure 16, p. 65) found in these burials originated with them. However, more recentury excavations, especially at Deir el-Balah, located on the coast some 25 miles south of Ashkelon, have shown that the tradition of burial in anthropoid clay coffins came from Egypt and preceded the arrival of the Sea Peoples. All of this implies that the Philistines adopted this burial practice very quickly, just as they did other aspects of the local culture.

Architectural remains

The clearest examples of Philistine architecture have come from the excavations at Tell Qasile, Ashdod, Ashkelon, and Ekron. While final conclusions must be made with caution due to limited exposure of Philistine strata, enough has been found to conclude that the Philistines imposed upon their new homeland building styles which they brought with them. At Ashkelon, L. Stager has discovered a public building that went through several phases, similar to such buildings found at Ashdod, Tell Qasile, and Ekron. The remains of over 150 clay spool weights suggest a weaving industry was located here.

At Ekron, the site reflecting the clearest example of Philistine architectural planning, public buildings have been found in the center of the site. What has been described as a "well-planned monumental building" and identified as possibly a governor's residence or palace was found in Field IV, located in the center of the city. This building contained several rooms, two of which have been associated with cultic practices. Of particular interest is the remains of a round hearth that was found in a courtyard connected to the above two rooms (see Figure 37, p. 114). Such hearths are thought to have been the main architectural feature of megaron buildings found in the Aegean world. Only in two other Philistine sites have such hearths been discovered: Tell Qasile and Ashkelon.

What have been identified as remains of private houses have been discovered at several sites, including Ashdod and Tell Qasile. They were built of mud brick and consisted of several rooms each. At Tell Qasile there is evidence of a pillar building. Since this site was first occupied by the Philistines, such an architectural style may have been brought with them. Similar pillar buildings have been found at other sites not normally associated with the Philistines such as **'Ai**, **Bethel**, Raddana, and **Gibeon**. 'Ai and Raddana are of particular importance since both sites are sealed loci stratigraphically with no preceding Late or Middle Bronze Age remains. Such evidence, along with other artifacts, implies that the occupants of these Iron Age I Central Highland villages had more in common with the Philistine inhabitants of the coastal region than with desert nomads from the east.

Philistine religion

Except for the brief and inconclusive biblical texts mentioned above, the only other evidence for Philistine religion is in the archaeological evidence, especially evidence from Ashdod, Tell Qasile, and Ekron. From Ashdod comes the now famous "Ashdoda" (see Figure 7, p. 34) a small female figurine attached to a table (throne?) representation. This object, along with other broken heads and chairs of similar figurines, led the excavator to conclude that during the first half of the twelfth century BCE, the Philistines still worshiped the so-called "Great Mother" of the Mycenaean world. Other finds are clay figurines interpreted as "mourning" women. How such items were actually used, if at all, in Philistine cultic practices is not known. From Tell Qasile comes the only completely excavated temenos (sacred area) of a Philistine site. During the twelfth and eleventh centuries (Str. XII–X), the buildings in the sacred area underwent constant changes. What has been identified as a large temple (25.5 × 28 feet, outer dimensions) in Stratum XI consisted of several rooms and a large courtyard. In the courtyard was found a pit that contained many bones as well as discarded vessels, many of which were characterized as "cultic." The excavator concluded that the architectural styles involved in this complex are unknown in Canaanite structures.

Among the cult objects recovered is a plaque with representations of what have been identified as goddesses, an anthropomorphic female libation vessel, a lion-shaped cup, cylindrical stands decorated with animal and human motifs, as well as offering bowls decorated with images of birds. However, there was no trace of the "Ashdoda" cult found at Tell Qasile. Another interesting object is a bimetal knife (the blade is of iron, while the rivets that attached it to its handle are of bronze) with an ivory handle. A similar knife has been discovered at Ekron. With the destruction of Stratum X, perhaps by David, the hey-day of the Philistine city came to a close.

At Ekron (Tel Miqne) a major Philistine city has come to light (see chapter on Ekron/Tel Miqne). Fortified with a mud-brick wall over 10 feet thick, the city covered over 50 acres and included an industrial zone; an area with public buildings, including one identified as a sanctuary; and a domestic area. In the sanctuary building, which went through two phases, was found the hearth, mentioned above, and many small objects, some of which have been linked to the Philistine cult. Among these objects are three bronze wheels with spokes and part of a frame with a loop interpreted as a hole for an axle. Unique among finds in Israel, such objects have been discovered in Cyprus. T. Dothan has pointed out that the description of the laver stands made for Solomon by Hiram, King of Tyre (1 Kgs. 7: 27–33) includes a reference to "bronze wheels and axles of bronze" (v. 30). Another important discovery is the bimetal knife similar to that from Tell Qasile mentioned above. What cultic or ceremonial significance it may have had is not clear. Three other handles dated to the first half of the twelfth century BCE were also found. During the last phase (Str. IV – late eleventh to early tenth century BCE) of this building, the hearth was no longer used and many small finds point to increased Egyptian influence. By the time of its destruction in the first half of the tenth century, Ekron had already lost a lot of its Philistine distinctiveness.

The end

From the textual and archaeological evidence, it can be concluded that the Philistines were a highly organized, militarily superior, and economically sophisticated people for a hundred and fifty years whose cultural achievements far exceeded that of any other known group in

Israel during Iron Age I. Their ceramic, architectural, and industrial remains testify to a highly industrious and artistic people which once and for all should destroy the popular connotation of cultural backwardness associated with the word "Philistine." Furthermore, what is known of their burial practices and domestic remains indicate they often achieved wealth and status, for only such people could have afforded the kind of houses they lived in and the tombs they were buried in.

Even though it is now known both archaeologically and textually (Jer. 25: 20; Zeph. 2: 4; Zech. 9: 5–8) that the Philistines existed throughout the Iron Age II period, by the middle of the tenth century, if not earlier, they seemed to have lost most of their cultural uniqueness. Beginning with such wealth, craftsmanship, political and military superiority, how did this happen? Part of their demise, no doubt, was brought about by their defeat by the Israelites. But this in itself seems insufficient to explain their rapid decline. The clue, I think, lies in the two things known the least about them: their original language and religion. While ethnic identity is a complex subject, certainly language and religion play a role. The Philistines seem to have been as eclectic in these areas as they were with their pottery styles. This eclecticism enabled them to assimilate fairly rapidly to Canaanite culture, but such assimilation also robbed them of much of their original identity. The land which they shared with the Israelites ultimately became their cultural grave. Fittingly enough, the name by which this land has been known for at least 2,000 years, "Palestine," stands today as their epitaph.

Further reading

Dothan, Moshe. "Archaeological Evidence for Movements of the Early 'Sea Peoples' in Canaan." *REI*. S. Gitin and W. G. Dever, eds. Winona Lake, Indiana: Eisenbrauns (1989): 74–81.

Dothan, Trude. *The Philistines and Their Material Culture*. Jerusalem: IES, 1982.

—— "The Philistines Reconsidered." *BAT*: 165–76.

—— and Moshe Dothan. *People of the Sea: The Search for the Philistines*. NY: Macmillan, 1992.

Singer, I. "Egyptians, Canaanites, and Philistines in the Period of the Emergence of Israel." *FNM*: 282–338.

Stone, Bryan Jack. "The Philistines and Acculturation: Cultural Change and Ethnic Continuity in the Iron Age." *BASOR* 298 (1995): 7–32.

APPENDIX B
A NOTE ON CHRONOLOGY

The dates of the various archaeological time periods have been debated from the very beginning. The problems and differences of opinion are so great, that this field of research has become a specialized study in and of itself. One should not be discouraged when one reads different dates in other publications. The important thing here is for the reader to become conversant with the terminology used to identify these time periods and their approximate, if not exact, dates.

For the most part, I have followed the suggestions in the *OEANE*, vol. 5, p. 411 and/or in the *NEAHL*, vol. 4, pp. 1529–1531.

Prehistoric periods

Paleolithic	1400000–18000 BCE
Mesolithic	18000–8500 (8000) BCE
Neolithic	8500–4500 (4200) BCE
Pre-pottery Neolithic (PPN)	8500 (8300)–6000 (5500) BCE
Pottery Neolithic (PN)	6000 (5500)–4500 (4200) BCE
Chalcolithic	4500 (4200)–3300 BCE

Historic periods

Early Bronze Age 3300–2200 (2000) BCE

Early Bronze Age I	3300–3000 BCE
Early Bronze Age II	3000–2700 (2800) BCE
Early Bronze Age III	2700–2200 (2800–2400) BCE
Early Bronze Age IV (Middle Bronze I)	2200–2000 (2400–2000) BCE

Middle Bronze Age 2000–1550 (1500) BCE

Middle Bronze Age I (Middle Bronze Age IIA)	2000–1800 (1750) BCE
Middle Bronze Age II (Middle Bronze Age IIB)	1800–1650 BCE (others date Middle Bronze Age IIB from c.1750–1550)
Middle Bronze Age III (Middle Bronze Age IIC)	1650–1550 BCE

Late Bronze Age 1550–1200 BCE

Late Bronze Age I	1550–1400 BCE
Late Bronze Age IIA	1400–1300 BCE
Late Bronze Age IIB	1300–1200 BCE (others see Late Bronze Age II as one period – 1400–1200)

Iron Age 1200–587 (540) BCE

Iron Age I	1200–1000 BCE (others divide Iron Age I into two periods: IA: 1200–1150; and IB: 1150–1000)
Iron Age IIA	1000–923 BCE (1000–900 in others)
Iron Age IIB	923–700 (900–700)
Iron Age IIC	700–540 BCE (others date this period from 700–586)

Babylonian and Persian 586–332 BCE

Hellenistic 332–63 BCE

Early Roman 63 BCE–132 CE

(Herodian Period 37 BCE–70 CE)

Late Roman 132–324 CE

Byzantine 324–638 CE

Early Islamic (Umayyad and Abbasids) 638–1099 CE

Middle Islamic (Crusader and Ayyubid) 1099–1291 CE

Late Islamic (Fatimid and Mamluk) 1291–1516 CE

Ottoman 1516–1917 CE